MACMILLAN LAW MASTERS

Land Law

Third Edition

Kate Green
LLB, PhD
Principal Lecturer in Law, University of East London

Law Series Editor: Marise Cremona
Senior Fellow, Centre for Commercial Law Studies
Queen Mary and Westfield College, University of London

First edition 1989 (reprinted twice)
Second edition 1993 (reprinted four times)
Third edition 1997

Published by
MACMILLAN PRESS LTD
Houndmills, Basingstoke, Hampshire RG21 6XS
and London
Companies and representatives
throughout the world

ISBN 0–333–69180–6

A catalogue record for this book is available
from the British Library.

This book is printed on paper suitable for recycling
and made from fully sustained forest sources.

10   9   8   7   6   5   4   3
06   05   04   03   02   01   00   99

Printed in Malaysia

To all my students, who have taught me so much

Contents

Part IV   TRUSTS OF LAND

Part V   LAND LAW, PAST AND FUTURE

Table of Cases

Table of Statutes

Preface to the Third Edition

This book is intended to be a clear and straightforward explanation of basic land law rules, a text which both introduces the subject and will be referred to during a land law course. It is only an introduction, of course, and has to gloss over many of the difficult problems presented to the law by people's dealing with land. A further aim is that the book should remove the unwarranted reputation of land law as a difficult and abstract subject. I hope to encourage students to consider the role of land law in their own world, and I wish all who read it a lasting interest in land law and its concerns.

Since the last edition, there have been two revolutionary changes in land law, both the result of Law Commission recommendations. The Landlord and Tenant (Covenants) Act 1995 abolished the test of 'touch and concern' in leases, and removed the continuing liability of the original tenant. The Trusts of Land and Appointment of Trustees Act 1996 abolished trusts for sale (and the doctrine of conversion) and strict settlements, replacing them with simple 'trusts of land' with power to sell or retain the land. Both of these major reforms will no doubt inspire a whole new line of cases for future editions: in this edition, a noticeable new feature is the Court of Appeal case law on the formality of land contracts under s.2 Law of Property (Miscellaneous Provisions) Act 1989.

Of course, the content of the subject 'Land Law' is merely a group of statutes and cases collected together as a result of historical accident and practical convenience. Outside the text books, the academic divisions between subjects are non-existent: land law is inextricably tangled with administrative and inheritance law as well as contract, tort, family law, equity and – above all – conveyancing. Most land law courses stay fairly close to the old syllabus originally devised by practitioners whose aim was to train conveyancers, and to provide a commentary on the important reforms of the 1925 legislation; even today, the need to prepare efficient conveyancers is seen as the main object of the most influential texts. As a result, the rules covered are for the most part those which concern property owners, that is, the 'haves' rather than the 'have nots'. This book covers the main areas in most courses, with the exception of future interests and the law against perpetuities.

I refer to a limited number of cases because understanding a few is of greater value to a law student than being able to drop a case-name at the end of every sentence. The number of cases referred to by land law textbooks is notorious; no one has ever been expected to remember a tenth of them. Rather than drowning in the flood of precedents, it is best to rely on a good knowledge of a few important cases which illustrate several points or difficulties with the law. There are also some pairs of cases which neatly demonstrate the working of a rule and these are useful too.

The standard forms found in many books are omitted here as these are more useful as 'live' teaching aids; in a textbook they often confuse more than they assist. On the other hand, there are figures and tables to provide alternative methods of analysis.

It will probably be noticed that 'she' and 'he' feature in alternate chapters. This method was chosen as it is no longer acceptable for women to be 'invisible men', and the 's/he' convention is clumsy and becomes very repetitive. The first chapter is in 'her' mode since 'she' won the toss!

My thanks are due to all my colleagues, and to all my land law students.

The law is stated as at 1 January 1997.

KATE GREEN

Part I

Introduction

1   Introduction to Land Law

1.1   How to Study Land Law

Land law is a fascinating and challenging subject, involving profound questions about the way we choose to live our lives, for land is vital for human life. In any society, even our technological, high-speed one, the use of land is of the utmost importance; where the supply is limited, as in England and Wales, the problems are acute. The dry and legalistic façade created by the artificial language and technical concepts of land law tends to conceal the fundamental issues: land law is really just about the sharing out of our limited island.

Land law has been developing in this country ever since people got ideas about having rights over certain places; this probably came about when women began cultivating crops. Through the long process of development there have been periods of gradual change, and more dramatic times, such as the Norman conquest of 1066 and the property legislation of 1925. By and large, lawyers have, over the centuries, continued to use the words and ideas of their predecessors. However, although land law has kept its feudal roots and language, the substance of today's law is fundamentally changed. The law can certainly seem obscure – cloaked in the fog, rather than the mists, of time – so it is wisest to treat learning it initially like a foreign language. The vocabulary soon becomes natural, especially through reading about the same topic in different books.

The law is often further distanced from real life by historical introductions which serve to conceal more than they reveal. Lawyers' history tends to be of the 'century per paragraph' variety and is often coloured by unspoken political opinions. Such history should be treated with caution.

As explained further below, lawyers are concerned with various rights to land, called 'interests in land'. They might talk about someone 'owning land' but really they mean someone owning *an interest in* the land; these interests are not the land itself. the earth and the buildings, but abstract concepts, like the fee simple and the lease.

The first thing to do when starting to study any interest in land is to grasp the definition thoroughly. This helps to avoid two of the most depressing things that can happen to land law students: the first is staring at a problem without having even an idea of what it is about, and the second – possibly worse – is recognising what the problem concerns, but feeling incapable of writing anything down. If in doubt, start with the interests in the land.

The rules which constitute land law are like a complicated machine; moving one lever, or adjusting one valve, changes the end-product. Some authors compare the subject with playing chess; there are various 'pieces' (which correspond to interests in land) and they can be moved about according to strict rules. The owner of an interest in land has limited freedom of action, and one small change in her position can affect the relative value of other interests in the land.

In practical terms, the complicated connections within the machine mean that one part of the subject cannot be fully grasped until *all* the others have been understood. There is no single starting place: it is necessary to watch the machine, bit by bit, until the connections become clear. It is useful, from the beginning, to ask, 'What would happen if . . .?'; if one lever is moved, what interests will be affected, and why?

As a consequence of the complex definitions and the interdependent rules, land law may only make sense when the course is nearly complete. However, in the meantime, it is necessary to make mistakes in order to grasp the way the rules relate to one another. It *will* eventually come together, with hard work in faith and hope: the charity, with any luck, will be provided by the teacher.

The language used by land lawyers expresses the way they think they see the world. This is a world in which people's relationships to land can only occur within the legal structure of interests in land, so lawyers squeeze the facts of ordinary life into the pre-existing moulds of 'the interests'. A land law student's job is to learn the shapes of the moulds, and imitate the squeeze; then she will be able to operate the whole machine. Finally, armed with this knowledge and skill, she may begin to question whether land law really does operate like this in practice.

1.2   Land Law Rules

Land law is made up of rules in statutes and cases; case law rules are further divided into legal and equitable rules. That is, the rules were created, if not by an Act of Parliament, either by a court of 'law' or by a court of 'equity'. The development of these two sets of rules is well described by others (for example, Murphy and Roberts, 1987), and is merely outlined here.

The customs which became known as the 'common' law were enforced with extraordinary rigidity by judges who followed the strict letter of the law. Aggrieved citizens – in the absence of crusading television journalists – wrote begging letters to the king. These were replied to by his 'secretary', the Chancellor, who employed the king's power to override the decisions of the king's judges. Appealing to the Chancellor's conscience, to 'equity', grew in popularity and from about 1535 the chancellor's court, Chancery, was regularly making decisions overriding the law in the king's court.

However, this new system of justice did not set out to replace the rules of law, but merely to intervene when conscience required it: *equity came not to destroy the law but to fulfil it*. The common law and Chancery courts existed separately, each with its own procedures and remedies, to the great profit of the legal profession. Eventually things became intolerably inefficient and the two courts were merged by the Judicature Acts 1873 and 1875 but, even today, lawyers keep the legal and equitable rules and remedies separate (and see 1.5 below).

Most land law statutes are dated 1925, an emotive date for land lawyers. The law was actually changed by a very large Law of Property Act in 1922, but that Act was not brought into force, being divided up into the various 1925 Acts. The main statutes of that year are:

Administration of Estates Act (AEA)
Law of Property Act (LPA)
Land Charges Act (now 1972) (LCA)
Land Registration Act (LRA)
Settled Land Act (SLA) (now see Trusts of Land and Appointment of Trustees Act 1996)
Trustee Act (TA)

They contain many radical reforms and also 'wordsaving' provisions, some of which had previously appeared in earlier statutes. In the good old days, conveyancers were 'paid by the yard', so the more words they used the better for their bank balances, but interfering politicians ensured that many common promises in land transactions no longer need to be spelt out in full, being implied by statute: in effect, the customs of careful conveyancers become enshrined in statute.

The aim of the 1925 legislation was to make conveyancing (buying and selling land) simpler in order to revive the depressed market in land. It is impossible to say whether it had this effect. Certainly, the increase in home ownership is not connected, for many American states share English common law – they do not have any statutory equivalent to the 1925 statutes – but conveyancing is cheaper there. In addition, some of the 1925 reforms were, as it will appear, inappropriate to the modern world.

Few examiners expect an encyclopaedic knowledge of the statutes. Referring to the important sections is impressive, but mostly this is gained from studying the law and not from learning by rote.

1.3   Land Law Today

At the most basic level, human beings are land animals; they need somewhere to put their bodies, a piece of land on which to 'be'. On the emotional plane, humans must have contact with land, their roots in the earth. Physically, they need air to breathe and space in which to move about, food and shelter; all these are provided only by land.

As a resource, land also has other special characteristics. Except in the rare cases of land falling into or being thrown up by the sea, it is geographically fixed (you cannot move it about); it is also ultimately indestructible. Its nature means that the boundaries between one piece of land and another are normally touching, so neighbouring owners are aware of one another's business. Further, to its occupant one piece is never exactly the same as another, each is unique; even in a regimented tower block each floor has its own particular characteristics.

However, these rigid features of land are matched by its flexibility, for it has an infinite number of layers. Land is really 'three-dimensional space' which can be used by a number of people in different ways simultaneously: one person can invest her money in a plot, while two or more live there, a fourth tunnels beneath and half a dozen more use a path over it as a short-cut, or graze their cattle on a part of it.

It can be shared consecutively as well as simultaneously; that is to say, people can enjoy the land one after another. The great land-owning families traditionally created complicated 'settlements' of their estates, whereby the land would go down through the succeeding generations as the first owner desired. Each 'owner' only had it for a lifetime, and could not leave it by will because, at death, it had to pass according to the directions in the settlement (see Chapter 11).

Each society develops its own cultural attitudes to its land. These attitudes are coloured by the kind of land (for example, desert or jungle) because this determines the uses to which it can be put. The view taken of land is also influenced by its scarcity or otherwise, and by the economic system. In places where land was plentiful, it was not normally 'owned'. When the white woman arrived in America, the Indians said:

'The earth was created by the assistance of the sun, and it should be left as it was . . . The country was made without lines of demarcation, and it is no man's business to divide it . . . The earth and myself are of one mind. The measure of the land and the measure of our bodies are the same . . . Do not misunderstand me, but understand me fully with reference to my affection for the land. I never said the land was mine to do with as I chose. The one who has the right to dispose of it is the one who created it.' (Quoted by T. C. McLuhan, *Touch the Earth*, Abacus (1972) p. 54)

Similarly, native Australians regarded the land with special awe; as concluded in one of the cases about aboriginal land claims, it was not so much that they owned the land, but that the land owned them (*Milirrpum* v. *Nabalco Pty Ltd and the Commonwealth of Australia* (1971) 17 FLR 141 and now see (1995) Conv. 33). The traditional African view was that the land was not capable of being owned by one person but belonged to the whole tribe:

'land belongs to a vast family of which many are dead, a few are living and countless numbers still unborn.' (West African Lands Committee Cd 1048), p. 183)

In early English land law, the fundamental concept was 'seisin'. The person who was seised of land was entitled to recover it in the courts if she were disseised. Originally, according to Simpson, 'the person seised of land was simply the person in obvious occupation, the person 'sitting' on the land' (1986, p. 37). Seisin thus described the close relationship between a person and the land she worked and lived on. This simplicity was, over centuries, 'refined, modified and elaborated', and the concepts of ownership and possession took over. Nevertheless actual possession or occupation can still be of great importance in land law, for example, in adverse possession (see Chapter 3).

Over the last three or four hundred years, our land law has been developing alongside the growth of capitalism and city-living. There has been a huge population increase: in 1603, there were about 4 million people in Britain, while today there are over 55 million on the same area, about 200 000 square kilometres (that is, about 3500 square metres of surface area per person). More recently there has been an enormous increase in the ownership of land by ordinary people; it has more than doubled over the last 30 years, from 30 per cent to over 70 per cent (although it cannot grow much more as probably about 25 per cent of the population will never be able to afford it). Despite this increase, people are often less aware than, say, American Indians of their personal relationship with land.

However, although British people no longer expect to live in one place for more than a few years, most can say where they were born and have lived, and moving house is often a memorable experience. For the majority of adults the land they own (although subject to a huge debt) is both home and investment. It is an expression of their personality and a retreat from the world; at the same time it represents a status symbol and – they hope – an inflation-proofed savings bank. For other people (for example, those whose home is rented weekly) 'home ownership', with its apparent psychological and financial advantages, may be only a hope for the future. In the meantime, their relationship with their land may be less secure, subject to the authority of a landlady. However, in a lawyer's view tenants are also in theory 'land owners' (see 1.4 below).

Some authors interpret the modern law as treating land merely as if it were money, but a law which actually dealt with land in this way would not fulfil the needs of our society. Most of the difficult issues in land law today focus on the informal arrangements of people who – unlike the landowners of previous centuries – do not see the need to transact their family business via a lawyer. Take the following situation as an example: Jane lets Raj share her house in exchange for his paying the mortgage, and later she sells the house to Chris. Chris wants to live there by himself, but Raj does not want to leave. This kind of problem, where a transaction between buyer and seller involves a third person's interest in land, appears in various forms throughout this book. It is a kind of eternal triangle, as in Figure 1.1.

It is often said that land law disputes centre on the conflicting require-ments of the market in land. In order to maximise the value of land, ownership must be capable of being freely and safely traded, while people who have lesser interests in the land must also feel secure. In 10.9 below I suggest that, where land is registered, these two principles are now out of balance.

The market certainly seems to have an influence on the development of the law. One of the most influential factors in the attitudes of judges to difficult decisions is their view of the state of the market. When there was a slump at the end of the last century they tried to ensure that liabilities attached to land (that is, the lesser, third-party interests) were minimised so that the land would be attractive to buyers. In the 1960s and 1970s there

Figure 1.1   *'The Eternal Triangle'*

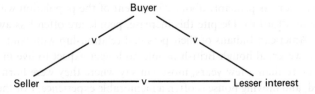

were booming prices in most areas of the country, and a greater interest in the security of 'non-owners', like Raj. The falling market of the early 1990s produced its own response, and this was significantly influenced by the interests of the building societies and banks (see Chapter 6).

1.4   'Land'

Definitions of land

At common law, land means the soil, the rocks beneath and the air above (see 4.4 below). It includes things growing on, and buildings 'attached' to, the land. If Jane sells her land to Chris, she is selling not merely the surface, but also the grass and trees, and the bricks, tiles and chimney-pots of the house. The extent to which things fixed onto a building, or cemented into the ground, are 'fixtures', part of the land itself, is a question of fact in every case.

In *Berkley* v. *Poulett* (1976) 120 Sol Jo 836, the eighth Earl Poulett sold his estate and took with him some pictures which had been screwed onto panelling as well as a marble statue of a Greek god. The buyer sued him, claiming that the items were part of the land. The court held that two questions had to be asked: first, to what degree was the item attached to the land, and second, why had it been attached? It was held (by a majority in the Court of Appeal) that neither the pictures nor the statue were fixtures. The pictures were not part of the intrinsic design of the room, and the statue – unlike its plinth, which the earl had left behind – was not essential to the landscaped garden.

This can be a very important question at the end of a lease because anything that the tenant attaches to the land may become part of the land, and thereby the property of the lessor. Similarly, if a bank repossesses a house because the mortgage is unpaid, the carpets, gas fires and kitchen units may have become 'land', and they can be sold by the creditor and the proceeds put towards paying off the debt. In addition, a person who supplies goods which become attached to land may not be able to take them back again if the buyer fails to pay for them, as happened in the case of *Aircool Installations* v. *British Telecommunications* [1995] (Curr Law December 1995) in relation to air conditioning units.

Land is also defined in s.205(1)(ix) LPA:

'Land includes land of any tenure, and mines and minerals . . . buildings or parts of buildings . . . and other corporeal hereditaments; also . . . a rent, and other incorporeal hereditaments, and an easement right, privilege, or benefit in, over, or derived from land.'

Thus both freeholds and leases are 'land', so a person who buys a lease (that is, becomes a tenant) is a buyer of *land*. The term 'corporeal hereditaments' is an ancient way of referring to the land and fixtures, while 'incorporeal hereditaments' are the invisible interests in land, such as mortgages and easements (rights of way, for example). Thus a person who buys a right of way over her neighbour's land is also buying 'land'.

Types of 'land'

Since 1925 all titles to land in England and Wales are either 'unregistered' or 'registered'. Although people often refer to 'registered land', and the main statute in question is the LRA 1925, technically it is the *title* which is registered, not the land.

The aim of simplifying conveyancing was ultimately to be achieved by registering all titles to land in a central registry (see Chapter 10), but even now, although most titles have been registered and all land must be registered on sale, about 30 per cent of titles are not yet registered.

The two regimes have different procedures and rules, which occasionally produce different results. Therefore the very *first* question to ask when faced with any land law issue is:

**QUESTION 1: 'HAS THE TITLE
BEEN REGISTERED YET?'**

1.5 Estates and Interests in Land

Estates and interests

It has already been mentioned that the land lawyer views every piece of land as potentially fragmented into an infinite number of interests. For historical reasons, she sees people owning an abstract estate or interest in land, not the land itself. The lesser interests are carved out of the major ones called the 'estates'. This word 'estate' has a long lineage; it means 'an interest in land of some particular duration' (Megarry and Wade, 1984, p. 38), but today this definition is an academic relic, of no practical importance. All that is necessary to know is that there are now two estates

– the freehold and the leasehold – and a third, called 'commonhold', may soon be introduced (see below, 5.11).

The term 'interest in land' is significant to land-lawyers because it shows that the rights and duties of the people concerned are not merely personal or contractual. These rights and duties are 'glued' to the land itself and they automatically pass to anyone who buys or inherits the land; they can therefore be transferred to other people and bind third parties. In lawyers' vocabulary, interests in land are 'property' (see below, 13.1, 13.7).

On reading land law problems, it is crucial to develop an instinct for the various interests so that you can immediately cry out, 'Aha! This looks like an easement.' The *second* question to ask in problem-solving is therefore:

QUESTION 2: 'WHAT INTERESTS MAY EXIST HERE?'

Legal and equitable interests

The courts of *law* recognised various estates and interests in land and would enforce the rights of a legal owner; the courts of *equity* might override this in favour of a person with, in its view, a stronger moral right to the land. The owner of the legal interest was deemed by equity to hold it on behalf of (on trust for) the person who had the better right. Today there are many pieces of land where legal title and equitable enjoyment are divided in this way.

This can be illustrated by the famous case of *Bull* v. *Bull* [1955] 1 QB 234. A son and mother both contributed to buying a house on the outskirts of London, but only the son's name appeared on the conveyance (the deed) so he was the legal owner. He then married and tried to get rid of his mother, but the Court of Appeal held that he could not simply evict her. She had a share of the equitable title because of her contribution to the purchase, so the son held the legal title on behalf of the equitable owners (himself and his mother). Another way to express this is to say that the son is a trustee for himself and his mother; they share the 'beneficial' interest. Equity normally recognises a trust relationship like this when the apparent owner *ought* to hold the land wholly or partly for the benefit of someone else. The trust is a useful, and very common, device by which land can be shared (see Chapters 11 and 12).

There are therefore many legal interests in land and, in a kind of parallel universe, many equitable interests. As a general rule, anyone who buys or inherits land owns it subject to any interests which had been created by previous owners of the land. However, this rule has numerous exceptions.

Enforcing interests

There are two main reasons why it is still important to label interests as 'legal' or 'equitable'. The first is that equitable interests depend on equitable remedies and these depend on the court's discretion: the court of equity, being 'a court of conscience', only grants a remedy if the claimant has behaved fairly. (Legal remedies on the other hand (damages, for example), are available 'as of right'; a plaintiff is entitled to damages if her strict legal rights have been infringed, whether or not this is fair.) Thus the mother in the *Bull* case, who was relying on an equitable interest, could not have succeeded if she had been deceitful or had delayed unreasonably. This is expressed in the maxim, '*she who comes to equity must come with clean hands*'. (A modern version might be, 'Keep your nose clean'.) An example of unacceptable delay is *Tse Kwong Lam* v. *Wong Chit Sen* [1983] 1 WLR 1349 (see below, 6.3).

The second reason to distinguish between legal and equitable interests is that the courts of equity could not bring themselves to enforce equitable rights against a completely innocent and honest legal buyer. Therefore, the rule was established that the owner of an equitable interest in land would lose it if someone paid for the legal estate, in good faith and without notice of the equitable interest. This rule about the good buyer (the 'bona fide purchaser') is also called the 'doctrine of notice'.

Before the many changes made in 1925, the rule was that an equitable interest did not bind:

> **THE PURCHASER IN GOOD FAITH OF THE**
> **LEGAL ESTATE FOR VALUE WITHOUT NOTICE,**
> **ACTUAL, IMPUTED OR CONSTRUCTIVE**

Proof of any one of the three kinds of notice would mean that the buyer was bound by the equitable interest. If she actually knew about, for example, the mother's interest in *Bull* v. *Bull* (above), or if her agent knew about it ('imputed notice'), she would step into the son's shoes and would be bound by the mother's rights. Under 'constructive notice' (also known as the rule in *Hunt* v. *Luck* [1902] 1 Ch 428), the buyer was taken to know – whether or not she did – anything a prudent purchaser would have discovered by inspecting the land and the title deeds to the land. Any buyer of the bungalow in the Bull case would probably have discovered, had she looked around it carefully, that someone other than the son and his wife lived there; she would have had constructive notice of the mother's right and would have been bound by it. The 1925 legislation made important differences to the doctrine of notice (see Chapters 9 and 10).

Another way to express the difference between legal and equitable interests in land is to say that legal rights are effective against anyone in the world, but equitable rights are only 'good' against certain people. Equitable interests bind everyone except the bona fide purchaser of the legal estate for value without notice, and then only if the claimant has behaved well. The *third* question therefore that must be asked about a land law problem is:

QUESTION 3: 'IS THIS INTEREST LEGAL OR EQUITABLE?'

The answer will be very important in determining the relative rights of the various parties.

Equitable interests and conveyancing

As part of the reforms directed at making conveyancing simpler, legal rights to land were strictly limited in 1925; many interests could no longer be legal but could only be equitable . The section which establishes this is 'the cornerstone' of the legislation:

LPA 1925

S.1 **(1)** The only estates in land which are capable of subsisting or of being conveyed or created at law are:
   (a) An estate in fee simple absolute in possession [the freehold];
   (b) A term of years absolute [a lease].

   (2) The only interests or charges in or over land which are capable of subsisting or of being conveyed or created at law are:
   (a) An easement, right, or privilege in or over land for an interest equivalent to an estate in fee simple absolute in possession or a term of years absolute [rights of way, for example];
   (b) A rentcharge in possession issuing out of or charged on land being either perpetual or for a term of years absolute [a kind of rent without a lease];
   (c) A charge by way of legal mortgage;

    (d) [A tithe] [effectively repealed]

    (e) Rights of entry exercisable over or in respect of a legal term of years absolute [a landlady's right to end a lease].

(3) All other estates, interests, and charges in or over land take effect as equitable interests.

Thus, whatever the historical position, since 1 January 1926 there are only two estates (freehold and leasehold), and five interests which are capable of existing *at law;* all the rest must be equitable. Such equitable interests, however, would be insecure because of the doctrine of notice – there is always the threat of a 'purchaser of the legal estate in good faith for value without notice'. The 1925 scheme therefore provides ways to protect these equitable interests against unscrupulous legal owners (see especially Chapters 9–12).

It must be emphasised that s.1 LPA does not say that the fee simple and the lease *are* legal, merely that they *may* be. Whether or not an interest is legal is an interesting question: the answer will be clearer after reading the next chapter.

1.6 Comment

It can be seen, even from this brief introduction, how land law works within a special language, using a set of abstract interests as the basis for the ownership and enjoyment of land. The language, abstractions and interdependent rules can cause difficulties initially, but perseverance overcomes these. The fascinating history of land law can, if there is time to read in depth, provide a more profound understanding of the roles played by the law and by lawyers in relation to people sharing their space.

Summary

1 Land law is fundamentally about how people share land.
2 In approaching land law, it is essential to grasp the language and definitions of interests in land as well as the rules about them.
3 'Land' means the physical land and fixtures and includes any interest in land; land may be either registered or not yet registered.
4 There are many interests capable of existing in a piece of land; these interests must be identified as either legal or equitable.
5 Land law was reformed in 1925 and a number of legal interests was limited to two estates, freehold and leasehold, and five interests.

6   Legal interests would bind anyone who owned the land; equitable interests would bind everyone except a buyer of a legal estate in good faith for value without notice, actual, imputed or constructive.
7   In analysing a land law question, the following three primary questions should be asked: is the title registered or not yet registered? What interest may exist here? Is the interest legal or equitable?

Exercises

1   Is an equitable interest as good as a legal interest?
2   Why does it matter whether land is registered or not yet registered?
3   Why is s.1 LPA 1925 important?
4   How does a lawyer define land?
5   Is land law difficult so far?

2   Buying and Selling Land

2.1   Introduction

This chapter explains the normal process of buying and selling land and the effects of the sale, including the rules about the creation and enforcement of contracts for the sale of land, and about deeds. These rules are crucial to land law because, if they are not observed, there may not be a contract, or the buyer may only obtain an equitable interest which may be insecure, as explained in 1.5 above.

First, it is important to remember that 'land' includes all interests in land (see 1.4 above) and:

> 'purchaser means a purchaser in good faith for valuable consideration and includes a lessee, mortgagee or other person who for valuable consideration acquires an interest in property.' (s.205(1) (xxi) LPA 1925)

Therefore, the rules in this chapter control the creation and sale of leases and mortgages, for example, as well as of freehold land.

The transfer of a form of property which is financially and emotionally so important is bound to be the subject of some ritual and, therefore, of technical rules. These conveyancing rules are also, to a large extent, a recognition of the good practices of conveyancing lawyers: Parliament's and the courts' role can often be seen as retrospectively approving the accepted practice of the experts. All land in England and Wales must now be registered on sale, and therefore every sale today is subject to at least some of the rules about registration of title (see Chapter 10).

In 1989, the Law of Property (Miscellaneous Provisions) Act provided completely new rules about how a contract for the sale of a legal interest in land must be made. The old law (including the 'written memorandum' of a contract, 'subject to contract' and 'part performance', and the old definition of a deed) is now largely of historical interest, for as time passes old contracts are decreasingly likely to be the subject of legal action. However, some of the old principles, and the problems they caused, may help predict how the courts will decide disputes under the new law. For these reasons, this chapter refers briefly to the old law as well as the new.

As in all areas of land law, the rules on which this chapter focuses are affected by other rules. The most important are those about registered and unregistered land but, in addition, legal title can also be obtained by long use and equitable title by means of a trust. Given the interdependent parts of the land law machine, it is only possible fully to understand the rules about buying and selling land when the rest of land law is also understood.

2.2 A Typical Domestic Sale

The usual procedure

The box opposite shows the important steps in a typical conveyance of freehold land. (A conveyance is a document which transfers property and includes a deed, also called a 'grant'; the word 'grant' is sometimes used by cruel examiners to trap students who have not attended lectures.)

The Bs want the legal title to the bungalow. In unregistered land, legal title must initially be transferred by a deed and then the title must be registered. If title is already registered, its transfer must be recorded at the Land Registry in order for legal ownership to be changed.

However, during the several weeks of negotiation necessary before the legal title is finally transferred, neither side can be sure of completing the sale. The Bs might fail to get their loan, or might decide that the bungalow is too expensive, or the Ss could decide to withdraw from the market until prices pick up. Each side would like the other to be bound as soon as possible, but is wary of committing himself too soon.

2.3 Transfer of the Equitable Interest

Fortunately, the parties to a sale of land can usually feel secure some time before the final transfer of legal ownership. The rules of equity provide that a contract can be enforced before the deed is executed ('completion' of the contract) because equity provides a remedy for breach of contract: 'specific performance'. The remedy is available because *equity looks on that as done which ought to be done*. As an equitable remedy it is discretionary and will only be ordered if the claimant has behaved properly (see 1.5 above).

If equity is prepared to grant specific performance of the contract, the sellers become, effectively, trustees for the new equitable right of the buyers to become the legal owners when the contract is completed. There is some sort of trust relationship between the Bs and the Ss although the Ss do retain some rights to enjoy the land.

Mr and Mrs B want to purchase a bungalow from Mr and Mrs S:

Time	Facts	Law
About 8 weeks	Negotiation of price, fittings, etc. Conveyancers negotiate legal details, check with Local Authority regarding planning, etc. Survey and finance arranged. Draft contract (2 copies) prepared by Ss' conveyancers, agreed by all.	None of these steps has any legal or equitable implications: there is *no contract* (s.2, 1989 Act), but note estoppel
About 4 weeks	Contracts containing all the terms of the contract are signed by both sides and exchanged.	The contract is made (s.2, 1989 Act)
	Final checks of title and searches for land charges.	(Land Charges Register for unregistered land; Land Register for registered land.)
	'Completion' by execution of the deed and payment of the remainder of the price.	Legal title is transferred in unregistered land (s. 52, LPA)
	Land transfer received at the Land Registry.	Legal title transferred in registered land.

	Negotiation	**Exchange**	**Completion/registration**
Legal title	Sellers	Sellers ⟶	Buyers
Equitable title	Sellers ⟶	Buyers	Buyers

Figure 2.1   *Transfer of legal and equitable titles*

The case of *Walsh* v. *Lonsdale* (1882) 21 Ch D 9 (see also 5.5 below) is an example of the rule that an equitable interest in land is created as soon as there is a contract. In this famous old case, Lonsdale made a contract to grant a seven-year lease of a mill to Walsh, but the parties never completed the deed necessary for transfer of the lease, the legal estate. Jessel MR said:

'The tenant holds under an agreement for a lease. He holds therefore under the same terms in equity as if a lease had been granted, it being a case in which both parties admit that relief is capable of being given by specific performance.' (at p. 14)

Thus equity recognised the contract, and Walsh had a seven-year equitable lease. One might have expected him to be delighted with this result, but unfortunately for him it meant that he had to observe all the terms of the lease, including payment of rent in advance: he owed Lonsdale £1005.

A written contract for the sale of land is therefore an equitable interest in land, and is called an 'estate contract'. In addition, because of the rule that the equitable interest passes as soon as there is a contract, the buyers have the responsibility for insuring the land (against the risk of fire, for example). The Law Commission (No. 191, 'Risk of Damage After Contract for Sale', 1990) has concluded that, subject to the intentions of the parties, the risk should only pass at the time of completion. Such a rule, they say, would have 'the merits of universal application, fairness and consistency with reasonable expectations' (para. 3.8). Although the recommendation has not yet become law, in practice a term to this effect is now usually inserted into a contract for the sale of land.

2.4   Enforcing the Contract

Under the old rules, replaced by the 1989 Act, a contract for the sale of any interest in land was not enforceable until there was some evidence of it either by writing, or by part performance. The original rule that contracts for the sale of land had to be evidenced in writing originated from s.4 Statute of Frauds 1677, designed to reduce the 'frauds and Perjuryes' committed by people trying to enforce alleged oral contracts. In 1925, the old section was restated in s.40 (1) LPA.

The old law about contracts in writing

S.40(1) applied to all agreements for the sale of any interest in land made before 27 September 1989, but is irrelevant to any contract made on or after that date. The old law may still arise today in rare cases of options to purchase made before then.

The wording of s.40(1) was clear but somewhat misleading:

'No action may be brought upon any contract for the sale or other disposition of land or any interest in land, unless the agreement upon which such action is brought, or some memorandum or note thereof, is in writing, and signed by the party to be charged or by some other person thereunto by him lawfully authorised.'

There need not be what most people would think of as a memorandum or note; not all the terms had to be written down; it did not need the actual signature of the party to be charged (usually the defendant or his agent) although it is likely that the signature would be there. On the other hand, case law spelt out the implicit need for the writing to show that a contract had been made. The modern requirements of S.40(1) were: (a) writing (possibly in several different but related documents); (b) details from which the essential terms of the contract could be ascertained; (c) in some way acknowledged by the defendant; and (d) an indication that an agreement had been reached.

These requirements were decorated by many case law rules. For example, it was held that the important terms of the contract usually included: the identities of buyer and seller, the property, and the price, and, in the case of a lease, the beginning and ending of the term. However, it was not actually necessary for all to be written in full. A useful maxim here, as in other areas of land law, is: '*that is certain which can be made certain*'. (For wrinkled readers, the Latin is *Id certum est quod certum reddi potest*.) It was enough to satisfy the statute if the essential terms could be deduced from the written description without relying on oral evidence, and this was a question of fact in every case.

In *Tiverton Estates Ltd* v. *Wearwell Ltd* [1975] Ch 146, the Court of Appeal chose to follow an old line of cases which held that if the writing, however formal and clear, contained the words 'subject to contract' then the writing could not be evidence of a contract: 'subject to contract' indicates that no final agreement has been reached so there is no contract yet. (This magic formula is less important since the 1989 Act because it is now much less likely that the necessary paperwork for a contract will come into being unintentionally.)

Under the old law, only the person who acknowledged the contract by 'signing' the document was liable to be forced to go through with it. It was therefore possible under s.40 to have a contract which was enforceable by one side only. The acknowledgement, however, need not be a full signature; initials would be enough. Thus, it was quite possible under s.40 for a person inadvertently to become liable on a contract as in *Dewar* v. *Mintoft* [1912] 2 KB 373, where the defendant's angry letter repudiating the contract claimed by the plaintiff was enough to make him liable (which probably made him even angrier).

Modern requirements for the contract

The world of buying and selling land is today very different from that of 1677 but the aim of the modern law is still to ensure that ordinary people's expectations are fulfilled, and that they are not caught out by legal technicalities. The Law Commission (No. 164, 'Formalities for Contracts for Sale etc. of Land', 1987) concluded that special formality is appropriate for transfer of a property with such significance in people's lives, both in order to avoid inadvertent transfers and to ensure that people do not unfairly escape their moral obligations. However, the Act does not match exactly the recommendations of the Commission and therefore cannot wholly be relied on in deciding what the new law means.

S.2 Law of Property (Miscellaneous Provisions) Act 1989 states:

'A contract for the sale or other disposition of an interest in land can only be made in writing and only by incorporating all the terms which the parties have expressly agreed in one document or, where contracts are exchanged, in each.'

(For the impact of this section on mortgages, see below 6.2.)
It therefore requires:

> **ALL THE TERMS**
> **IN WRITING**
> **SIGNED BY BOTH BUYER AND SELLER**

In brief, under s.2 Law of Property (Miscellaneous Provisions) Act 1989 there is no contract at all until there is a signed document containing all the agreed terms. It is no longer a question of a contract being merely unenforceable (as under s.40(1)) without written evidence; now, there *cannot be any contract without writing.* Further, the requirements of the new statute are far stricter than the old law.

S.2 has, inevitably, induced an increasing flow of case law, much of which reflects the same problems as faced the courts under s.40. Initially, the judges appeared reluctant to find that an apparent agreement was not, under s.2, a 'contract', and sought to hold people to their word; more recently, a stricter view seems to be emerging, in which the courts are readier to find that there was no contract because of s.2.

Very soon after the section came into force, in *Tootal Clothing Ltd* v. *Guinea Properties Ltd* (1992) 64 P & CR 452, the Court of Appeal held that s.2 does not apply to contracts which have already been completed. In this case, where a long lease had already begun, s.2 could not be invoked to make the lease non-existent. More recently, in *Singh* v. *Beggs* (1996) 71 P & CR 120 the Court of Appeal held that s.2 does apply to a contract for the sale of an interest in land even though the seller does not at the time own the relevant interest but is hoping to buy it in the future. Here, therefore, by s.2 the oral 'agreeement' that Beggs would sell Singh the freehold of her rented flat for £10 000 as soon as he had acquired it could not be enforced because by s.2 it was not a contract.

An early case on s.2 of the 1989 Act, *Spiro* v. *Glencrown Properties* [1991] 2 WLR 931, concerned an option to purchase land and raised the question of whether the letter giving notice that the buyer was going to exercise the option and buy the land had to satisfy the section by containing also the seller's signature. Hoffmann J held:

> 'Apart from authority, it seems to me plain enough that section 2 was intended to apply to the agreement which created the option and not to the notice by which it was exercised . . . The exercise of the option is a unilateral act. It would destroy the very purpose of the option if the purchaser had to obtain the vendor's countersignature to the notice.' (p. 933)

The only document which needed both signatures was the contract creating the option, and it did. Therefore again here the buyer was entitled to demand enforcement of the contract.

Already, three Court of Appeal cases have been concerned with the question of the circumstances in which more than one document can satisfy the section. The section states that the terms must be 'contained in one document, or, where contracts are exchanged, in each.' Further, in s.2(2), the terms may be contained in a separate document from the one that is signed by both parties, but then the signed document must refer to the document containing the terms. In *Hooper* v. *Sherman* (1994) NPC153, it was held that an exchange of informal letters, each containing the terms but signed by one of the parties, could amount to 'an exchange of contracts'. Here, as part of a separation agreement, Hooper agreed to transfer his share of a house to Sherman in exchange for her paying the mortgage. Due to the building society's delay in approving this arrangement, Hooper tried to get the house sold to someone else, claiming that s.2 was not satisfied so there was no contract preventing him. Two of the judges held that in fact the two letters could be joined together and therefore the section was satisfied: all the terms were in writing and signed by both parties. The third judge dissented, however, on the ground that these letters would have been enough for s.40 but were not sufficient for the clear terms of the new law.

Soon afterwards, in *Commissioner for New Towns* v. *Cooper (GB) Ltd* [1995] Ch 259 (and see [1995] Conv 319) the parties were in dispute as to the terms of payment for building work as part of a complex of various land agreements. They reached an agreement, subject to the approval of the plaintiff's directors, the terms of which were included in an exchange of faxes. One side claimed that this amounted to an 'exchange of contracts' for s.2, but the Court of Appeal of Appeal unanimously held that it did not, because 'exchange of contracts' in the section refers to the exchanging of identical documents, a formal process which indicates the intention to enter a contract:

'. . . where there has been a prior oral agreement, there is only an "exchange of contracts" when documents are exchanged which set out or incorporate all of the terms which have been agreed and when, crucially, those documents are intended, by virtue of their exchange, to bring about a contract to which section 2 applies.' (Evans LJ at p. 295)

The Court decided that *Hooper* v. *Sherman* was not binding as the facts were different in this case.

In the third case, *Firstpost Homes* v. *Johnson* ([1994] 4 All ER 355, the owner of farm land orally agreed to sell it to the plaintiffs. She sent them a letter containing the orally agreed terms which had the plaintiff's name typed on it as addressee and also her name typed but without her signature, paper-clipped to a plan of the land. The plaintiff signed the plan, and returned it to the seller, who signed her name above the plaintiff's signature on the plan and dated it. The seller then died, and the plaintiff sought to enforce the 'contract' but the personal representatives claimed there was no contract because s.2 was not satisfied.

On appeal it was held that the two documents could not be joined as one since the plan – the only signed document – did not 'incorporate' the letter just by being in the same envelope with a paper clip. Further, there was no indication in the letter that there was an intention to enter a contract and the typed names on the letter did not amount to signatures. The judges thus refused to follow the old cases on s.40 which suggested that this could be enough; indeed, Peter Gibson LJ remarked that he did not think it right to 'encumber the new Act with so much ancient baggage', suggesting that s.2 should be read in its own, radical, terms. Perhaps this indicates that in future, the courts will prefer to adopt the direct interpretation of 'exchange of contracts' in the *Firstpost* case, rejecting the softer approach in *Hooper* v. *Sherman*.

S.2 poses problems for conveyancers since, as is clear from the cases above, conveyancing is not always as tidy an operation as the section suggests and contractual terms are often agreed and added over a period of time. The Law Commission which preceded the 1989 Act suggested that the solution to this gradual agreement of terms could lie in the doctrine of 'collateral contracts' (contracts 'on the side'):

> 'A collateral contract is, as its name suggests, a separate contract which is in some way related to the main contract. It must be a true contract, that is, there must be an agreement supported by consideration and it must be intended to be binding. Often the consideration will be that, without the promise contained in the collateral contract, a party would not enter into the principal contract . . . The collateral contract seems to us to be a useful conceptual tool to assist in analysing what may be a complicated situation.' (para. 5.8)

This is what happened in *Record* v. *Bell* [1991] 1 WLR 853. Here contracts had been signed but then an additional term was agreed in another document. In this second document the seller, Record, promised that there were no unforeseen burdens in the land register (this was necessary because of delays in the registry). After this the buyer, Bell, then changed his mind about buying the house, and argued that there was no contract under s.2 since not all the terms were written either in one document or incorporated in one document: that is, the second document did not refer back to the first one. The seller, however, claimed that the additional term was a collateral contract and asked for specific performance of the original agreement of sale.

Judge Baker QC held that the additional term was indeed a collateral contract; there was an original contract for sale and an additional one, under which the buyer had effectively agreed to complete the original contract in exchange for the seller's extra promise. This was therefore not a case where the writing failed the s.2 test, and Bell was bound to complete his purchase (and see R. J. Smith 108 LQR (1991) 217). Under the old law too, Bell would probably (depending on the operation of 'subject to contract') have been liable to complete the contract.

The question of terms not included in the exchanged documents has also arisen in two more recent cases. In *Robert Leonard Developments Ltd* v. *Wright* [1994] March 23 contracts were exchanged for the sale of a show flat, but the contracts omitted the term that the furnishings would be included in the sale (they were not fixtures, see 1.4 above). It was held by the Court of Appeal that the exchange of contracts did not satisfy s.2 since an essential term had been omitted, and therefore, it would appear, there was no contract. However, the Court agreed that the document could be rectified to include the term, thus satisfying the statute.

This convenient escape from the rigours of s.2 was not available in the the second case, *McCausland* v. *Duncan Lawrie Ltd* [1996] June 6 Lexis. Here the exchanged contracts set completion of the contract for a Sunday, and then re-arranged it for the preceding Friday by an exchange of letters by the solicitors. There was no completion, and it was held by the Court of Appeal, allowing the appeal, that s.2 was not satisfied here and there was therefore no contract. The completion date was an essential term and it was fatal to the 'contract' that it had not been included in the exchanged documents:

'The choice lies between permitting a [later, oral] variation, however fundamental, to be made without any formality at all and requiring it to satisfy s.2. In my view it is evident that Parliament intended the latter. There would be little point in requiring that the original contract comply with s.2 if it might be varied wholly informally.' (Morritt LJ)

Remedies

If s.2 is satisfied, then the buyer or the seller will be entitled to specific performance if the other defaults. If the plaintiff, however, does not come with clean hands, the remedy may be denied. Also, wherever a person is entitled to specific performance, the court may award damages instead if it would be fairer.

If s.2 is not satisfied, there is no contract and there can be no contractual remedy. There might be a claim for the equitable remedy of rectification to correct the writing as in *Robert Leonard Developments* above. Other remedies may also be available, as the 1987 Law Commission noted, and the most obvious is proprietary estoppel (see 2.6 below). Alternative remedies may include suing for a lost deposit under quasi-contract, or suing for deceit in tort.

Where writing is not necessary

S.2(5) of the 1989 Act lists certain contracts which do not need to be made in writing:

1   contracts to grant three year, or shorter, leases (which by s.54(2) Law of Property Act 1925 can be legal without a deed: see 2.7 below); and
2   contracts made in a public auction (because the public nature of the agreement is sufficient evidence); and
3   contracts regulated under the Financial Services Act 1986 (which governs investments such as shares, which may include interests in land).

The rule that there is no need for writing for a contract for a short lease is a new one (in s.2(5) of the 1989 Act), to tidy up the old law which was illogical since s.40(1) had required written evidence of a contract for a lease which was itself legal by s.54(2) even if created orally.

In addition, s.2 has no effect on the creation or operation of 'resulting, implied or constructive trusts' (see below, 11.4). This provision was unnecessary under s.40 which relied on part performance to mitigate the writing rule, but the new, stricter rule will have to be mitigated in some cases by the creation of a constructive trust through proprietary estoppel (see 2.6 below).

2.5   The Intervention of Equity

Within ten years of the Statute of Frauds 1677, it was apparent that, far from preventing fraud, it merely provided a different loophole for liars. Whereas before 1677 a rogue could unfairly force a sale by buying witnesses to give false evidence of an oral contract, after that date he could unfairly escape a contract if there was no writing to satisfy the statute. Therefore the court of equity provided a remedy on the basis of the maxim, '*equity will not allow a statute to be made an instrument of fraud*'.

Equity would accept evidence that the plaintiff had performed a part of (or had done some other act showing the existence of) the unwritten contract and that the defendant knew of this. This 'part performance' of the contract by the plaintiff enabled the court of equity to enforce it although there was nothing in writing to satisfy the statute, for otherwise the defendant would be using the statutory rule in order to cheat. This equitable doctrine was expressly preserved in 1925 by s.40(2) Law of

Property Act but is repealed by the 1989 Act; there can be no part performance of a non-existent contract.

An uncontroversial example of the old doctrine was *Rawlinson* v. *Ames* [1925] 24 Ch 96. Mrs Rawlinson was converting a large house into flats and Miss Ames orally agreed to buy a 21-year lease of one of them. She sent a letter which would have been sufficient for s.40(1) except that it did not specify the starting date of the lease. Rawlinson carried out Ames's substantial and detailed construction and decoration requirements but then Ames changed her mind. The construction and decoration at her request were held to be acts of part performance by Rawlinson who was therefore entitled to an order of specific performance to enforce the contract.

Generally, however, the courts had a great deal of difficulty with the doctrine and the Law Commission had no hesitation in recommending its abolition. They were clear that the existing equitable doctrine of proprietory estoppel could supplement s.2 to prevent rogues taking unfair advantages.

2.6   The New Law: The Extension of 'Proprietary Estoppel'

The essence of proprietary estoppel is that the court stops someone enforcing a legal right to land because, if he were to exercise his legal rights, it would be unfair to the plaintiff. In relation to s.2, the argument would be that, although there is no contract because of the absence of the signed document, nevertheless for reasons of conscience one party should be prevented from relying on their legal rights. For example, in the *McCausland* case (2.4 above), there was no contract because of the informal variation of the completion date, but the question of estoppel was left open.

Although the Law Commission expected part performance to be replaced by proprietary estoppel, they did not envisage frequent resort to equity:

'In putting forward the present recommendation we rely greatly on the principle, recognised even by equity, that "certainty is the father of right and the mother of justice".' (Law Commission No. 164 (1987), para. 4.13)

An advantage of the new law is that all the old controversial cases on part performance can now be forgotten. However, the doctrine of estoppel is not always clear; indeed, it sometimes seems as though estoppel is becoming the modern resort of lawyers with difficult cases. This is probably because of the attractiveness of its simple moral basis, but the case law is by no means as simple: the courts do not override statute without careful consideration, and proprietary estoppel is only granted if certain requirements are fulfilled.

The essence of the doctrine arises, as defined by Snell:

'[when] one (A) is encouraged to act to his detriment by the representations or encouragement of another (O) so that it would be unconscionable for O to insist on his strict legal rights.' (p. 558)

The three separate but interdependent elements are:

> **PROMISE**
> **RELIANCE**
> **DETRIMENT**

Inwards v. *Baker* [1965] 2 QB 29 provides an example. A father encouraged his son to build a bungalow on the father's land, promising him that it would be his (the son's) own. The son built the bungalow but when the father died his heirs claimed the land. The Court of Appeal held that the father would have been estopped from going back on his promise, since the son had acted in reliance on it, and the heirs were in the same position as the father. The son kept his home. Clearly, proprietary estoppel might have provided a remedy in *Rawlinson* v. *Ames* (2.5 above); Ames made a promise to buy the land and stood by while Rawlinson acted to her detriment in relying on the promise.

The requirements of proprietary estoppel have changed over the years, from a fairly strict set of requirements (the 'five points' of *Wilmott* v. *Barber* (1880) 15 Ch D 96) to the more flexible modern approach of Oliver J in *Taylors Fashions Ltd* v. *Liverpool Victoria Trustees Co Ltd* [1982] 1 QB 133:

'I am not at all convinced that it is desirable or possible to lay down hard and fast rules . . . [T]he more recent cases indicate, in my judgment, that the application of the . . . principle . . . requires a very much broader approach which is directed rather at ascertaining whether, in particular individual circumstances, it would be unconscionable for a party to be permitted to deny that which, knowingly or unknowingly, he has allowed or encouraged another to assume to his detriment than to inquiring whether the circumstances can be fitted within the confines of some preconceived formula serving as a universal yardstick for every form of unconscionable behaviour.' (pp. 149, 151–2; approved by the Privy Council in *Lim Teng Huan* v. *Ang Swee Chuan* [1992] 1 WLR 113)

✳The question therefore is whether it would be 'unconscionable' if someone were to go back on their assertion or encouragement. In the *Taylors Fashions* case two tenants had claimed that their landlord stood by while they spent large sums in reliance on the expectation that they had the right to renew the leases. No one knew until later that the right to renew was void because of the Land Charges Act (see below, 9.3). Oliver J held that it would be 'conscionable' for the landlord to refuse to renew the first tenant's lease because it was not clear that the tenant really had relied on any assertion by the landlord when he installed the lift 18 years before; it was more likely that he had relied on his own solicitor's statement that the lease was renewable. However, the landlord had directly encouraged the second tenant to spend money in reliance on the mistaken belief concerning the option to renew. As regards the second tenant, therefore, the landlord was estopped from denying the tenant's right to renew the lease.

Most reported cases concern family disputes; the following three indicate the kind of problems faced by the courts when people make oral agreements, and the solutions the courts find for them. In the first, *Re Basham (decd)* [1986] 1 WLR 1498 a daughter successfully claimed proprietary estoppel against her step-father's estate. He had promised her that if she looked after him he would leave the house, formerly her mother's, to her. In reliance on his promise, over many years she had cooked for him, maintained the house, taken legal action for him in relation to a boundary dispute and her husband had refused a better job elsewhere. It would therefore be unconscionable for him to deny his promise. As a result, his heirs were estopped from relying on their legal right to inherit.

Another case, *Matharu* v. *Matharu* [1994] 2 FLR 597 concerned a dispute within an extended family. A daughter-in-law relied on the assurance of her husband (who represented her father-in-law, owner of the house) that the house was as much hers as his and consequently abandoned her divorce proceedings and spent money on the property. The father-in-law had known of this reliance. The Court of Appeal held that she had succeeded in her claim to a share of the house by proprietory estoppel and refused to grant a possession order to the father-in-law (and see 13.6 below).

In the third case, *Wayling* v. *Jones* (1993) 69 P & CR 170 (and see Davis (1995) Conv 409), two men cohabited for about 16 years, and the plaintiff worked for very little payment in his (much older) friend's business on the understanding that he would receive some of the property on his friend's death. At first instance, the plaintiff failed because, although he had proved the detriment and assurance, he had not proved reliance; the judge found that there were other reasons for his contribution to his friend's businesses, such as their mutual affection. The Court of Appeal allowed the appeal on the basis that the judge had come to the wrong decision on the evidence given by the plaintiff in the case: the promises do not have to be the sole inducement for the detriment. Here, since the promised land had already been disposed of, the plaintiff was awarded the value of the land in compensation.

The remedy for proprietary estoppel is not limited to specific performance and/or damages but will vary with the circumstances. In some cases, such as *Basham*, the claimant won the fee simple, but others, like *Matharu*, have merely won the right to remain on the land until death. The issue for the court is now 'how best to satisfy the equity' and the court will order whichever remedy is fair. Often, a constructive trust is imposed (see 11.5 below).

2.7   Transfer of the Legal Interest

The deed

As mentioned already, a deed is normally necessary to transfer a legal estate or interest. (When the land is registered the deed is a Land Transfer form from the land registry.) S.52(1) LPA states:

'All conveyances or land or of any interest therein are void for the purpose of conveying or creating a legal estate unless made by deed.'

Before 31 July 1990, a deed was a document that was 'signed, sealed and delivered'. Now, the ancient requirement for a seal is replaced by the need for a witness. Under s.1 Law of Property (Miscellaneous Provisions) Act 1989, a deed is defined as:

---

1   A DOCUMENT WHICH MAKES CLEAR ON ITS FACE THAT IT IS A DEED;
2   SIGNED AND WITNESSED;
3   DELIVERED.

Although a deed is not required to *create* a short lease under s.54(2) LPA, a deed is always necessary to *assign* (that is, transfer) a legal lease.

This was restated in *Crago* v. *Julian* [1992] 1 All ER 744 where a husband transferred his weekly tenancy to his wife when their marriage ended. Ten years later, the landlady discovered this and sought possession against the wife. The husband's legal tenancy was not statutorily protected because he was not living there, and the wife had no legal tenancy, so the landlady won. (The wife might have had some right in estoppel against her husband, but this would not have affected the landlady who had not made any promise to her at any stage.)

Signature and witnessing
The signature must be by the person who is 'executing' (that is, making) the deed, and in this case the signature must be in the presence of one witness who also signs. Alternatively, the deed can be signed 'at his direction and in his presence' by another person, and in this case there must be two witnesses present who also sign the deed.

Delivery
A deed is 'delivered' when the 'grantor' (the person executing the deed) does or says something to 'adopt the deed as his own'. In practice, solicitors usually treat a deed as delivered at the moment they add a date to a document which has already been signed and witnessed; this is said to show that they adopt it.

Where a deed is not needed

There are a number of circumstances where a legal interest can be obtained without a deed. These are:

1 *short leases* (s.54(2) LPA, and see 2.4 above): a lease is legal without *any* formality (even writing) if it does not exceed three years, the tenant moves in straight away (that is, the lease 'takes effect in possession') and it is at a market rent. There is no need for any special formality for a short lease where the tenant is in possession and is paying rent because there is little risk that a buyer would be caught out by this interest in the land – the tenant would be present on the property. However, somewhat illogically, a deed is still needed to *transfer* any tenancy (even a weekly one) at law, as shown in *Crago* v. *Julian* (above).
2 *long use*: using someone else's land for a minimum of 12 years can ensure that the user cannot be defeated by anyone; effectively, he becomes a legal owner (see Chapter 3). Also, long use of an easement

or profit (for example, a right of way or a right to fish) can create a
legal right (see below, 7.5).

3   *personal representatives' assent* (s.36(1) AEA 1925): if a landowner dies,
his land automatically goes to ('vests in') his legal representatives.
When they have completed their administration of the estate, they
transfer the land to the heir(s). Writing, but no deed, is necessary to do
this; it is called an 'assent'.

4   *trustee in bankruptcy's disclaimer*: where a landowner goes bankrupt,
the land automatically vests in his trustee in bankruptcy. If the land is
more trouble than it is worth (for example, a lease with a high rent) the
trustee can disclaim it in writing; a deed is not necessary.

5   *court order*: a court can order land to be transferred.

The effect of a deed

The deed not only transfers the interest but also any advantages which
belong to the land, unless the parties show that they intend otherwise; s.62
LPA states:

> 'A conveyance of land shall be deemed to include and shall by virtue of
> this Act operate to convey, with the land, all buildings, erections,
> fixtures, commons, hedges, ditches, fences, ways, waters, watercourses,
> liberties, privileges, easements, rights, and advantages whatsoever,
> appertaining or reputed to appertain to the land, or any part thereof,
> or, at the time of conveyance, demised, occupied, or enjoyed with, or
> reputed or known as part or parcel of, or appurtenant to, the land or
> any part thereof.'

In addition, by s.76 LPA, the use of a deed ensures that the buyer
will also automatically get the benefit of any promises made about the
title to his predecessor. Ss.78 and 79 ensure that he will automatically
have the right to enforce, and will be bound by, any valid restrictive
covenant over the land. (These four sections are some of the 'wordsaving
provisions' mentioned in 1.2 above. There is more about them in
Chapters 3, 5, 7 and 8.)

2.8   Comment

The rules relating to the buying and selling of interests in land are, in
general, formalistic and detailed, but, in an area where the law is seeking
to achieve a simple resolution of complicated and dynamic human

relationships, this is hardly surprising. Recent cases on s.2 suggest that not all the problems have been solved by the new law, but the judges do now seem to be recognising that it is a radical departure from the old s.40 LPA, and are beginning to enforce it more strictly.

In the compromise between the need for a clear rule, and the need to make sure people do not unfairly take advantage of one another, there is clearly emerging a tendency towards a more ruthless simplicity, but this may change according to the state of the property market, and according to the attitude adopted towards s.2's flexible friend, proprietory estoppel. In any event, despite the nature of the rules, many thousands of interests in land are successfully conveyed each year; the state of the property market is far more important to most non-lawyers than the technical rules.

In the future, the law will increasingly have to come to terms with developments in new technology. Already, faxes and computer communications are the subject of new rules of contract law and these will also have their effect on the conveyancing of land. In the conveyancer's office of the twenty-first century, paper may be obsolete, and so would be the 1989 Act.

Summary

1 The normal procedure for buying and selling interests in land is governed by rules relating to the need for formality in land contracts, by writing and by deeds, and is supplemented by equity.
2 Since 1989, as soon as there is a contract for the sale of an interest in land, the buyer effectively becomes the equitable owner of the land, provided the discretionary remedy of specific performance is available.
3 In order for there to be a contract for the sale of an interest in land, normally all the terms must be in writing and signed by both sides.
4 If there is no contract under statute, equity may nevertheless enforce the 'agreement' under the doctrine of proprietary estoppel if it would be unconscionable for the defendant to deny that he made a promise to transfer the interest, provided that the plaintiff acted to his detriment in reliance on the promise.
5 A deed, signed, witnessed and delivered, is now normally necessary to create or transfer a legal interest in land. It also transfers benefits attached to the land.
6 Some legal leases not exceeding three years (or a contract to grant one) may be created, but not assigned, without any formality.

Exercises

1 When did ss.1 and 2 Law of Property (Miscellaneous Provisions) Act 1989 come into effect? Why does it matter?

2 When is an equitable interest in land transferred, and why?
3 What is necessary today for proprietary estoppel?
4 What is a deed? Why is the definition significant?
5 William owned the freehold of a house. Last September, he was short of money so when his friend Debbie arrived from Australia he agreed that she could have a tenancy of the ground floor of the house for £100 per week.

Six months later, still short of cash, he advertised the house for sale for £100 000. Ajay arrived and looked around the house. That evening he telephoned William and offered £90 000 if certain repairs, costing about £10 000, were done. William agreed, and has carried out all the repairs. Ajay has now decided not to buy the house because prices have fallen.

Advise all the parties.

3 Adverse Possession

3.1 Introduction

The last chapter explored the rules governing the formal transfer of interests in land, and was concerned with land which clearly belonged to a particular person. This chapter investigates the issues which arise when it is not clear to whom land belongs because the apparent owner has not been in possession for many years. Nowadays a typical example would concern a narrow strip of land between two houses, where one householder has not taken care of her boundaries and the other has encroached.

Adverse possession is part of the general law of limitation of actions, now contained in the Limitation Act 1980, and there is special provision for adverse possession in registered land (see below, 10.5 and 10.8). The basic principle is straightforward and quickly grasped: through adverse possession, a person can effectively become the legal owner of land solely because of her occupation of it. The 'real' owner cannot bring an action against the user so, after (usually) twelve years, a person using land may have a better title to it than anyone else simply because no one can remove her. Her title may eventually 'ripen' into a fee simple or registered title and she will be able to sell it like any other property.

The statute provides the structure of the rules, but the cases are of great importance because the essence of adverse possession is a question of fact: one has to examine very carefully all the details of each individual story in order to decide whether a person has adversely possessed the land for the limitation period. The cases also help in grasping the way the judges see the issues: they are often dealing with disputes between neighbours (almost as difficult as family arguments), and the various demands of public policy may conflict.

3.2 The Basic Issues

The fundamental reason for the rule that court cases may not be brought after a certain length of time ('time-barred') is that, in the interest of certainty and the market in land, there must be an end to 'stale claims'. In addition, deeds can get lost and people can forget what they own, but the land itself remains. If the law did not provide for cases where there is no formal proof of title, areas of land would be 'outside the law' and unmarketable. Adverse possession thus provides a way of curing defective titles for, after the required period of possession, the squatter cannot be evicted by the 'paper owner'.

The law of adverse possession inevitably causes problems for people who think that legal title to land – private property, for which the owner has probably 'paid good money' – ought to be protected by the law, come what may. However, in real life few titles to land are perfect. Innumerable difficulties arise when a title needs to be traced to its origin. In *Johnston* v. *O'Neill* [1911] AC 581, a case involving eel-fishing rights, title to land in Northern Ireland had to be traced back to 1605. Lord Macnaghten said:

> 'My Lords, I will not weary you by recapitulating or reviewing what has been called the paper title . . . Infinite labour and excellent learning have been expended on the law relating to grants from the Crown, on patents, on commissions, and on inquisitions . . . I must say I am rather surprised to find the title as complete as it is. At the same time, I have no doubt that lawyers less learned than those to whom we have had the pleasure of listening would not have much difficulty in picking holes in it here and there, either because there may be something missing which cannot be supplied after the lapse of centuries, or because it is not proved that formalities, adjudged necessary in other cases, have been duly observed in this.' (p. 580)

It is normally sufficient to prove a good title (the 'root of title') going back only fifteen years to satisfy a purchaser of land (s.23 Law of Property Act 1969, and see M. Dockray (1985) 49 Conv 272). However, if it were not for adverse possession, many pieces of land would be waste, forgotten by the paper owner and worthless to anyone else.

It is unusual to see Parliament and the judges helping a person who in some lights appears to be a common thief, but there are good reasons to do so. The need to end stale claims and the inadequacy of formal titles may be the main practical reasons, but there is also the ethical issue of the neglectful owner belatedly trying to evict an industrious and careful squatter. Land is, after all, a national resource and, if the paper owner has so little interest in her land that she cannot be bothered even to walk around it once in twelve years, should the law protect her rights against someone who has invested labour in improving the land? Clearly, protecting private ownership is only one of the policy considerations.

The case of *Williams* v. *Usherwood* (1982) 43 P & CR 235 illustrates the interplay of the various policies behind the law. Here, adjoining suburban houses, which were built in 1934, shared a drive; the legal arrangement was that each owner had title to the half running alongside her house and an easement over (a right to use) the other's half. For convenience, the fence between the houses was built close to Number 33, and it therefore looked as if the drive belonged to Number 31. As it happened, the owner of Number 33 never did use the drive and, from 1952, never even had access to her strip. The people who bought Number 31 in 1962 used it for parking their cars and paved it.

In 1977, the Williams family moved into Number 33 and decided to pursue their apparent legal right, as the 'paper owner', to half the width of the drive. They lost. The owners of Number 31 successfully argued adverse possession (by earlier owners of the house) so that the Williams could not enforce any remedy against them. In this case, the land was registered and therefore it was necessary for the judge also to order that the Land Register should be corrected to show the owners of Number 31 as owners of the whole drive (see 10.8 below).

The arguments in favour of the Williams family are that they were the legal owners of the strip of land – the original title deeds stated it clearly – and they ought therefore to be entitled to legal protection against trespassers. From their point of view, the law of limitation of actions is a 'cheat's charter' (McCormick (1986) 50 Conv 434). On the other hand, the earlier owners of that house 'slept on their rights'; should the Williams family, decades later, be allowed to pursue such an old claim? The owners of Number 33 had neglected the land; the owners of Number 31 had repaved it, 'at some expense, which went beyond any normal maintenance requirements'. Most people agree that the Court of Appeal came to a sensible decision here.

3.3   The Basic Rules

The period

S.15 (1) Limitation Act 1980 provides:

> 'No action shall be brought by any person to recover any land after the expiration of twelve years from the date on which the right of action accrued to him, or, if it first accrued to some other person through whom he claims, to that person.'

The section states clearly that the paper owner cannot bring an action if twelve years have passed since the right to do so arose: that is, since the squatter – by definition, a trespasser – moved onto the land. The statute does not operate to transfer the paper owner's title to the adverse possessor but, by refusing any remedy, merely ensures that no one can remove her.

By s.38 Limitation Act, 'land' means more than just the fee simple absolute in possession; it includes, for example, the equitable fee simple and also legal and equitable leases (see 3.5 below). It is possible therefore to obtain title to a long lease as well as to freehold land.

There are special rules for adversely possessing Crown land and for special classes, such as between trustees and their beneficiaries (s.21 Limitation Act). In *Pollard* v. *Jackson* [1994] 67 P & CR 327, the heir of a freeholder returned from Canada to claim her inheritance – fifteen years after the death of her father. She found that the tenant of the ground floor flat in the house had taken over the whole of the house when the old man, who lived upstairs, had died, and was claiming adverse possession of it. In her claim for possession, she argued, amongst other things, that the tenant had become a constructive trustee (see 11.5 below) of the freehold since he knew that the land must, from the time of the death, be held on trust. As a constructive trustee, she said, he could not deny her beneficial right to possession of the land. However, the Court of Appeal rejected this because it would mean that in any case where a paper owner died during the twelve year period, and the squatter knew of the death, adverse possession would be impossible. The tenant therefore won the case.

It is important to remember that, as the squatter herself is not a 'purchaser' of land, she is, like someone who simply inherits land, bound by *all* earlier interests in the land, whether they are legal or equitable, and whether or not they were registered or she had notice of them.

Continuous possession

The squatter must prove that, for at least twelve years, the paper owner has been continuously dispossessed: there must not have been any 'interruptions'. If the use has been for an occasional activity, such as parking a car, this may rather give rise to a claim for an easement by long use (see 7.5 below).

In *Edginton* v. *Clark* [1967] 1 QB 367, the claimant had occupied bombed land in the East End of London for about seven years and then offered to buy it from the owner. No sale followed and, after a further ten years, he claimed adverse possession. It was held that the offer to buy was an acknowledgment of the owner's title and that therefore the possession was interrupted. Since there was not twelve years' continuous dispossession the paper owner won.

No concealment or fraud

In addition, under s.32 of the Act, the adverse possessor must prove that she did not deliberately conceal her activities or keep her possession through fraud. If there is any deception, the twelve years starts to run from the date when the paper owner 'could with reasonable diligence have discovered it'. Concealment was argued in *Rains* v. *Buxton* (1880) XIV Ch D 537; the adverse possessor had occupied an underground cellar, and the paper owner – 60 years later – said that the possession had been concealed. However, as the door to the cellar was clearly visible from the basement area and was used without secrecy, this argument was rejected. The squatter here obtained title to a layer of the land – the cellar – leaving the paper owner's rights above (and below) undisturbed.

A succession of squatters

The twelve years' adverse possession need not have been by one squatter. In *Williams* v. *Usherwood* (1982) (see 3.2 above), there were several different owners of Number 31 who, in succession, adversely possessed the land continuously for the period.

A person who succeeds against a paper owner's action for possession might yet be vulnerable to being sued by a previous squatter. If, for example, Joe took possession of Chan's land in 1976, and (without any interruption) Neeta took over the land in 1984, then Chan would find himself without a remedy after 1988. However, Neeta could be sued by Joe, and could not defeat him until 1996. This clearly demonstrates how all titles to land in English law are relative.

As in all legal disputes, the claimant must be careful not to lose her claim in negotiations after the event (see 2.6 above). In *Colchester Borough Council* v. *Smith* [1992] 2 WLR 728 it seemed as if the squatter had gained adverse possession by farming about 15 acres of the council's agricultural land after fifteen years of use (although the council argued that they had given him permission to occupy). Finally, it was agreed in negotiations that the council would lease the land to the claimant if he gave up his claim to adverse possession. The Court of Appeal held that the would-be adverse possessor was estopped from going back on this freely entered agreement.

The possession must be adverse

The most important rules in this area of law concern the nature of the possession by the squatter. Four rules can be identified from the cases:

REQUIREMENTS OF ADVERSE POSSESSION

1 IT MUST BE A REAL POSSESSION of the land, as shown especially by improving the land (for example, paving it or levelling a slope).
2 THE POSSESSION MUST BE ACCOMPANIED BY AN INTENT TO POSSESS, the *animus possidendi;* this is particularly important in cases where the acts of possession are marginal.
3 POSSESSION MUST BE ADVERSE to the paper owner but not necessarily hostile; the owner must have been excluded by the squatter's possession.
4 POSSESSION MUST NOT HAVE BEEN BY PERMISSION.

3.4 Cases on Adverse Possession

These five cases have been selected because together they best illustrate briefly the kinds of problems which may arise and the operation of the rules.

Hayward v. *Chaloner* [1968] 1 QB 107 (CA)

About a quarter of an acre was let to whomever was the rector of a small village, but from 1942 no rent was paid so there were at least twelve years of possession without acknowledgment of the paper owners' title. The rector decided to sell the land as his own and the paper owners decided to fight him; they had failed to collect the rent not because they forgot, but because of 'their loyalty and generosity to the church'. The rector won by a majority decision in the Court of Appeal, although all the judges regretted it:

'The generous indulgence of the plaintiffs and their predecessors in title, loyal churchmen all, having resulted in a free accretion at their expense to the lands of their church, their reward may be in the next world. But in this jurisdiction we can only qualify them for that reward by allowing the [Rector's] appeal.' (Russell LJ, pp. 123–4)

Treloar v. *Nute* [1977] 1 WLR 1295 (CA)

In 1961, the adverse possessor's father bought land adjoining a derelict part of Mrs Treloar's farm. Father and son used this derelict land for grazing; they fenced it in with the father's own land and filled in a ten-foot-wide gulley (that is, they improved the land). After twelve years the son began building a bungalow and Mrs Treloar went to court for a possession order.

The Court of Appeal felt that the acts in this case just about amounted to actual possession: the most influential was the filling-in of the gulley. They quoted with approval Lord O'Hagan in an old case concerning Scottish salmon fishing rights:

> 'As to possession, it must be considered in every case with reference to the peculiar circumstances. The acts, implying possession in one case, may be wholly inadequate to prove it in another. The character and value of the property, the suitable and natural mode of using it, the course of conduct which the proprietor might be expected to follow with a due regard for his own interests – all these things, greatly varying as they must, are to be taken into account.' (*Lord Advocate* v. *Lord Lovat* (1880) v. AC 273)

Here, given that the squatter had possessed the land, it was enough that he did so exclusively and with the necessary intention. Contrary to the earlier decision of the Court of Appeal in *Wallis's Cayton Bay Holiday Camp Ltd* v. *Shellmex and BP Ltd* [1975] QB 94, the Court here held that the squatter did not need to prove that he had inconvenienced or ousted the paper owner in order to show that he did not act under 'an implied licence':

> 'It is not permissible to import . . . a requirement that the owner must be inconvenienced or otherwise affected by that possession. Apart from the cases relating to special purpose no authority has been cited to us which would support the requirement . . . On the contrary, so far as our own experience goes, the typical instance in which a possessory title is treated as having been acquired is that in which a squatter establishes himself upon a piece of land for which the owner has no use. Indeed, if inconvenience to the owner had to be established it would be difficult ever to acquire a possessory title since the owner if inconvenienced would be likely to take proceedings.' (Sir John Pennycuick, p. 102)

The 'implied licence' in *Wallis*'s case was examined by the Law Reform Committee (Cmnd 6923, 1977) and, as a result, the 1980 Act (Schedule 1 para 8(4)) states that there is no *legal* presumption of an implied licence whenever a paper owner has an ultimate purpose for her land. The courts are to find an implied licence only where the *facts* suggest it.

Boosey v. *Davis* (1988) 55 P & CR 83 (CA)

The Booseys claimed that they had gained adverse possession of a strip of waste land, of which the Davis family were registered proprietors. Since 1963, they had cleared the land of bushes and had grazed their goats; they had also replaced a fence. Although they won at first instance, they lost in the Court of Appeal. Slade LJ said:

'The cutting down of the scrub was merely to facilitate the minimal use by the goats – it was not for any wider purpose. Moreover, although in some cases the erection of a fence can be very significant, it seems to me that that was not so here. The fence . . . did not in any event enclose the disputed land.' (p. 87)

Buckingham County Council v. *Moran* [1989] 2 All ER 225 (CA)

From 1971 Moran used as an extension to his garden a patch of land owned by the council; his predecessor had probably done the same since 1967. Moran built a new fence, enclosing the land, and added a new gate and a lock. The council finally noticed him in 1985 and sued for possession. It had originally bought the land to use as a road, so it argued that it had not been dispossessed because impliedly they gave permission to Moran (and his predecessors) to use the land until they needed it themselves. The court took the opportunity to explain its view as to the modern importance of the 'implied licence':

'If in any given case the land in dispute is unbuilt land and the squatter is aware that the owner, while having no present use for it, has a purpose in mind for its use in the future, the court is likely to require very clear evidence before it can be satisfied that the squatter who claims a possessory title has not only established factual possession of the land, but also the requisite intention to exclude the world at large, including the owner with the paper title . . . In the absence of clear evidence of this nature, the court is likely to infer that the squatter neither had nor had claimed any intention of asserting a right to the possession of the land.' (Slade LJ, p. 235)

The Court of Appeal also further defined the intention necessary for a squatter to succeed as:

'an intention *for the time being* to possess the land to the exclusion of all other persons, including the owner with the paper title'. (at p. 278)

Moran succeeded. This was very much a case on the margins, and Moran was lucky to have able counsel on his side against the council.

East Sussex County Council v. *Miller* (26 April) (CA)

The council owned a shop and the flat above; eventually, they intended to demolish it in order to extend what was then Brighton Polytechnic. Over fourteen years, a succession of squatters lived in the flat. They changed the locks and repaired the premises; they paid the rates (local taxes) and offered to pay rent but the council refused to give them the status of tenants.

At first instance and in the Court of Appeal the council won its order for possession. As far as comparison with *Moran* above is concerned, Farquharson LJ said that the situation is different with a different kind of land: a suburban garden is not the same as a flat 'in a metropolitan context such as one finds in Brighton'. The main difference between the cases is that here the squatters seemed really to have seen themselves as occupying the flat until the council needed it, *with the council's permission*. In *Moran* the successful adverse possessor saw himself as occupying *without permission*, even if only until the council built the road.

3.5 Leases

The rules about leases and adverse possession are complex, and only brief details are given here.

If a person takes possession of land when it has been leased, the possession is adverse to the tenant; that is, it is the tenant who loses her interest in the land, not the landlady. This is because the tenant, not the landlady, is entitled to possession; the landlady is only entitled to the rent. The landlady will lose her right to the land against the tenant only when a period of twelve years has expired since the lease ended. During the lease itself, a squatter is in the same position as the paper tenant and her right to possession must end when the lease ends.

A tenant cannot adversely possess against her landlady during the lease because a tenant is not allowed to deny her landlady's title. A tenant who remains in possession without permission for twelve years after the lease has ended may, however, succeed as in *Hayward* v. *Chaloner* (1967) (see above). However, if a person in possession of leased land is actually a licensee, then there can be no adverse possession (see *Onyx (UK) Ltd* v. *Beard* [1996] EGCS 55, 5.4 below).

There have recently been several cases on adverse possession of leased land. In *Price* v. *Hartley* [1996] EGCS 74 a weekly tenant stopped paying rent in 1971 and never acknowledged the paper owner's title after 1973 but remained in occupation and improved the property – probably spending more on it than he would have paid in rent. The former tenant's heir successfully claimed adverse possession against a new paper owner of the freehold in 1996. In *Lodge* v. *Wakefield* MDC [1996] EGCS 136 the question of a tenant's intention arose. In line with *Moran*, above, the Court of Appeal held that a tenant can gain adverse possession so long as she 'intends to possess' the land, even if she actually believes during the limitation period that she is only a tenant.

Where a tenant adversely occupies neighbouring land during her lease, she may only get a leasehold title to it; when the lease ends, any rights arising from adverse possession may have to be surrendered with the lease.

If a tenant is dispossessed by a squatter, the tenant can only claim possession within the twelve years while the lease continues; if the lease ends, so do the tenant's rights to possession. However, in *Chung Ping Kwan* v. *Lam Island Development Co Ltd* [1996] 3 WLR 448) the Privy Council held that a tenant who had the right to renew the lease could do so and thereby extend the period within which an action for possession could be brought. In such a case, the tenant must renew the lease within the limitation period, that is, within 12 years (in Hong Kong, 20 years) of the end of the original lease.

Where land has been leased and a person who is not the lessor receives the rent, this can amount to adverse possession of the freehold. This line of argument failed in *Pulleyn* v. *Hall Aggregates (Thames Valley) Ltd* (1992) 65 P & CR 276, where the claimant adverse possessor had merely received gifts at Christmas from the occupier of the land. The Court of Appeal said that it would be very difficult ever to prove adverse possession in circumstances like these where the land was occupied by a third party with the permission of the paper owner.

3.6   Rights against Trespassers

Until the squatter has successfully completed the limitation period, without interruptions, she can be dispossessed as a trespasser. The paper owner can do-it-herself, or go to court for an order for possession: a special fast procedure is available.

Merely entering land as a trespasser can in some circumstances be a crime. For example, the Criminal Law Act 1977 created several crimes of trespass, including the offence of failing to leave *premises* when required to by the resident owner who has been displaced (s.7). S.39 Public Order Act 1986 (directed against 'New Age' travellers) created the crime of failing to leave *land* after a proper direction to do so.

3.7   Comment

The law of adverse possession further demonstrates land's permanence, its uniqueness and its value. The difficulty in identifying what can amount to possession also illustrates the character of land as property, for physical control requires frequent attention. It also illustrates that no title is sacred, that all titles to land under English law are relative for, unlike legal systems based on Roman law, there is no theoretical concept of title as 'dominium'; an English court simply assists the stronger of the two parties in the case before it.

Finally, the study of adverse possession demonstrates again that an understanding of one part of land law requires a knowledge of many other areas. To grasp fully the rules relating to adverse possession, it is also necessary to have grasped rules relating to easements, estoppel, trusts and leases.

Summary

1 Adverse possession allows a weak title to be cured as time passes and prevents ancient claims being revived.
2 Twelve years' unconcealed adverse possession, without interruptions, prevents the paper owner repossessing the land.
3 The squatter's possession must be real, adverse, with intent and without permission.
4 Each case on adverse possession is decided on its own facts.

Exercises

1 What may a land owner do to get rid of a trespasser?
2 What intention is required by an adverse possessor?
3 In what ways is the nature of the piece of land relevant to an adverse possession dispute?
4 When may an apparently successful adverse possessor lose the land?
5 Olwen owns a 300-year lease in Animal Farm, the registered proprietor of which is a pension company called Trusties. At one corner of the farm there lies a small triangle of woodland of about one-third of an acre. Here Kate, an eccentric old woman, lives in a barrel with her tame goat, Peter, who finds his food in the wood. They have lived there since the Falklands War. She moved into the barrel after the death of Mumtaz, who had lived there, he had claimed, since well before 1960. Mumtaz had originally been a weekly tenant but had never paid rent after the first week.

Olwen has just been offered an excellent price for her lease, if she can deliver vacant possession within a month. She wishes to sell but, on being asked to leave, Kate refused. Olwen claims that, although she never gave permission for anyone to live there, she did not really mind as it was so far from the house. She had no particular use for the woodland although, if she could have got a grant, she would have cut down the trees and erected battery hen units. Kate says that it is her woodland now and points out that her boundary was marked out by large boulders and electric cable (hung between the trees) by Mumtaz. She claims that Olwen has not been allowed in the woodland for years and years.

In an action for possession, who will win? Who should win?

The Estates and Interests

Part II

The Estates and Interests

4   Freehold Land

4.1   Introduction

In English land law, the 'biggest and best' way of owning land is to own the 'freehold estate'. At this point, the ancient historical roots of modern English land law show through the ground: the origins of freehold land can take lawyers straight back to the conquest of England by William of Normandy in 1066. In theory, all the land in England and Wales is still owned by the Crown, with individuals holding interests in the Queen's land.

There used to be many different legal estates, with different rules about inheritance and transfer, but only two of these remain: *freehold* is a holding 'for ever', and *leasehold* is a holding 'for a fixed time'. Because of the reforms of 1925, the legal freehold estate is the basic concept of land ownership but, in registered land, the 'registered proprietor' holds a new kind title, the statutory equivalent of the legal freehold (see 10.3 below). The Law Commission in 1987 proposed a new estate in land called *commonhold*. This would be a land ownership intermediate between freehold and leasehold for buildings in which separate parts, such as flats, are owned by different people (see below 5.11).

4.2   Definition of the Freehold Estate

The fee simple is the only surviving legal freehold estate; its proper name is *fee simple absolute in possession*. Each of these words has a particular significance.

Fee: This word comes from 'fief' (*feudum* in Latin), the basic concept of the feudal system. A fee had by the sixteenth century come to be recognised as an estate which could be inherited because it did not automatically return to the feudal landlord when the tenant died.

Fee simple: The fee is 'simple' because it does not suffer from the complications of the other fee, the fee tail or 'entail', which has to go to a particular kind of heir when the owner dies. The fee simple can be inherited by anyone the owner wished, but the fee tail has to pass to a direct descendant (child, grandchild and so on), and it could be restricted to, for example, a male child (a 'tail male').

Fee simple absolute: The word 'absolute' is used to distinguish this fee simple from others which are limited in some way. For example, there is a 'fee simple upon condition'; an example is where a mother gives land to her son *but if* he marries a solicitor, the land will go to his cousin. This must be distinguished from the 'determinable fee simple', which is created by words such as '*until* he marries a solicitor': a very subtle difference. It is important because, although in 1925 only the fee simple absolute could be a legal estate (s.1(1) LPA, see 1.5 above), a special exception was made in 1926 for conditional fee simples: these can now be legal, but the other limited fee simples (including determinable fees) have to be equitable.

Fee simple absolute in possession: All interests in land can be 'in possession', 'in remainder' or 'in reversion'. In possession means that the owner is entitled to enjoy the interest (occupy the land or collect the rent and so on) *now*; the other two mean that the owner will have the right to enjoy the interest after another interest (for example, an interest for life) has ended. In the example above therefore, the son has a conditional fee simple in possession, and the cousin has a fee simple absolute in *remainder*. However, if it were settled that the land was to go back to the mother if the son did the unthinkable, the mother would have a fee simple absolute in *reversion*.

4.3   Legal and Equitable Freeholds

Out of all the possibilities raised in the sections above, only the fee simple absolute in possession can be a legal estate (subject to the exception for conditional fees), because of s.1 LPA (see 1.5 above). The fee tail therefore can only be equitable, held behind a trust.

4.4   The Rights of the Freeholder

In theory at common law the owner can do whatever he likes with his land: he owns everything under, above and on his land, down to the centre of the earth and up to outer space (of which there is no agreed definition, but which probably starts 100 km above sea level: see He Qizhi (1982) 2 Jo Space Law 157).

In 1885, Challis wrote that ownership of the fee simple 'confers . . . the lawful right to exercise over, upon, and in respect of the land, every act of ownership which can enter into the imagination.' However, even then this was not true because the law of tort could be used (to prevent a nuisance, for example). Today, legislation has imposed great limitations on the owner of land, so that, for instance, he cannot prevent aeroplanes from flying above his land, may not mine coal, demolish a listed building, kill protected species or pollute water; he must also observe building regulations and licensing laws.

The Town and Country Planning Acts impose probably the most famous, or notorious, limitation on land-owners. When the first was passed, in 1948, it was suggested by some that the fee simple had been destroyed by the powers taken by the government to control land use. Few people would say so now, since most land-owners appreciate the fact that the value of their land is maintained for them by the local authority, which can forbid their neighbours to open an amusement arcade or a garage for example.

4.5 Comment

This chapter has given a glimpse of the ancient law hidden within the modern rules; even the basic concept of today's law, the fee simple, can only be explained by reference to events which took place nearly 1000 years ago. However, although we may use the same words as lawyers in the eleventh or fifteenth centuries, the meaning and context is quite different: our forebears might recognise the terms but they would not understand our law.

Part of the fascination of the history of land law is the tracing of threads which link us to very different worlds. Many people find the history interesting for its own sake but the methods of historians can also be used to illuminate our own world: historians explain changes in land law by reference to the political, economic and social events of the time, and modern cases and statutes, which appear as merely technical rules, should be viewed in the same light (see for example Anderson (1984) Curr LP 63).

Summary

1 The basic unit of ownership in modern land law is the legal fee simple absolute in possession which originates in the feudal system imposed after 1066.
2 'Fee simple absolute in possession' means an interest in land which can be inherited by anyone, is not restricted by some future event and which is enjoyed at the moment.
3 Although it has been asserted that the owner in fee simple absolute in possession has unlimited powers over his land, both common law and statute have greatly restricted his freedom of action.

Exercises

1   Does the history of land law matter?
2   Which is more important, planning law or the doctrine of estates?
3   What is special about a fee simple upon condition?
4   What is an entail? Can it be legal?

5 Leases

5.1 Introduction

As already seen (in 1.5 above), freehold (fee simple absolute in possession) and leasehold are currently the only estates in land which can be legal. A lease was originally a contract for the occupation of land, and it was only in the sixteenth century that leases were recognised as 'interests in land' so that the rights and duties of the parties were no longer merely contractual, but became glued to the land. However, much of the law of leases is still contract law, with statutory additions.

The commercial advantages of the lease are obvious. A land-owner can let other people use her land for a certain period of time – to farm, mine for gravel, or live there – in exchange for a regular income. She can make rules about the kinds of things that are – or are not – to be done on the land and, at the end of the period, she will get the land back. Great cities like London were developed in the eighteenth and nineteenth centuries through building leases. The ancestors of the Duke of Westminster, for example, owned large estates in London and they granted long leases to speculative builders, subject to strict rules about the density and type of housing. The builders made their profit, the Dukes enjoyed the rent, and at the end of the period the valuable housing estates were to revert to the descendants of the first Duke (but see 5.9 below). Thus London and other cities grew through the carefully planned, high quality developments of farsighted land-owners – and also, of course, through get-rich-quick rented slums.

Today, leases play a much smaller part in controlling large building developments – that role has largely been taken over by public authorities – but leasehold arrangements are still very important. In financial terms, the most significant use of leases is in the business world, such as office blocks, warehouses and so on. In addition, many of the urban houses built on building leases are still leased; other people now leasing property to live in are home buyers with long leases (often 99 years). Owners of homes in multi-dwelling blocks probably own long leases, but this may change if commonhold is introduced (see 5.11 below).

There are also many other tenants, poor or temporary occupants, with much shorter leases (the last group comprises about 8 per cent of the population). Short leases for housing have been greatly affected by Acts of

Parliament since 1915 because of the social and economic importance of decent housing for the community as a whole. Parliament has also intervened to restrict sex and race discrimination in rented housing. Statutes concerning rent control, security and repairs were 'originally passed to help poor tenants, unable to protect themselves by negotiating . . . the kinds of protection usually found in properly drawn leases' (Partington, 1980, p. 43), but they now extend to most short-term tenants. They are usually outside the scope of land law courses and are only referred to very occasionally in this chapter.

5.2   The Vocabulary of Leases

There are several words to describe a lease, including tenancy, letting, demise and term of years absolute (see 5.3 below). All these words have the same meaning, but lawyers use 'tenancy' and 'letting' for a short period and 'lease' or 'demise' for a long one.

The following story is typical of leases: Louise let the basement flat in her house to Teresa, for three years at £200 per month. Teresa decided to live elsewhere and sold ('assigned') her lease to Ahmed who then rented two of the rooms in the flat to Sam for six months. Then Louise decided to move, and sold her whole house (including the freehold, the 'reversion', of the flat) to Robert.

This story could be continued indefinitely but thus far it illustrates the possibilities of leases, and is shown diagrammatically in Figure 5.1 below. (These diagrams are very useful for sorting out the characters in a problem on leases; leases are always shown as vertical lines and assignments as horizontal lines, and, as in real life, the landlady is always on top.)

Figure 5.1   *Leasehold relationships in diagram form*

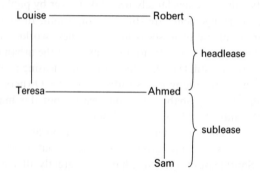

Louise owned the freehold; she is the original landlady (lessor, owner of the freehold, owner of the leasehold reversion). Robert is the new landlord (lessor, landlady's assignee – pronounced 'ass-eye-knee' – or assignee of the reversion). Teresa is the original tenant (lessee, owner of the lease). Ahmed is the current tenant (lessee, owner of the headlease, tenant's assignee, assignee of the headlease). He is also the landlord in the middle, the mesne (pronounced 'mean') landlord. Sam is the subtenant (sublessee, owner of the sublease).

The difference between an *assignment* and a *sublease* is that Teresa assigned (sold the *whole* of her remaining interest to Ahmed) but Ahmed sublet (only sold a *part* of his interest to Sam, retaining the rest for himself). The difference between them can be important, but whatever word – 'assignment' or 'subtenancy' – is used by the parties, the judges in deciding what a transaction is look to the substance of the arrangement.

5.3 Definition of a Lease

The term of years absolute

This is the phrase adopted in the 1925 legislation and is defined at great length in s.205(xxvii) LPA 1925. Basically:

> **A TERM OF YEARS ABSOLUTE HAS:**
> **A FIXED BEGINNING AND A FIXED END**
> **AND**
> **GIVES EXCLUSIVE POSSESSION TO THE TENANT**

(For more on exclusive possession see 5.4 below.)

The period can be anything from thousands of years to a few hours. The beginning and end must be stated at the outset but the lease may end ('determine') earlier.

Some leases do not state a fixed beginning and a fixed end but the facts nevertheless may be fitted into the definition of a 'term of years absolute', as in *Prudential Assurance Co Ltd* v. *London Residuary Body* [1992] 3 WLR 279 (HL). Here, a London council let land in 1930 until the land would be needed for widening a road. The Court of Appeal had held that there was insufficient certainty about the date of the lease's ending and therefore it was not a valid term of years absolute. However, they found instead that this was a lease 'from year to year' (a periodic legal tenancy:

see below) which could only be ended by the council if it were going to widen the road. The effect of the decision was that, since the road would not now ever be widened, the tenant could enjoy the land indefinitely at £30 per year while the current market rent would be £10 000 per year.

The House of Lords allowed the appeal. They agreed with the Court of Appeal that the original agreement must have created an implied legal yearly tenancy but they held that the council's successor in title was able to give 6-months' notice as normal under a yearly tenancy: the term that the landlord could only give notice if the land were needed for widening the road was inconsistent with a yearly tenancy and therefore invalid (see Sparkes 109 LQR (1993) 93).

The certainty of leases rule may be due for some reconsideration. Lord Browne-Wilkinson said:

'This bizarre outcome results from the application of an ancient and technical rule of law which requires the maximum duration of a term of years to be ascertainable from the outset. No one has produced any satisfactory rationale for the genesis of this rule. No one has been able to point to any useful purpose that it serves at the present day.' (p. 287)

However, no statutory change has yet been proposed.

Within the definition of a lease as providing a fixed period and exclusive possession, there is a great range of types of leases. The start can be set for a date in the future, but it must start within 21 years (s.149(3) LPA); this is called a *reversionary* lease.

A lease for a specific period such as a week, which can be continually repeated until one side gives notice, is called a *periodic* tenancy. A weekly or monthly period is common for furnished accommodation and a yearly for agricultural tenancies. If a person uses land and regularly pays money to the owner, then – provided the tenant has exclusive possession (see 5.4 below) – the common law implies a periodic tenancy, unless the parties intended something else. The period of the tenancy is decided by the period by which rent is assessed, not by the period of payment; thus, if the rent is '£1000 per year, payable monthly', there is an implied legal yearly tenancy.

Another lease which continually repeats itself is the *perpetually renewable* lease. It is different from the periodic tenancy because here the lessor cannot give notice; the lease continues as long as the lessee chooses. This kind of arrangement was common in agricultural lettings with absentee lessors. They were anomalous within the 1925 structure of land ownership, so s.145 LPA 1922 automatically converts them into lease for 2000 years, with special rules for giving notice. At first the courts interpreted the section literally and a lessor with a carelessly drafted lease suddenly might find herself saddled with a lessee for 2000 years, but the judges now 'lean against' this interpretation.

Leases for life

Before 1925 there were two types of lease: the term of years absolute and the lease for life (or until marriage), and both could exist as legal estates. Since 1925, s.1 LPA, only the first of these can be legal. Because some people with legal leases for life or marriage would have suddenly found themselves to be merely equitable lessees on 1 January 1926, s.149(6) LPA converts their interests into legal leases for 90 years, provided the lessee pays rent. Such a lease can be determined by one month's notice at the death or marriage.

5.4 Leases and Licences

Normally, if a person occupying another's land does not have exclusive possession (the right to keep the owner out), she is not a tenant but only a lodger, or a licensee. The word licensee describes anyone who has a permission to be on land, such as readers in a library; these 'non-interests-in-land' are discussed in more detail in Chapter 13. A licence can be created by contract, with a regular payment of what looks like rent, and then it may closely resemble a lease. However, leases are 'interests in land', while licences are merely 'personal': they cannot usually be transferred and will probably not bind a buyer of the land.

The difference between a lease and a licence is 'notoriously difficult' (Bridge (1986) Cony 344); there are hundreds of pages of judgments devoted to explaining what the difference is. It used to be very important because many residential tenants had statutory protection of their occupation and could claim a fair rent, while 'mere licensees' enjoyed neither of these statutory protections (but see also 13.5 below for implied terms in licences). However, this difference has been eroded for residential leases/licences created since 15 January 1989 (s.34 Housing Act 1988). The case law nevertheless remains relevant to commercial agreements and for any occupation agreements made before that date.

The decision of the House of Lords in *Street* v. *Mountford* [1985] AC 809 was a milestone in the case law on the lease–licence distinction. Mr Street (a solicitor) let Mrs Mountford live in his house in return for a weekly payment. In a written agreement, headed '*Licence*', she accepted rules about visitors and heating, and eviction if the 'licence fee' was more than a week late. Mr Street reserved the right to enter the house to inspect it. Such agreements had been assumed to be licences, since this seemed to be the clear intention of the parties. However, the House of Lords held that this was a weekly tenancy and so Mrs Mountford won a fair rent.

Lord Templeman was clear that an occupier of residential land must be either a tenant or a licensee, and that:

'A tenant armed with exclusive possession can keep out strangers and keep out the landlord.' (p. 816)

The normal test of a tenancy is the factual question of 'exclusive possession'; the intention of the parties is irrelevant:

'The occupier is a lodger [licensee] if the landlord provides attendance or services which require the landlord or his servants to exercise unrestricted access to and use of the premises . . . If on the other hand residential accommodation is granted for a term at a rent with exclusive possession, the landlord providing neither attendance nor services, the grant is a tenancy . . . The manufacture of a five-pronged implement for digging results in a fork even if the manufacturer, unfamiliar with the English language, insists he intended to make, and has made, a spade.' (pp. 817–18, 819)

The case was held to apply to all occupation agreements, including shops and agricultural land. It soon became clear, however, that multiple occupation, as is common in rented flats, posed different problems. In *A. G. Securities* v. *Vaughan, Antoniades* v. *Villiers* [1988] 3 WLR 1205 the House of Lords held, in the first of this pair of cases heard together, that a group of four people who shared a flat could not be tenants because they did not fulfil the requirements of a 'joint tenancy', the only way by which people can legally share land (see Chapter 12). They did not all arrive at the same time, and so they did not share 'unity of title': they were merely licensees. In the second case, however, a 'Licence Agreement' which seemed to give the owner the right to sleep in the tiny flat with a cohabiting couple was held to be a tenancy; the term looked as if it denied exclusive possession to the couple but it was a sham, inserted in the agreement merely to avoid giving Rent Act protection to the occupants, and it had no effect.

These cases, and the many subsequent decisions, cannot provide all the answers. Essentially, the question is whether the agreement itself gave exclusive possession to the tenant (or the tenants jointly) so that they had the right to keep the owner out. However, it is often impossible to decide what the agreement means or whether a term in it is a sham without looking at the facts of the whole case. Thus, the House of Lords decided in *City of Westminster* v. *Clarke* [1992] 1 All ER 695 that a person given temporary occupation by a local council did not have a tenancy but only a licence. Lord Templeman held that this was 'a very special case' (p. 703), quite different from private lettings. He held that there was no exclusive possession here because of the purpose of this agreement: a term that the occupant could be moved at any time to another room was not a sham because the council needed it in order to fulfil its statutory duty to vulnerable people.

There are three standard exceptions to the *Street* v. *Mountford* rule that exclusive possession normally creates a lease. The first is where services (such as breakfast) are provided, the second where there is an 'act of generosity', and the third where the tenant is an employee. In *Bostock* v. *Bryant* (1991) 61 P & CR 23, a family lived in a house belonging to 'Uncle Joe'. The family paid the bills, but no 'rent'. There was exclusive possession, but it was held by the Court of Appeal that this was an 'act of generosity'; there was no intention to create legal relations and no tenancy, only a licence which did not protect the occupants when Uncle Joe died. In *Norris* v. *Checksfield* [1991] EGCS 45 a man was employed on condition he got a coach-driver's licence, and was given a house to live in to make his job easier. He was disqualified from driving so he lost the job, and the Court of Appeal held that, although he had exclusive possession, he was merely a licensee in the house because he was only there in connection with his employment.

The recent decision in *Onyx (UK) Ltd* v. *Beard* [1996] EGCS 55 (and see 3.5 above) illustrates several of the rules about leases and licences. Here Michael Hart QC had to decide whether a club, which had occupied for nearly 30 years land now owned by the plaintiff, had successfully gained rights of adverse possession. He held that they had not, because they had been licensees rather than tenants without a rent. The absence of rent in the agreement was ambiguous, but this arrangement had been an act of generosity, the period was not sufficiently certain, the 'tenant' was a shifting group of club members, and they did not have exclusive possession. For these reasons, they could not remain in possession of the land against the real owner. Further, there was no evidence of estoppel (see 2.6 above) in the case, because the owner had not promised them a legal interest in the land.

5.5   The Creation of Leases

Legal formalities

The rules for the creation of legal interests in land were set out in Chapter 2. Briefly, a deed is necessary to *create* a legal lease, unless it is within the exception in s.54(2) LPA for short leases (see 2.7 above). A deed is always required to *assign* a legal lease (see *Crago* v. *Julian* (1992), 2.7 above). When the land is registered, special rules apply to leases over 21 years (see 10.4). If there is no deed where one is needed (or the registered land procedure is not followed), then only an equitable interest is created or transferred.

Equitable leases

It can be very important to know whether a lease is legal or equitable because:

**AS BETWEEN THE ORIGINAL LANDLADY AND TENANT,
AN EQUITABLE LEASE IS PROBABLY
AS GOOD AS A LEGAL LEASE
BUT
WHEN THE LEASE OR REVERSION HAS BEEN ASSIGNED,
IT MAY NOT BE**

This was shown in *Walsh* v. *Lonsdale* (1882) 21 Ch D 9 (see above 2.3), where the landlord of the mill could enforce the 'rent-in-advance' term in the equitable seven-year lease against the tenant. The tenant had moved in and was paying a yearly rent, so there was also an implied legal periodic (yearly) tenancy. This parallel relationship is relatively common; landlady and tenant effectively have two sets of rights and duties, legal and equitable.

Walsh v. *Lonsdale* is authority that, as between the original parties, the terms in the equitable lease normally prevail; but this may not be so if either the lease or the freehold is assigned. The most important rule here is that legal interests bind the world, but equitable interests are subject to the doctrine of notice and its statutory replacements (see the rules about estate contracts in Chapters 9 and 10). In addition, the rights and duties in an equitable lease may not pass with the land (see 5.7 below). Whether an equitable lease (or a contract for a lease) is as good as a legal lease is an ancient essay question; useful cases are given in Cheshire (1994) pp. 379–82.

Where s.2 of the 1989 Act is not satisfied, for example because there was only an oral agreement for a five year lease, there is no 'contract for a lease'. However, the courts may decide that proprietory estoppel may allow the lease to be enforced in equity (see above 2.6).

Statutory conditions

The owners of property are not allowed to discriminate on the grounds of sex or race in choosing a tenant (s.31 Sex Discrimination Act 1975 and s.24 Race Relations Act 1976). The only common exceptions concern small houses or flats where the landlady lives on the premises. Such discrimination is a civil wrong and the victim can take action for damages, an injunction and/or a declaration.

5.6 Covenants in Leases

Commonly found covenants

'Covenant' is the general name given to promises in contracts concerning land; they may be express (written or spoken) or implied (either by common law or by statute). Several covenants are commonly found in leases.

COMMONLY FOUND LEASEHOLD COVENANTS

By the lessor
not to derogate from her grant;
for the lessee's quiet enjoyment;
to repair.

By the lessee
to pay rent (sometimes also land taxes and/or a service charge);
to repair;
to permit the lessor to enter to inspect (or repair);
to insure;
not to alter the structure;
not to assign or sublet without permission;
not to use the premises except for a specific purpose (for example, as a private dwelling house).

The most important are explained here.

Covenants for quiet enjoyment and non-derogation
These are the essence of the lease, the counterpart of the tenant's right to exclusive possession. If they are not expressed in the lease, they are implied

by common law. First, the landlady promises not to interfere with the tenant's enjoyment of the land: this means much more than merely keeping quiet, but refers to the tenant's right to take possession as promised and to be able to enjoy all aspects of her possession without interference. Second, the landlady promises not to take back what she has given. These two promises are very closely connected and whether or not the covenants have been breached is a question of fact.

In *Browne* v. *Flower* [1911] 1 Ch 219, the tenants of a ground floor flat complained that a new outside staircase, which ran alongside their bed-room windows, invaded their privacy and breached the covenants. As regards the covenant for quiet enjoyment, Parker J said:

> 'there must be some physical interference with the enjoyment of the demised premises and . . . a mere interference with the comfort of a person using the demised premises by the creation of a personal annoyance such as might arise from noise, invasion of privacy, or otherwise is not enough.' (p. 228)

On non-derogation, he held that a breach only occurs if property is 'rendered unfit or materially less fit to be used for the purpose for which they were demised' (at p. 226). The tenants here lost both arguments; after all, the rooms could still be used as bedrooms if they drew the curtains. (If they had wanted *private* bedrooms they could have made sure a covenant to that effect was put in the lease.)

Browne v. *Flower* may be contrasted with two other cases. In *Mira* v. *Aylmer Square Investments Ltd* (1990) 22 HLR 182 repairs which seriously interfered with occupation (including dust, noise, loss of privacy, holes in the ceiling and water penetration) gave the tenants the right to damages (including loss of subletting rent) for breach of the covenant for quiet enjoyment. There was also a breach of the covenant not to derogate from grant in *Harmer* v. *Jumbil (Nigeria) Tin Areas Ltd* [1921] 1 Ch 200: land was leased expressly for the storage of explosives and then the landlord decided to build on his neighbouring land, which would have made the storage illegal. The tenant was able to prevent the building.

These common covenants are reinforced by s.1 Protection from Eviction Act 1977, amended by s.29 Housing Act 1988. This section creates a *crime* of harassment where a landlady 'does acts likely to interfere with the peace or comfort of the residential occupier' or refuses any facilities (such as the electricity supply) knowing or believing that this will discourage the occupier from enforcing her rights. (This section protects residential licensees as well as tenants.)

An example is *Cardiff City Council* v. *Destrick* [1994] April 14, a landlord cut off the gas and electricity of a flat rented by a young couple with a young baby. He was charged with the crime of doing an act with intent to cause the occupier to leave (s.1(3)), and also with doing an act which was likely to make the occupier leave (s.1(3A)), but was acquitted of both charges. He had argued that he had no intent to force them out (it was summer, not winter), and, further, that it was reasonable (under s.1(3B)) to act as he did because the tenants were behind with their payments. The magistrates agreed with him. On appeal, the judges recognised that Parliament's intent was to protect tenants by ensuring that if a landlord wants to get a tenant out, he has to go to court: he is not entitled to rely on self-help and eviction, or to 'indulge in harassment'. However, they found that the magistrate's decision had not been so irrational that it should be overruled.

This case may have opened a useful escape route for lessors, but it will be a question of the evidence of the reasonableness of the lessor's conduct in every case.

S.27 of the 1988 Act also creates a *tort* of 'unlawful eviction' with potentially very large damages to be awarded against the landlady (under s.23). *Tagro* v. *Cafane* [1991] 2 All ER 235 is 'a cautionary tale for landlords who are minded unlawfully to evict their tenants by harassment or other means' (Lord Donaldson MR at p. 236). The landlord here harassed the tenant and eventually 'totally wrecked' her room and possessions. The tenant won £31 000 damages (see too Bridge 57 Conv (1993) 84).

Covenants to repair
Either landlady or tenant, or both, may have duties to repair various parts of buildings (but see 5.12 below). A covenant to keep the property in repair is breached as soon as a repair is needed and not carried out (*British Telecommunications* v. *Sun Life Assurance plc* [1995] 4 All ER 44, where the lessor was liable as soon as the cladding of the office block started to bulge outwards).

It is normal for there to be an express term in long leases that the lessee should leave the property in a good state at the end of the lease; what this means in practice depends on the locality, character and age of the premises, subject to 'fair wear and tear'. If there is nothing expressed in the lease, under common law a periodic tenant with a year's term or less probably just has to use the premises in a 'tenant-like manner'. This is a vague expression but Lord Denning MR has given some examples. A weekly tenant must, for example, clean windows and unblock sinks:

'In short, he must do the little jobs about the place which a reasonable tenant would do. In addition, he must, of course, not damage the house . . . But . . . if the house falls into disrepair through fair wear and tear or lapse of time, or for any reason not caused by him, then the tenant is not liable to repair it.' (*Warren* v. *Keen* [1954] 1 QB 15, p. 20)

At common law, a furnished dwelling must be fit for habitation at the start of the lease; a famous breach of this implied covenant occurred where a house was leased and found to be full of bugs (*Smith* v. *Marrable* (1843) 11 M & W 5. Statute (currently s.8 Housing Act 1985) requires the landlady of a dwelling let at a very low rent to keep it fit *throughout* the lease. In addition, ss.11–14 Landlord and Tenant Act 1985 impose a duty on the landlady of any dwelling (for a term less than 7 years) to keep certain items in order, including the external structure, heating and water and sanitary services.

A tenant may win damages for the lessor's failure to repair (or for badly carried out repairs which breach the lessor's covenant for quiet enjoyment, as shown in the *Mira* case, above): general damages are assessed according to what is needed to put the tenant in the position she would have been in had the repair been properly carried out, and the court may also award special damages. For example, in *McGuigan* v. *Southwark LBC* (1995) Curr L 154 a tenant whose flat had been appallingly infested by cockroaches for 5 years won £17 000 general and £11 000 special damages after she had had to move out for medical reasons and abandon all her belongings – even her phone – because of the infestation.

Covenant not to assign or sublet
Theoretically, lessors and lessees have an unlimited right to sell their interests, and the lessee also may sublet. In practice, the lessee often promises not to assign or sublet, and not even to 'part with possession', unless the lessor consents. If this kind of covenant (a 'qualified' covenant) is in the lease, s.19 Landlord and Tenant Act 1927 provides that the consent cannot be unreasonably withheld, 'notwithstanding any provision to the contrary'. S.1 Landlord and Tenant Act 1988 placed the burden of proof on the landlady to show that her refusal of consent was reasonable, and *Midland Bank plc* v. *Chart Enterprises* (1991) 44 EG 68 held that the landlady is entitled, if she suspects something which would make her refusal reasonable, to take reasonable time to investigate it.

The Landlord and Tenant (Covenants) Act 1995 (and see below) s.22 has amended these rules for new leases. It provides that, in the case of leases made after 1995, the lessor who gives consent can demand that the tenant guarantees her assignee's performance of the covenants. It allows *business* lessors and lessees to specify in the lease in what circumstances consent to assignment may be refused, and in that case the courts may not inquire into the reasonableness of a refusal. This provision is likely significantly to alter commercial negotiations for future leases, but as far as any pre-1996, or non-business, leases are concerned, s.19 of the 1927 Act remains the law.

If the consent is unreasonably withheld, the tenant can go ahead and assign or sublet regardless. If she is not sure whether the landlady is being reasonable, she can go to court for a declaration. If a tenant wrongly assigns or sublets, she may lose her lease (see 8.2 below).

What is reasonable is a question of fact in every case. As Lord Denning MR remarked:

'No one decision will be a binding precedent as a strict rule of law. The reasons given by the judges are to be treated as propositions of good sense – in relation to the particular case – rather than propositions of law applicable to all cases.' (*Bickel* v. *Duke of Westminster* [1977] QB 517, p. 524)

A useful test can be found in *International Drilling Fluids Ltd* v. *Louisville Investments (Uxbridge) Ltd* [1986] Ch 513, where it was said to be a question of whether the lessor's decision was one 'which might be reached by a reasonable man in the circumstances'. Reasonable refusals include the unsatisfactory references of the proposed tenant and the fact that the subletting would create a tenancy protected by statute. Unreasonable refusals include a proposed assignee's diplomatic immunity and a prejudice against a person's sex or race (Sex Discrimination Act 1975 and Race Relations Act 1976). (There is a long list of reasonable and unreasonable refusals in Yates and Hawkins (1986), pp. 310–11.)

The Court of Appeal was faced with an interesting issue in *Olympia and York Canary Wharf Ltd* v. *Oil Property Investments Ltd* [1994] EG 121 where the lessor was refusing leave to an assignee of the lease who wanted to sell it to the original tenant of the lease. The reason for refusal was that the original tenant had the personal right to end the lease (and this would reduce the value of the lessor's interest by £6 million). The Court held that this was a reasonable ground to refuse consent to assignment. Since the 1995 Act this kind of case is unlikely to arise in new business leases since the parties can now specify the conditions for assignment in advance.

The 'usual covenants'

The 'usual covenants' is a technical expression, quite different from the list of common covenants above. This set of covenants (see box) is implied into a lease if the lease states that the parties will be bound by the 'usual covenants', or if the lease is silent as to most matters (as is common in short periodic tenancies). These usual covenants are also implied in a contract for a lease, unless the parties intend otherwise.

THE USUAL COVENANTS

By the tenant: to pay rent;
                    to pay land taxes;
                    to repair;
                    to allow access to the landlady to repair.

By the landlady: quiet enjoyment and non-derogation from grant;
                    right of re-entry for non-payment of rent.

Other covenants may be 'usual' in the circumstances, for example, because of local or trade customs.

5.7   The Transfer of Rights and Duties under a Lease

It is the automatic transfer ('running with the land') of both parties' rights and duties under the lease which makes leases so useful; anyone who buys either the lease or the reversion has the benefits and burdens of covenants in the lease. ('Benefit' means a right to sue and 'burden' a liability to be sued). Thus, a person who buys the freehold and becomes the new landlady can sue for the rent; one who buys the lease can sue for repairs. In 1995 the Landlord and Tenant (Covenants) Act revolutionised this area of the law but the old rules still apply to all leases (and contracts for leases) made before 1 January 1996.

The old law for pre-1996 leases

Under the old law, the original parties to the lease are bound by their contract and, with some exceptions in the case of the landlady, remain liable for the whole period of the lease, whether one month or 99 years. Once the lease or reversion is sold, however, in order to enforce a leasehold covenant the plaintiff has to prove:

PRIVITY OF ESTATE
AND
THE COVENANT 'TOUCHES AND CONCERNS' THE LAND

The present authorities for the rules are as shown in Table 5.1. Privity of estate means that there is a current *legal* relationship of landlady and tenant between the parties. A sign of privity of estate is that one person pays rent to the other, so there is therefore no privity of estate between head landlady and subtenant. In order to identify privity of estate, it is necessary to know (1) the formality rules in Chapter 2, and (2) the difference between the assignment of a lease and the creation of a subtenancy (see 5.2 above).

'Touches and concerns' is the sixteenth-century phrase used by the courts to decide whether promises ought, as a matter of public policy, to be glued to the land. In the LPA, 'touch and concern' is replaced by 'has reference to the subject matter of the lease' (ss.141 and 142) but the meaning is identical. The test is easy to explain but harder to apply; the basic question is whether the promise really affects the parties in their roles as tenant and landlady, or whether it rather affects them in their personal capacity. In Cheshire's terms, 'the promise must be reasonably incidental to the relation of landlord and tenant' (1994) at p. 446.

All the commonly found covenants in 5.6 above do touch and concern the land, and the benefits and burdens under them automatically pass with the reversion and the lease to the new landlady and the new tenant. Other examples are covenants for the tenant to buy petrol for the leased petrol station only from the landlady, and for the landlady to supply water to the leased premises. Examples of covenants which do not touch and concern the land are: to build a wall on the landlady's other land, and not to complete with the tenant's business on the leased premises (a pub) within half a mile. In Cheshire (1994) pp. 446–7, there are long lists of covenants which do, and do not, touch and concern the land.

As already indicated, the original landlady and tenant have promised to obey the covenants for the whole lease and in theory they (or their heirs) may be able to sue – and may be liable – for the whole period; of course, they are very unlikely to sue once they have parted with their interests, but the liability to be sued for unpaid rent may be a nightmare for the original tenant of an expensive commercial lease.

The rules are different for the original lessor and lessee. If the *original lessor* assigns the reversion, because of the wording of ss.141 and 142, she can only sue and be sued by the original lessee and not by any other holder of the lease. The *original tenant* however can sue, and will be liable to, any

Table 5.1

	Benefit	Burden
Landlady	s.141 LPA	s.142 LPA
Tenant	–	Spencer's case (1583) –

assignee of the freehold, providing there is privity of estate and the covenant touches and concerns the land. Unlike the original landlady, therefore, the original tenant remains liable when she sells her interest: any owner of the reversion can choose to sue the original tenant of a lease rather than the present one for any breach of leasehold covenant.

Case law is still developing here. For example, in *City of London Corporation* v. *Fell* [1993] 3 WLR 1164 the House of Lords offered 'a meagre crumb of comfort to the unfortunate original tenant' (Bridge [1994] CLJ 28), in this case a firm of solicitors. It held that the original tenant was not liable for rent unpaid by a later assignee of the lease in the case of a tenancy continued after the end of the term by the provisions of Part II of the Landlord and Tenant Act 1954.

Now, by s.17 Landlord and Tenant (Covenants) Act 1995, the lessor of any lease (whenever created) must give a 'problem notice' to the original lessee if she is planning to sue her for money unpaid by a current tenant. If the original tenant pays the sums due, then she is now entitled to an 'overriding lease' which places her between the lessor and current lessee, thus gaining some potential relief in exchange for her liability. However, if no notice was given, the original tenant escapes all liability for that debt.

If the original tenant is sued, the common law provides that she can claim an indemnity from the current tenant. If the present tenant is not worth suing (as is likely), she can (by s.77 LPA which is implied into all leases since 1925) choose to sue the person to whom she assigned her interest. As a further protection, when a business lease is assigned, the proposed new tenant will probably have to obtain a guarantor (a 'surety'). If the new tenant fails to pay the rent, the guarantor may also be sued for it.

There are different rules for equitable leases because in such cases there is no privity of estate: privity of estate depends on a *legal* relationship. Due to the wording of ss.141 and 142, the benefits and burdens of all covenants which touch and concern the land pass to *any landlady*, whether legal or equitable. As far as the *equitable tenant* is concerned, the benefit of covenants which touch and concern may pass, but it seems that the burden may not (but see below for equitable leases made after 1995).

The operation of the old rules

Take the following leasehold story: Alpha Co granted a 99-year lease of the top-floor flat in a large block to Bella in 1928. Alpha covenanted to keep the roof in repair and Bella covenanted to pay £500 per year rent and to use the premises as a private dwelling house only. There was a provision for forfeiture for breach of any covenant. Alpha went into liquidation and the reversion was conveyed to Bravo Co and then to Charlie Ltd. Bella died and her executors conveyed the lease to Gerald who then sold it to

Dino. The roof is now leaking badly. Dino is running an umbrella repairing service from the flat, and is in arrears of rent. The lease and all assignments were made by deed (see above for equitable leases).

The rights and duties of the various people in this tale obviously change as time passes. The present situation is as shown in diagram form in Figure 5.2.

1   As regards the leaking roof, there is privity of estate between Dino and Charlie and the covenant to repair touches and concerns the land: Dino can sue Charlie because the covenant was breached as soon as the roof leaked.

2   As regards the arrears of rent and the umbrella business, there is privity of estate and the covenants touch and concern the land: Charlie can sue Dino. Alternatively, Charlie could sue Bella as the original tenant – but only so long as a problem notice is served in respect of the unpaid rent. Bella, if liable, could sue either Gerald (s.77 LPA) or Dino (common law). (The original tenant's liability is only likely to arise in practice when money is a suitable remedy; an injunction against the business use of the flat would not be granted against the original tenant because she is no longer in control of the flat.)

Once Alpha and Bravo have assigned the lease they cannot be sued by anyone. If there were a subtenant, she could neither sue Charlie Ltd (the head-lessor) nor be sued by them because there would be no privity of estate between them. The position of head landlady and subtenant is the same as if they were neighbouring freeholders, and the enforcement of covenants in the headlease depends on the rules about freehold covenants (see Chapter 8).

The new law

From 1 January 1996, 'a statute without precedent . . . will have an untold impact on . . . commercial leases in this country' (Bridge [1996] CLJ 313).

Figure 5.2

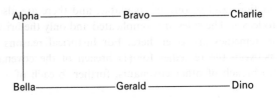

The Landlord and Tenant (Covenants) Act was passed as a result of a Law Commission Report (1988, No. 1974), the commitment of a single MP, and lessor and lessee lobbies (see Davey 59 MLR (1996) 78). It (1) abolishes the test of touch and concern (s.3), so that all benefits and burdens automatically pass when the lease or freehold is assigned, unless they are specifically expressed to be 'personal'); (2) abolishes the continuing liability of the original tenant; and (3) applies the same rules to all legal and equitable leases (s.28). By s.11 the rules only operate in 'lawful' assignments (that is, assignments with any necessary consents).

The Act contains a number of highly detailed and complex provisions for the new regime which will no doubt keep lawyers busy for many years to come. The negotiations around the new law resulted in a series of hurriedly drafted provisions to effect compromises between lessor and lessee lobbies. Thus, the original tenant escapes future liability in exchange for the possibility of having to guarantee the next tenant (s.22, above). The original lessor now becomes liable for the whole term of the lease, but may obtain a release from the current lessee in order to avoid this (s.6), and business lessors may agree with the tenant conditions for consenting to assignment, thus avoiding disputes as to the reasonableness of a refusal to consent.

The effect of many of these new rules in practice will depend on the relative negotiating strengths of the parties, itself influenced by the state of the property market. If the lease between Alpha and Bella (above) were made in 1996, the position might therefore depend more on negotiations between the parties. However, it is probable that Alpha, the original lessor, would be liable to repair the roof as well as the present lessor, but Charlie could no longer sue Bella, the original tenant, for rent unpaid by Dino.

5.8   Remedies for Breach of Covenant

Covenants, conditions and rights of re-entry

The important question for a practical lawyer is always, 'What remedy is available?' As a lease is a contract, normal contractual remedies (damages, injunctions and so on) are available, and there are also remedies particular to leases. The rules are complicated and only the briefest details of the main remedies are given here. For historical reasons there is a difference between the remedies for (1) breach of the covenant to pay rent, and (2) breach of other covenants; further, breach of a landlady's repairing covenant is the subject of a wide range of possible remedies. First, however, it is necessary to distinguish between covenants and conditions.

If a promise in a lease is called a 'condition', or is clearly intended to be a condition of the lease, then the landlady can automatically take possession of the land if the condition is broken. This is called repossession (or re-entry, or forfeiture). If the promise is not a condition, but merely a covenant, there is no such automatic right and the landlady can forfeit the lease (re-enter) or give notice to quit only if there is a covenant to that effect.

If the usual covenants (see 5.6 above) are implied, then there will be a provision for forfeiture for non-payment of rent but not for breach of any other covenant.

It is very important to be aware of the doctrine of waiver. If a landlady accepts rent knowing of a breach of covenant or condition, she will be taken to have waived her right to take action for the breach. Any lessor wishing to enforce a forfeiture must avoid any action by which she indicates to the tenant that the lease will continue, but there is no waiver if the lessor did not know of a breach when she indicated the continuance of the lease.

Non-payment of rent

The possible remedies are forfeiture, distress and an action of recovery of rent. The landlady can only choose one of these at a time.

Forfeiture
Forfeiture provisions are contained in every carefully-drafted lease. First, the landlady cannot re-enter if she waives her right (above). The clearest example of this would be if Charlie in the story above accepted rent from Dino after discovering the umbrella business.

The right to re-enter makes it sound as if the landlady can just barge in, but because of statutory limitations it is much safer for her to go to court for an order for possession in the case of residential property, otherwise she might well commit a crime under s.6 Criminal Law Act 1977 or ss.1–3 Protection from Eviction Act 1977, or become liable in tort under s.27 Housing Act 1988 (see 5.6 above). Once the landlady has gone to court, the tenant might be able to claim 'relief' against forfeiture for non-payment of rent under s.212 Common Law Procedure Act 1852 (in the High Court) or s.138 County Courts Act 1984 (in the County Court). This is exactly what it sounds like: very simply, if the tenant pays the arrears and costs, she may be reinstated. (The rules here are intricate and some-what illogical because of the interplay of equity, common law and statute.)

Distress
Since 1066 a landlady has been able to enter the premises between sunrise and sunset and 'levy distress': she may take the tenant's belongings and sell them if the rent is not paid within five days. Many items are supposed to be exempt from distress, for example, bedding and clothes. Only the landlady herself or a certified bailiff can levy distress.

In Report No. 194 (1991), the Law Commission concluded that distress for non-payment of rent is 'wrong in principle', and recommended its abolition.

An action for recovery
An action for recovery can be brought for arrears of rent. Only the last six years of rent can be recovered (s.19 Limitation Act 1980, and see Chapter 3.5).

Breach of other covenants

General remedies for breach of a tenant's covenant are forfeiture or damages or an injunction; a tenant may only be able to obtain damages or an injunction, but there is a suggestion (in *Hussein* v. *Mehlman* [1992] 2 EGLR 87, and see below) that a tenant might also be able to repudiate a tenancy.

Forfeiture
If there is a forfeiture clause, the landlady must give notice to the tenant by s.146 LPA:

THE S.146 NOTICE MUST SPECIFY:
1 **THE BREACH; AND**
2 **THE REMEDY (IF IT CAN BE REMEDIED); AND**
3 **THE COMPENSATION (IF APPROPRIATE OR REQUIRED).**

(S.146 notices do not apply in respect of non-payment of rent.)

If the notice is incomplete, it is invalid. The difficulty here is that some breaches of covenant cannot be remedied: for example, a wrongful subletting is irremediable, and so is a covenant not to use the premises for immoral purposes (unless the tenant is blameless and takes the appropriate action against her immoral subtenant).

It is essential to know which breaches can be remedied and which cannot, because if the covenant cannot be remedied, the s.146 notice need not specify a remedy. This area of law was examined in *Expert Clothing Service and Sales Ltd* v. *Hillgate House Ltd* [1986] Ch 340. In this case it had been agreed that the tenant should convert the premises but, because of lack of money, the tenant had not even begun the work by the date it should have been completed. Expert Clothing issued a s.146 notice, claiming that the breach was irremediable. The Court of Appeal held that the breach could be remedied; the test is whether the harm could still be put right and here the conversion work could still be done. The s.146 notice was therefore invalid.

If the tenant does not, or cannot, remedy the breach within a reasonable time, the landlady can go to court for an order of possession. Again, the tenant (or subtenant) can apply for relief. If the lease specifies that the landlady can re-enter if the tenant goes bankrupt, there is no relief for tenants of certain properties – pubs, for example, or furnished houses – and no relief for any tenant once a year has passed after the bankruptcy, unless the lease has been assigned during that time.

The House of Lords held in *Billson* v. *Residential Apartments Ltd* [1992] 2 WLR 15 that a tenant can apply for relief whether or not the landlady has actually re-entered the land, provided there is no final court older granting possession. Here the tenant was carrying out building work in breach of covenant so the landlord served a s.146 notice and then re-entered by changing the locks. Since there was no court order granting possession at this stage, the House of Lords sent the case back to the trial court for a decision as to whether relief was to be granted.

If the lease is forfeit, a sublease will also disappear since its existence depends on the headlease. Therefore, s.146(4) LPA allows the subtenant to apply for relief and, if she is successful, she steps into the shoes of the tenant but cannot gain a term longer than her original sublease.

Damages or an injunction
Either or both of these may be an appropriate remedy for some breaches, and may be available to both lessor and lessee. In the story in 5.7 above, Dino might claim damages for his carpets spoilt by the rain leaking through the roof, but only for damage which occurred since Charlie Ltd had been told of the need for repair.

The law concerning repairs to leasehold premises is immensely detailed and, as P. F. Smith commented, the 'problems are clear: the same cannot always be said of the solutions' (54 Conv (1992)). It is reported that more than one-fifth of private rented accommodation is unfit for human habitation, and the Law Commission has published a Report (No 238, 1996) recommending new implied terms in residential leases to the effect that lessors of seven years or less of residential property should be liable to maintain the premises in a fit state throughout the period.

At present, tenants often have very serious problems in persuading their landladies to carry out repairs; the problems of lessees in rundown mansion blocks is part of the reasoning behind the proposal for 'commonhold' (see 5.11 below). Tenants theoretically do have the ordinary remedies of damages and specific performance, or they may pay for the repairs and deduct the cost from the rent without becoming liable for non-payment (a 'right of set-off'). A recent example of damages for landlord's failure to repair is *Hussein* v. *Mehlman* [1992] (above); here the house was uninhabitable due to the lack of repair and the tenant not only won damages but was entitled to end the lease because of the fundamental nature of the lessor's breach of covenant.

Sometimes the tenant's best solution is to get the local authority to take action. There are many possibilities here. For example, in an extreme case where the disrepair amounts to a statutory nuisance (a threat to health) she may persuade the authority to serve an abatement notice, do the repairs and charge the landlady. In areas of very poor housing, the local authority has powers to declare a housing action area or a general improvement area and force landladies to act. It becomes interesting when it is the local authority itself which is the defaulting lessor as in the *McGuigan* cockroaches case (5.6 above). (There are full details of the law concerning leasehold repairs in Bright and Gilbert (1995), chapter 7.)

5.9   Determination of Leases

Since all leases must be only for a limited period, sooner or later they must end ('determine'). Most of the ways in which a lease can end have already been mentioned, they are:

1 *Forfeiture;*
2 *Expiry* (when the period ends);
3 *Notice* (for example, half a year's notice for yearly tenants, or as specified in the lease);
4 *Surrender* (where the tenant gives up the lease); this does not affect the rights of any existing subtenant, but a periodic subtenancy can be determined by the appropriate notice;
5 *Frustration* (very rarely: for example, where there is some physical catastrophe);

6 *Merger* (where the tenant obtains the freehold). There are statutory rights for certain tenants to buy their freehold: council houses are one example. Another example is very long leases; the Duke of Westminster in 1986 lost an action in the European Court of Human Rights against a lessee who, under the Leasehold Reform Act 1967, had claimed the freehold of a lease; see Gray (1994), p. 769. Merger does not affect a subtenant's rights.

5.10   Some Odd Kinds of Leases

Tenancy at will

This is very like a licence; the 'tenant' occupies the land but either side can end the arrangement at any time.

Tenancy at sufferance

This arises if a tenant remains in occupation ('holds over') after the lease has expired, without the landlady's agreement. The landlady can claim compensation for use of the land and can evict the tenant at any time. The tenant may also be liable to a penalty under statute for holding over wrongfully.

Tenancy by estoppel

If a person grants a lease which she could not grant because she was not herself sufficient owner, she is estopped from denying her tenant's rights against her. This is part of the ordinary principle of estoppel.

Lease of the reversion

Where a landlady creates a lease of *her* remaining interest, she is leasing the reversion; it is also called a concurrent lease. The tenant of the reversion has the right to collect rent and enforce other covenants against the tenant of the lease. (Compare the *reversionary* lease explained in 5.3 above.)

Time share

A contract to occupy land for 'two weeks per year for 50 years' may also create a legal lease even though the 'period' is discontinuous. These agreements are subject to the Timeshare Act 1992.

5.11   Commonhold

The Law Commission (Report Cm. 179, 1987) recommended common-hold as a new scheme of land ownership to 'regulate relations between owners of separate properties which lie in close proximity to each other and are interdependent', and a new draft bill was published in 1996. It would enable 'co-operation between owners in a defined area' by allowing a developer to set up a commonhold scheme, or existing lessees (with leases of more than 21 years) of a block of flats to take control of their building. The 'commonholders' would become registered proprietors of their own fee simple and would share ownership of the common parts of the building through a commonhold association registered on a Common-hold Constitution Register.

The advantage of the commonhold scheme is that it allows positive covenants to pass with freehold land (see Chapter 8), thus getting rid of the need to create leases in shared buildings, and the associated problems of landladies failing to repair and the difficulties of getting mortgage finance in the last years of the lease. Of course, as the Law Commission remarked, the new scheme will not by itself solve the problems: neighbours will not always co-operate, and buildings cannot be repaired for ever. Nevertheless, the proposals do represent a new flexibility for land owners in planning land use to maintain peoples' homes and the value of their land (see Clarke 58 MLR (1995) 486).

5.12   Comment

In many ways, the most interesting aspect of the lease is its enormous flexibility. Leases can control housing development, provide long- and short-term housing, allow land to be used to raise capital and income, and provide for the changing needs of businesses. This is a vast area of law, with many detailed rules and areas of uncertainty and, as already indicated, the Law Commission has made many reports on the area and is working on a codification.

Balancing the interests of landladies, tenants and society in general has never been simple. To some degree, the history of this area of law demonstrates the failure of judges and legislators to resolve political, social and economic problems; the passage of the Landlord and Tenant (Covenants) Act 1995 demonstrates the powerful interests which influence the making of new laws in this area.

The post-war consensus about the need to protect tenants' security seemed to end in the 1980s: statutory protections for residential tenants decreased and public authorities became less able to provide adequate housing for those excluded from home-ownership. However, the different leasehold regimes in other EU countries, which generally offer greater and more effective protection to occupiers, may well gradually have an impact on English and Welsh law.

Summary

1 A lease must have a fixed beginning and a fixed end and the tenant must have exclusive possession; in deciding whether an arrangement is a lease or a licence, the court looks to the substance of the agreement, not the name given to it.

2 An equitable lease may be as good as a legal lease between the original parties but, once the lease or reversion is sold, an equitable lease may be less secure; if the lease was made before 1996, the terms of an equitable lease may be less enforceable.

3 Commonly found leasehold covenants include: the landlady's covenants for quiet enjoyment and non-derogation from grant; covenants to repair; the tenant's covenant not to assign or sublet without consent (such consent not to be unreasonably withheld).

4 In leases made before 1996, a covenant automatically runs with the land if there is privity of estate and the covenant touches and concerns the land; the original tenant remains liable on all the covenants but may claim an indemnity from her assignee or the current tenant.

5 In leases made after 1995, all covenants run with land; the original tenant ceases to be automatically liable for any breach after assigning the lease but the original landlady may remain liable, unless she obtains a release from the current tenant.

6 Remedies for non-payment of rent are normally forfeiture, distress or an action for recovery.

7 Remedies for breaches of other covenants include forfeiture, damages and injunction; breach of the landlady's repairing covenant may involve local authority powers or a tenant's right to repudiate the lease.

8 A new form of land ownership – commonhold – may be introduced.

Exercises

1 How certain must a 'term of years absolute' be?
2 What is the difference between a lease and a licence?
3 What is the difference between 'common covenants' and 'usual covenants'?
4 When may a landlady repossess her land?
5 In 1995 Grace agreed in writing with Han that Han would have exclusive possession of the top floor of Grace's house for £500 per month for three years; that Grace would keep the house in repair; that Grace would have a right of re-entry for breach of any covenant; that Han

would not assign, sublet or part with possession of the premises without Grace's consent. Han moved in straight away and started paying rent; a year later he assigned the lease to Thelma, with Grace's permission. Grace has now sold her interest to Anna who wants the top floor vacant. She has been threatening Han with physical violence, refuses to repair broken window frames and has refused to agree to Thelma's proposed assignment to James. The rent is three months in arrears.

Discuss.

Would it make any difference if the lease were made in 1996?

What differences would there be if all the recommendations of the Law Commission had all been implemented?

6 Mortgages

6.1 Introduction

Most of the rules in the law of mortgages are relatively straightforward and conform with common sense. However in this area of the law the language and the concepts are not quite as they might appear at first sight. It used to be said that a mortgage deed was 'a suppression of truth and a suggestion of falsehood', and this mismatch of expectation and theory can be unsettling. What is essential while learning mortgages is to keep hold of the rules while exploring the theory. As far as the poetic language is concerned, the easiest way to assimilate the technical terms (italicised on their first appearance in this chapter) is to try and explain them to your most tolerant friend.

The word mortgage is used in two senses by lawyers; first, it is a relationship between a landowner and a money-lender: the landowner transfers some interest in his land to the money-lender as security for a debt. The interest transferred may be a long lease; here, the money-lender is theoretically a lessee but does not live in the house and does not pay rent (the lease is just security for the loan). More often the security is a *charge* (a 'burden on land'): its proper name is 'a charge by deed expressed to be by way of legal mortgage'. Theoretically, this is not an 'interest in land' but the money-lender has all the rights he would enjoy if he had a lease (s.87 LPA).

The second use of the word 'mortgage' is as a way of referring to the interest – lease or charge – granted as security. Contrary to the way most people talk, the mortgage is the interest in the land exchanged for the money: a mortgage is *not* borrowed money. When the letter arrives to say that a building society will lend the money to buy a house, the borrower should not shout, 'Hooray – they're giving me a mortgage!', but rather, 'Well, well – they're letting me grant them a mortgage.' Thus, the *mortgagor* (the borrower) grants a mortgage to the *mortgagee* (the money-lender). (See Figure 6.1.)

Mortgage relationships have existed since Anglo-Saxon times but their form has changed a good deal since then. Since the seventeenth century, the harsh common law approach has been softened by equity which intervened in contracts between borrowers (typified as the poverty-stricken

Figure 6.1   *A mortgage agreement*

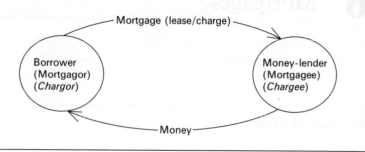

sons of the aristocracy) and money-lenders: this is one area of the law where freedom of contract did not operate.

The basic principle behind equity's intervention in mortgages is that one party (here, the lender) should not take an unfair advantage of the other (the borrower). In more recent times, statutes have been passed to protect borrowers; building society mortgages are all controlled by statute and the Chief Registrar of Building Societies, while second mortgages (from finance houses, banks and so on) may be subject to the Consumer Credit Act 1974. The terms of 'commercial' mortgages may be more negotiable and here the equitable jurisdiction is still important.

This area of land law illustrates very clearly the way in which land simultaneously fulfils several functions. It is used as a home by the borrowers and – they hope – at the same time it is their investment, an appreciating asset, although the assumption that land would always increase in value has now been shaken, some borrowers finding themselves with a debt larger than the value of their home ('*negative equity*', see below 6.4 and Martin [1993] Conv 59). About 40 per cent of householders are currently buying their homes on a mortgage and four out of five of them grant a mortgage to a building society.

The building societies started about 150 years ago and have increased in size and influence during the last 50 years, due at least in part to government support, including favourable tax laws. Mortgages also serve the building society investor (who may be a borrower at the same time). Because of the many functions which can be fulfilled by land – shelter, direct or indirect investment – it can be difficult to untangle the financial interests in disputes. Some building society cases, for example, concern the society coming into conflict with an owner of another interest in the land when the land is subject to a trust and a trustee has mortgaged it without declaring the equitable interest. Where the courts decide against the society, it is ultimately all the members (borrowers and investors) who foot the bill; where they decide against the beneficiary, he alone bears the cost.

There may be several mortgages created over one interest in land. Also, mortgages may be granted on any interest in land; thus, mortgages are frequently granted on leases (but only a long lease is sufficient security) (see 6.2 below). Land is often sold after a mortgage debt has been paid off (*redeemed*) but land may be sold subject to a mortgage, just as it may be sold subject to any other interest. There may also be mortgages of other property, such as company shares, and the same general rules apply. Some of the commercial cases in this chapter concern such mortgages.

Rentcharges are now relatively unimportant and are briefly explained at the end of this chapter.

6.2 Types of Mortgage (see Figure 6.2)

Legal mortgages

A mortgage by a long lease (often 3000 years) is often called a *demise*. A date is set for the money to be repaid (*the legal date of redemption*) and, when it is repaid, the lease is surrendered back to the borrower because

Figure 6.2 *Types of mortgage*

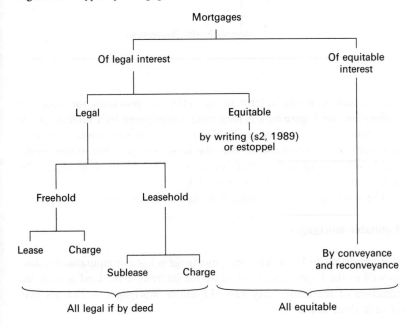

Figure 6.3 *Mortgage of a freehold by a long lease*

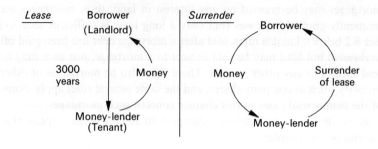

Figure 6.4 *Mortgage of a leasehold by a sublease*

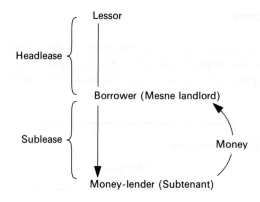

such a lease contains a term to this effect (a provision for *cesser on redemption,* see Figure 6.3). A long lease is mortgaged by a sublease, a few days shorter than the lease itself (Figure 6.4). If the borrower breaches a covenant of the headlease so that the lease is forfeit, the money-lender (sublessee) can apply for relief (see above, 5.8). All these mortgages by demise are now covered by ss 85–6 LPA.

The mortgage by legal charge was explained in 6.1 above.

Equitable mortgages

It is important to know whether a mortgage is legal or equitable because, as well as the lesser security of equitable interests if the land is sold, the remedies of the lender may vary. Equitable mortgages or charges may arise in three situations:

1 where an equitable interest is mortgaged; this can be done by conveying the whole equitable interest to the lender who promises to reconvey it when the debt is repaid. (Before 1925, this was the way legal estates were mortgaged; this is now impossible at law and any attempt to do it with a legal interest in land will instead create a 3000-year lease (or a sublease) instead (ss 85–6 LPA).)

2 where there is an express equitable charge (forerunner of the legal charge);

3 where there is a contract for a legal mortgage under s.2, 1989 Law of Property (Miscellaneous Provisions) Act, or by estoppel (see 2.6 above). Before 1989 an equitable mortgage could be created by depositing the title deeds or Land Certificate with the lender in exchange for the loan, but now that part performance has been abolished this method of creating a mortgage is obsolete, as confirmed by *United Bank of Kuwait plc* v. *Sahib* [1995] 2 All ER 973 (and see [1994] Conv 465). However, it is possible that an equitable mortgage might be created under the rules of estoppel (see 2.6 above).

6.3 The Position of the Lender

The legal lender

The lender (mortgagee) has remedies to enforce the payment of the money due to him (1–6 in the following list) and certain other rights (7–10). The legal mortgagee may:

1 take possession of the property;
2 sell the property;
3 appoint a receiver;
4 *foreclose*;
5 sue on the personal covenant;
6 *consolidate*;
7 hold the title deeds (or, in registered land, the Charge Certificate);
8 insure the property at the borrower's expense;
9 grant leases and accept surrenders of leases (ss. 99–100 LPA);
10 exercise rights in connection with a series of mortgages ('*tacking*').

The lender does not have to choose between these remedies: he can pursue several at the same time. They were developed when mortgages were not so commonly used for home buying and have been 'adjusted' by statute to protect the security of home buyers, just as tenants' security has been protected by modern legislation.

The issues which arise where there are several mortgages on the same land are referred to at p. 87 and in 6.6 below. Some of the other rights are examined here in a little detail, but first it is necessary to examine a problem which can particularly affect the rights and remedies of the lender: 'undue influence'.

Avoiding undue influence

A large number of cases have recently raised the question of undue influence in mortgages – a symptom of the increase in family home repossessions. Typically, a mortgagee institution seeks to repossess a home because of arrears, and one of the joint borrowers then claims to have signed the mortgage deed under the undue influence of the other (or one stands surety for the loan of the other because of his undue influence). If the institution did not take steps to ensure that the signature was properly obtained without any undue influence, the mortgage will be entirely void as far as the injured party is concerned. The two leading cases were decided in the House of Lords on the same day and provide guidelines to money-lending institutions which should enable them to ensure that any party involved in a loan on the security of land knows exactly what they are getting into and that they are making a free choice. (Some of the many of the cases reported since then concern mortgages taken out before the guidelines were laid down and are of limited precedent value.)

In the first of the Lords' decisions, *Barclays Bank plc* v. *O'Brien* [1993] 4 All ER 417, Mr O'Brien was the sole legal owner, but his wife had an equitable share. He told her he was borrowing £60 000 on mortgage for three weeks to save his business, so she signed all the surety forms at the bank without reading any of them and without any independent advice. In fact, the loan was for £135 000; within 6 months the repayments were seriously in arrears and the bank sought possession.

Mrs O'Brien successfully argued that the mortgage had been induced by her husband's undue influence – he was her trustee and yet he had 'abused the trust and confidence reposed' by her in him, and she could set aside the transaction as far as he was concerned. Further, the bank had constructive notice of the facts giving rise to her right to set the mortgage aside: a prudent bank would have made inquiries of a wife in this position because it was not to her financial advantage and there was 'a substantial risk' that the trustee – as he was her husband – might exercise undue influence over her. Therefore, the mortgagee bank could not take possession against her (and see 11.8 below). Lord Browne-Wilkinson stated that banks in this position should interview the wife separately, the whole transaction should be explained to her and she should be advised to take independent legal advice.

In the second decision, *CIBC Mortgages* v. *Pitt* [1993] 4 All ER 433 the facts were fairly similar but here Mrs Pitt, the wife, was a joint legal owner of the home. As joint legal owner she could be presumed to be benefiting financially from the mortgage loan (it was ostensibly to buy a second home, but her husband really wanted the money for gambling on the stock exchange) and therefore the bank was not put on notice to take steps to protect her position. Ironically, joint legal ownership of the land, which usually puts a person into a stronger position, gives less protection here because of the Lords' (possibly unfounded) assumption that a wife or cohabitee who is a joint legal owner is automatically going to gain a financial advantage from the loan, whereas one who is merely an equitable owner is not.

These two cases provide a basic rule, but many detailed questions remain, for example concerning the conduct of 'independent legal advisers' and the protection of non-cohabitees who are nevertheless in a close sexual/emotional relationship. Several recent decisions in the Court of Appeal show 'creditor-sympathetic outcomes' (Fehlberg, 59 OJLS (1996) 675); no doubt the story will continue.

Taking possession
In theory, because he has a lease, a lender has the right to '*go into possession before the ink is dry on the mortgage*'. (Building societies normally promise that they will not take possession unless the borrower fails to pay.) If the lender does take possession, he must not take any unfair financial advantage and must take care of the premises. It might seem extraordinary that the lender has the right to move in as soon as the mortgage deed is signed, but in practice this only happens if the borrower defaults. The lender then obtains a possession order before selling the property: it is important to take possession before sale to get the borrower out, since otherwise the land may be difficult to sell.

Where the property is (or includes) a home, s.36 Administration of Justice Act 1970 (as amended by s.8 Administration of Justice Act 1973) gives the court discretion, in a hearing for possession, to postpone a decision if the borrower is likely to be able to pay his arrears 'within a reasonable period'. In the harsh economic climate of the late 1980s and early 1990s, repossessions increased in frequency – doubling between 1989–91 – affecting the whole market in land. A number of cases have therefore focused on the issue of when the court might exercise the s 36 discretion; some have concerned the defaulting borrower's liklihood of finding employment and repaying arrears, and others on the chances of his being able to sell the land within a reasonable period.

The Court of Appeal stated in *Cheltenham and Gloucester Building Society* v. *Norgan* [1996] 1 All ER 449 that, although a 'normal' period of two years had become fairly established in judgments, 'a reasonable period' was not limited to any particular time span. Here, the mortgage term was to end 13 years from the time of the claim for a possession order, and the Court held that this could be a reasonable period within 'the logic and spirit of the Act'; they effectively asked the lower court to decide whether it could reschedule the debt over the whole repayment period. In future cases, such a rescheduling from the outset of the mortgagor's difficulties might avoid the continuing struggle and repeated orders and delays in repossession proceedings.

Sale

If the mortgage is made by deed, and unless there is a term to the contrary in the contract, the power of sale *arises* as soon as the legal date for redeeming the mortgage has passed (s.101 LPA). The legal date of redemption is usually set 6 months after the creation of the mortgage.

However, by s.103 LPA, the lender cannot *exercise* the power unless one of the conditions listed in the box is satisfied:

THE POWER OF SALE BECOMES EXERCISABLE IF:

1 **THE DEFAULT CONTINUES THREE MONTHS AFTER A NOTICE REQUIRING PAYMENT IS SERVED; OR**
2 **INTEREST IS TWO MONTHS IN DEFAULT; OR**
3 **THE BORROWER HAS BROKEN ANOTHER TERM OF THE MORTGAGE**

Although he only has a long lease (or sublease or charge), the lender may sell the borrower's whole interest as soon as one of the conditions has been fulfilled (ss.88–9). He does not need a court order (but he usually has one granting possession). Once the land is sold, the lender is under a *duty to account* to the borrower; this means that he must take reasonable care to get a good price when selling the property but he does not have to wait for an upturn in the market. (For building society mortgages, this rule is contained in s.13(7) Building Societies Act 1986.)

In a Privy Council case from Hong Kong, *China and South Seas Bank* v. *Tan* [1990] 1 AC 536, there was a mortgage loan of 30 million dollars on the security of shares. When the repayment became due, the shares were worth enough to repay the debt but by the time the mortgagee decided to exercise the power of sale the shares were worthless. The mortgage's surety argued that the mortgagee owed him a duty of care to sell as soon as possible, but this was rejected:

'If the creditor chose to exercise his power of sale over the mortgaged security he must sell for the current market value but the creditor must decide in his own interest if and when he should sell. The creditor does not become a trustee of the mortgaged securities . . .' (Lord Templeman at p. 545.

In another case from Hong Kong, *Tse Kwong Lam* v. *Wong Chit Sen* [1983] 1 WLR 1349, Tse had granted a mortgage to Wong in 1963 on a large development in Hong Kong. Three years later he was in arrears and the land was sold at auction to the only bidder, a company, owned by the lender and his wife and children. This in itself would not necessarily have been relevant, but the lender could not prove that:

'he protected the interests of the borrower by taking expert advice as to the method of sale, as to the steps which ought reasonably to be taken to make the sale a success and as to the amount of the reserve [minimum price].' (Lord Templeman, p. 1359).

The normal remedy in such a case is for the sale to be set aside, but here the Privy Council did not do so as the borrower had been 'guilty of inexcusable delay'; he had not pursued the matter for many years. He won the alternative remedy of damages, the difference between the price which was obtained and the price which should have been obtained.

The lender who has sold mortgaged property must also take care to protect the interests of others. He uses the proceeds of sale to pay his expenses and to pay himself the capital and interest due under the mortgage; he then holds the rest for whomever is entitled (s.105 LPA). This will usually be the borrower but it may be a second or subsequent mortgagee if there is more than one mortgage. Thus, although he is not a trustee of his *power* of sale, he is a trustee of the *proceeds* of sale and must act in good faith.

The buyer from a mortgagee must check that a power of sale exists but need not make sure that it has actually arisen. However, if he knows of, or suspects, any 'impropriety' he might not get a good title and for this reason he would be wise to ensure that the mortgagee has taken reasonable care, otherwise he might lose the land and have to try to get the purchase price back from the mortgagee.

Preventing sale
Sometimes, especially when the value of land has been falling, the mortgagee might seek to prevent, rather than to force, a sale of the mortgaged land. Where there is a negative equity, the borrower may be keen to sell the land and repay as much of the debt as possible to prevent

the interest due on the loan spiralling upwards while the lender may be as keen to prevent a sale, leasing out the land in the meantime in the hope that it might increase in value at some point in the future.

This arose in *Palk* v. *Mortgage Services Funding plc* [1993] 2 WLR 415 where the borrower had found a buyer for the land, but the price was about £50 000 less than the then mortgage debt. The interest on the debt was accumulating at a rate of £43 000 per year and an annual rent – as sought by the mortgagee – would not be more than about £13 000. The mortgagee argued that it could prevent a sale if the price was less than what was needed to repay the debt in full. Mrs Palk claimed, however, that under s.91 LPA (originally intended to facilitate sales in foreclosure proceedings) the court has a discretion to order a sale of mortgaged property. Here the Court of Appeal held for Mrs Palk: any borrower, even one suffering with a negative equity, can ask the court to order a sale because under s.91 the court has an 'unfettered discretion' here to prevent 'manifest unfairness'.

Appointing a receiver

A lender can appoint a receiver – who manages the land – in the same circumstances in which he has the power of sale (s.101 LPA). This can be very convenient in a commercial mortgage, for example, if the land is let to tenants and the mortgagee wants the rents to pay off interest which is due. The advantage of appointing a receiver rather than going into possession is that a mortgagee in possession is personally liable to the borrower for any loss but, if he appoints a receiver, the receiver must pay for his own mistakes. This is because, by s.109 LPA, the receiver is deemed to be the agent of the mortgagor (the borrower).

Foreclosure

This is an equitable order which ends all the borrower's rights to the land and is now extremely rare. Once the legal date of redemption has passed, the order is theoretically available, but it is only granted if the court is clear that the borrower will never be able to repay. In very special circumstances, the foreclosure order can be re-opened.

Suing on the personal covenant

The lender may sue the borrower for the debt, and if he succeeeds he can force a sale of *any* of the borrower's property.

Consolidation

In rare cases, where the lender owns mortgages granted by the same borrower over different pieces of land, he has a right to consolidate them. This means that he may join the various mortgages together; he can refuse to allow the borrower to redeem one of the mortgages without redeeming the other(s). Consolidation can be useful if one piece of land is not sufficient security for the debt. The right arises when the power is contained in the mortgage itself, and is exercisable only when the legal date for redemption has passed. There are a number of technical rules, very clearly explained in Fairest 1980, pp. 121–9.

Holding the title deeds
The first legal mortgagee of unregistered land is entitled to hold the deeds; if the title is registered, the Land Certificate remains in the Land Registry (see 10.7 below) and this makes it easier if the lender has to sell the property. It also means that, because the borrower does not have proof of his title, he is prevented from selling or re-mortgaging the land without admitting the existence of the mortgage.

The equitable lender

Both equitable mortgagee and equitable chargee can sue on the borrower's personal promise to pay but, apart from this, their rights differ.

The equitable mortgagee
If an equitable mortgage is not made by deed then there is no automatic power to sell or appoint a receiver, but the mortgagee can get a court order to do so (s.91 LPA). If there is a deed, the equitable lender generally has the same remedies as a legal lender but he must be careful to draft the document to give him the right to sell the legal estate. Case-law is not clear whether he has an automatic right to go into possession.

The equitable chargee
The rights of 'a mere equitable chargee' are fewer than those of other lenders. This kind of lender only has the remedy of sale or appointment of a receiver (both by court order).

6.4 The Position of the Borrower

As well as the rights which arise directly out of the lender's duties – for example to take precautions against undue influence and to obtain a good price on sale – the borrower has special rights to protection against oppression by a mortgagee, especially in relation to the terms of the contract and, in cases decided recently, in relation to the power to sell the land where there is negative equity (that is, when the mortgage debt exceeds the value of the land).

The equity of redemption

The *equity of redemption* is the name given to the whole bundle of rights which equity created to protect borrowers against exploitative money-lenders (and hence the term 'negative equity'). This is an equitable interest in land and can be sold, mortgaged and so on like any other interest in land. It can now be said to include:

1   the equitable right to redeem the mortgage;
2   the right to have oppressive terms removed from the contract;
3   the right to seek relief from an extortionate bargain under the Consumer Credit Act 1974.

Equity looks at the reality and not the name given to an agreement and, if it is actually a loan on the security of land, equity will recognise it as a mortgage and protect the borrower: '*once a mortgage always a mortgage*'. The rules are summarised in the expression that there must be '*no clogs or fetters*' on the equity of redemption. ('Clog' here is not a wooden shoe but a heavy piece of wood tied to an animal to prevent it wandering off.) The rules are explained in the following sections; it must be noted that some of the older cases cited in the books reflect a different financial world, and, furthermore, one in which the House of Lords was bound to follow its own earlier decisions. It is likely that modern judges will find a way around inconvenient precedents.

The equitable right to redeem

As mentioned in 6.2 above, mortgage agreements always specify a legal date of redemption. However, equity refused to enforce this and created an *equitable right to redeem*: the lender would be ordered by equity to accept the money if this was fair even after the legal date had passed.

The difference between (1) the equity of redemption and (2) the equitable right to redeem is that: (1) refers to all the borrower's rights, while (2) is merely one of these rights. (See Figure 6.5.)

Equity will make void any promise that a borrower will never redeem: for example, *Samuel* v. *Jarrah Timber and Wood Paving Co Ltd* [1904] AC 323 concerned a mortgage of company stock (a debenture). In the mortgage deed the borrower gave the lender an option to purchase; the lender could therefore choose to buy the stock from the borrower and the borrower might thus be prevented from redeeming the mortgage. The House of Lords declared the option void because it made the equitable

Figure 6.5 *Rights of the borrower (mortgagor)*

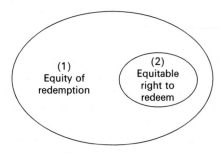

right to redeem 'illusory'. The decision was made very reluctantly – in 1904 the House could not reverse its own judgments – as the Lords felt that this arrangement, made by two large companies, was quite different from the kind of case for which the rule had been established:

> 'The directors of a trading company in search of financial assistance are certainly in a very different position from that of an impecunious landowner in the toils of a crafty money-lender.' (Lord Macnaghten, p. 327)

Modern decisions take into account the relative bargaining powers of the two parties and an agreement made by equals is likely to be enforced. If the parties today wished to create an option to purchase, they would probably be able to do so providing it was clear that the lender was not taking an unfair advantage of the borrower.

Any agreement which postpones the equitable right to redeem so that it effectively becomes meaningless will also be void. This occurred in *Fairclough* v. *Swan Brewery Co Ltd* [1912] AC 565, where Fairclough had a 17-year lease of a hotel. His lessor was the Swan Brewery, and they lent him money on the security of his lease. The legal date of redemption was fixed for a few weeks before the lease ended. As the equitable right to redeem does not arise until the legal date has passed, this postponement of the legal date of redemption made the mortgage effectively irredeemable and the promise was therefore held void. However, in *Knightsbridge Estate's Trust Ltd* v. *Byrne* [1939] Ch 441, a case between two large companies, the legal date for redemption of the mortgage (for £310 000) was set 40 years in the future. Given the relationship between the parties and the fact that the land was freehold, the Court of Appeal held that the term was enforceable. This was:

'a commercial agreement between two important corporations, experienced in such matters, and has none of the features of an oppressive bargain.' (Greene MR, p. 625)

Another of equity's concerns was the unfair advantage taken by a lender who restricted the borrower's commercial activities during the mortgage, such as a promise by a shopkeeper that he would only buy wholesale goods from the mortgagee. This is called a *solus agreement* and is subject to the law relating to restraint of trade.

Equity has also declared void any terms in the mortgage which would prevent the borrower freely enjoying his land after he has repaid all the money. An example of this is *Noakes & Co Ltd* v. *Rice* [1902] AC 24, where the owner of a 26-year lease of a pub mortgaged it to a brewery and promised he would buy liquor only from the lender for the whole of the lease. The House of Lords held that the promise was ineffective: the lender could not prevent him regaining his property free of ties when he repaid the loan. In *Kreglinger* v. *New Patagonia Meat & Cold Storage Co Ltd* [1914] AC 25, however, the House decided that a promise which was to remain after the mortgage had been redeemed was valid. This case concerned a loan of £10 000 and the security was a 'floating charge', an arrangement concerning company property which is very similar to a mortgage of freehold land. The promise was that the borrower would sell his sheepskins only to the lender for 5 years, regardless of when the loan was repaid. This was not a clog on the equitable right to redeem because it amounted to a separate arrangement; it was not invalid merely because it was contained in the same document as the mortgage.

The borrower's equitable right to redeem the mortgage does not last for ever. It ends when the property is sold by the lender, or if there is a foreclosure order. It will also be lost if it becomes unenforceable under s.16 Limitation Act 1980 (see Chapter 3).

Oppressive terms

Equity developed rules against other clogs on the equity of redemption, and declared void any other 'unconscionable or oppressive terms' in the mortgage. In *Multiservice Bookbinding Ltd* v. *Marden* [1979] Ch 84, the bookbinding company granted a mortgage as security for a loan of £36 000. The interest rate was linked to the Swiss franc, because the pound was very unstable. The fluctuation in the money markets meant that the borrower would have to pay £45 000 in interest. Browne-Wilkinson J held that this might be unreasonable but was not oppressive or unconscionable. For a promise to be struck out, it must be shown that the objectionable terms were imposed 'in a morally reprehensible manner . . . which affects his [the mortgagee's] conscience'. Again, the court showed its reluctance to intervene in a commercial agreement between equals, but the decision might have been otherwise had the borrower been an amateur and the lender a professional.

Extortionate bargains

The Consumer Credit Act 1974 replaced older statutes about money-lenders. It is a very important part of consumer law and is only briefly referred to here. (Details can be found in Gray (1993) pp. 964–8.) The Act concerns agreements between an individual (including an individual in the course of business) and anyone who lends money. Under s.137 the court can – amongst other powers – 're-open' the agreement if the payments are 'grossly exorbitant' or 'grossly contravene ordinary principles of fair dealing'. The Act mostly applies to second mortgages, because the court's powers do not apply to mortgage loans made by certain institutions (such as building societies and local authorities); banks' lending, however, is covered. Often these loans are for home improvements, like building an extension or installing central heating, but sometimes they are an act of desperation by a defaulting borrower and it is particularly here that the borrower needs protection in shark-infested waters. However, it seems that the courts have upset few agreements; this is because the more needy (and therefore weak) the borrower, the more justified is the lender in imposing a high interest rate because of the risk he is taking.

6.5 Discharge of Mortgages

A mortgage is ended when the lease, sublease or charge is removed from the title to the property. Normally in registered land the borrower obtains a signed receipt on the mortgage document; in registered land a form has to be sent to the Land Registry. In the case of a mortgage by a long lease, repayment of the loan means that the lease becomes a *satisfied term*.

6.6 Priority of Mortgages

The general rules

The rules about priority in mortgages are applied when there are several mortgages of one piece of land. If the borrower defaults and the land is not worth enough to pay back all the debts, then one or more of the lenders may lose money; the priority rules determine which of them is to be unlucky. There have been few cases this century on priorities but some land lawyers greatly enjoy creating and solving priority puzzles, especially concerning three or more mortgages. As the depressed land market of the early 1990s creates 'negative equities', any except the first mortgagee of a property with several mortgages is particularly at risk, and therefore new cases on priorities may be expected.

The basic rules are stated very briefly in the next sections; for further details see for example Cheshire (1994) pp. 719–30.

There are also special rules about the situation where there are several mortgages on one piece of land and a mortgagee owns two or more of them; he may be allowed to *tack*. This means that where (1) Oliver has borrowed money on a mortgage of his flat from Andy, and then (2) borrowed on a (second) mortgage from Belinda, if (3) Andy lends more money (by a third mortgage) on the security of the flat, Andy *may* be able to jump over Belinda's second mortgage and 'tack' (glue together) his first and third mortgages (compare consolidation of mortgages, 6.3 above). For the detailed rules, see Cheshire (1994) pp. 714–16.

Losing priority

A lender may lose his priority over other lenders if he is guilty of fraud, misrepresentation or gross negligence. Any lender who lies (expressly or impliedly) about his rights, and thereby enables the borrower to get another mortgage loan, will lose priority. Similarly, if he is grossly negligent and allows the borrower to get back his Land Certificate, so that the borrower can pretend the land is not burdened by a mortgage, the careless lender will not be able to defeat a subsequent mortgagee.

The set of rules to be applied depends first on whether the mortgage is of a legal or equitable interest (see 6.2 above), and second, on whether the land is registered or not.

Mortgages of a legal interest in unregistered land

The basic rules in unregistered land are the same as those which apply in any conflict between interests, but they have been complicated by the rules about registration of land charges (Chapter 9). Where a mortgage has to be registered, it ranks according to the date of registration, not the date of its creation. Briefly, subject to fraud or negligence, any mortgage *with* deposit of title deeds takes priority over all mortgages except any earlier mortgage which was properly registered; any mortgage *without* deposit of title deeds is subject to (a) any earlier mortgage with deposit of deeds, and (b) any other mortgage which was properly registered.

There is a wonderfully complicated situation, involving three or more mortgages, which creates a completely insoluble problem, but explaining it is not a priority of this book. (For details, see Cheshire (1988) p. 681–2.)

Mortgages of a legal interest in registered land

In registered land the general rule is that, once a mortgage or charge has been protected on the Register, it will defeat all later mortgages as well as earlier mortgages which have not been so protected. Thus the first mortgage entered on the Register ranks first and the remainder rank according to the date of their registration.

Mortgages of an equitable interest in any land

In the very rare case where the interest mortgaged is an equitable interest under a trust, the mortgages rank according to the order in which notice of the mortgage was given to the trustees, whether the title is registered (s.5 Land Registration Act 1986) or unregistered (s.137 LPA).

6.7 Rentcharges

A rentcharge is a right to a regular payment of money secured on freehold land; there is rent but no lease. If the money is not paid as due, the owner of the rentcharge can levy distress (see 5.8 above), sue for the debt, lease the land to trustees, or take possession of it.

Rentcharges used to serve several purposes, but now the only one possible is to attach to a piece of land a positive duty to do something. Thus, in a block of freehold flats, rentcharges can be used to make sure that all the residents contribute to a maintenance fund. These are called 'estate rentcharges'. Since the Rentcharges Act 1977, rentcharges (other than estate rentcharges) may be wound up according to a statutory formula. Their limited function today may be taken over by the proposed commonhold interest in land (see above 5.11).

6.8 Comment

The law of mortgages illustrates very clearly the difference between legal rules and what really happens: in every part of this area of law, theory and practice diverge. In 1991 the Law Commission (No. 204) recommended that the complex theoretical foundations and the miscellaneous protections offered by a random combination of common law, equitable and statutory rules should be completely replaced by new interests in land, called 'formal' and 'informal land mortgages'. The only function of these new interests would be to provide security for the loan, and some of the terms would be laid down in legislation. At the same time, the jurisdictions to set aside unfair terms would be codified.

The existing law, however, shows how it is possible to provide a flexible response to social and economic change behind the facade of unchanging concepts and rules, for cases such as *Palk* indicate how judges can readjust the balance between borrowers and lenders according to changes in lending practice and in the marketplace. On the other hand, the judges seem to be having more difficulty in adjusting to changing perceptions of the appropriateness of using a family home as security for business debt, as shown in *O'Brien* and *Pitt*. While they have ensured some limited protection for the partner who is merely an equitable, not a legal, owner, they have not yet sufficiently addressed the the shifting economic roles of husbands and wives or cohabitees. Nor has there yet been any judicial exploration of the complexity of the choices of emotional partners in financial difficulties as opposed to the decision-making processes of banks and other lenders who fit the contractual stereotype of the 'rational self-interested man'.

Summary

1   Legal mortgages are made by deed; they may be created by demise (or subdemise) or legal charge.
2   Equitable mortgages may be of a legal or equitable interest. Legal interests may be mortgaged equitably by a contract to grant a legal mortgage or by equitable charge. Equitable interests can also be mortgaged by conveyance and reconveyance.
3   The lender must take care to avoid constructive notice of undue influence of a mortgagee over a surety where there is a close emotional tie and the transaction is not apparently in the surety's financial interest.
4   The legal lender has the right to take possession of property but usually only does so when the borrower defaults; repossession of mortgaged homes is protected by statute.
5   In a legal mortgage, the power of sale (or to appoint a receiver) normally arises once the legal date of redemption has passed and becomes exercisable if s.103 is satisfied: the lender is then a trustee of the proceeds, not the power, of sale. The borrower may be able to sell despite a negative equity.
6   Equitable mortgagees and chargees may have fewer rights than legal lenders.
7   The borrower's rights (the equity of redemption) include the rights (reinforced by statute) not to have the equitable right to redeem

restricted, or to suffer unconscionable or oppressive terms; cases now depend on whether the lender has taken an unfair advantage.
8   Where there is a succession of mortgages, priority rules decide in what order the lenders should have their money repaid.

Exercises

1   Why are there legal and equitable rights to redeem a mortgage?
2   When does a mortgagee have a power of sale?
3   How may a legal lease be mortgaged?
4   Can there be a term in a mortgage which continues after the mortgage has been redeemed?
5   To what extent is a mortgage a trustee?
6   Clayton owns a freehold shop with a flat above where he lives with Emily who has an equitable share in the land. In 1994, in order to clear all his previous debts, he borrowed £100 000 on mortgage from Sharks Inc. who gave him documents for Emily to sign; she did so without reading them when he told her that they were 'just something about my will'. The interest rate was set at 5% above the bank rate.

Advise Emily in light of the fact that Clayton has fallen seriously behind with the repayments. He has a letter from his friend Pat who writes that he would buy the property for £80 000.

[handwritten margin note: benefit must be attached to the land]

7   Easements and Profits

[handwritten note: interests over someone else's land. easements are a right to do something on someone elses land.]

7.1   Introduction

Easements and profits are always linked together as interests 'over some-one else's land' (*in alieno solo*). Profits in medieval times were very nearly as important as the fee simple; the rules were settled centuries ago and have changed little. Easements are also ancient but they only achieved their present form within the last hundred years or so, after the enclosures of commonly held rural land and urbanisation. Easements are much more important than profits, which are now rarely created, having largely been replaced by contracts. Both profits and easements are generally liable to be affected by decisions in the law of tort; thus this chapter illustrates some of the interrelationships of the law of contract, tort and land.

The difference between an easement and a profit lies partly in the nature of the right enjoyed: easements are rights to *do* something on another's land, while profits are rights to *take* something from it. In addition, it seems that the benefit of an easement must be attached to land (must be 'appurtenant'), but a profit can exist without being connected to land ownership (may 'lie in gross'). There are also differences between them in the rules about acquiring such rights by long use.

The nature of land means that its value can often be increased by a right over neighbouring land; the most extreme example is the right to drive across a neighbour's field in order to reach land which is otherwise accessible only by helicopter. More common instances are the running of gas and water pipes, drains and electric cables from one house or flat to the next.

The essential problem for the judges in this area of land law – which is hardly touched by the 1925 legislation – is that they have to balance at least two conflicting demands. They would like to increase the value of land, for example by allowing a right to walk through a neighbour's garden as a short cut to a garage (see Figure 7.1), because this will make that land 'a better and more convenient property'. This will, however, decrease the value of the other land by reducing privacy and restricting what may be done there. As in the old rules about the running of leasehold covenants, the judges seek to ensure that the market in land is not depressed either by making agreed rights unduly insecure, or by unduly *[handwritten: If not easement - merely a license (personal)]*

preventing the exercise of other valuable rights. As well as these tensions between the interests of private landowners, and between them and the general public interest in the market in land, there is also the tension between private land ownership and land use by 'non-neighbours', but this latter question is not usually addressed in this country through the law of easements.

The general rule is that land owners cannot simply create easements as they will: 'Incidents of a novel kind cannot be devised and attached to property at the fancy or caprice of any owner' (Lord Brougham LC in 1834). At the same time, 'The category of . . . easements must alter and expand with the changes that take place in the circumstances of mankind' (Lord St Leonards LC in 1852). If a new right is, in the judges' view, not capable of being an easement or profit, it is only a licence. The significance of this is that a licence is said not to be an 'interest in land': the rights and duties are not glued to the land so that they pass automatically with it, but are only personal (see Chapter 13).

Easements and profits have the vocabulary appropriate to their great age, and some of the old terms have already been mentioned. 'Dominant tenement' and 'servient tenement' are most important. In the law of easements (and sometimes in profits), the claimed right to use the land of another must benefit ('accommodate') one piece of land, the dominant tenement; the land which provides the benefit ('serves') is the servient tenement (see Figure 7.l).

In problem questions, there are usually just two issues:

---

1 IS THIS AN EASEMENT (OR PROFIT)?
AND
2 HAS IT BEEN ACQUIRED HERE?

Figure 7.1 *An example of an easement of way*

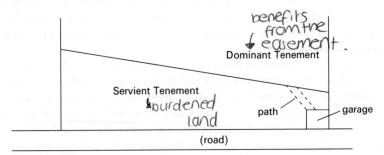

[handwritten: benefits from the ↓ easement.]
Dominant Tenement

Servient Tenement
[handwritten: ↳ burdened land]

path

garage

(road)

These problems are usually straightforward to answer, provided the two issues are tackled separately and in order, although in many decided cases the two issues are elided.

[handwritten: requirements :]

[handwritten: dominant + servient accommodation]

7.2   Easements

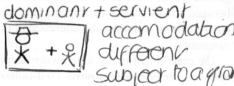

[handwritten: different subject to a grant]

The nature of easements

It is hard to define an easement but easy to give examples, or the standard list of the four requirements of an easement:

1   There must be a dominant and a servient tenement.
2   The easement must accommodate the dominant tenement.
3   The dominant and servient tenements must be owned or occupied by different people.
4   The easement must be capable of being the subject of a grant.

[handwritten: need to be an easement]

The authority for this list is *Re Ellenborough Park* [1956] Ch 131. Owners of houses near the Park (in a square near the sea at Weston-Super-Mare) had been granted the right to use it 'as a leisure garden', but during the Second World War it had been taken over by the government. By statute, individual land owners were entitled to compensation if they had been deprived of a legal right, and the only possible such right was an easement. Lord Evershed MR in the Court of Appeal reviewed the history of easements and affirmed that this was an easement.

Dominant and servient tenements

Clearly in *Ellenborough Park*, there was a servient tenement (the Park) and there were dominant tenements (the houses). Sometimes, however, this is not so obvious. In *Miller v. Emcer Products Ltd* [1956] Ch 304, a tenant had an easement to use the landlord's lavatory, and here the dominant and servient tenements were not two pieces of land, but two estates in land, the freehold and the leasehold; the tenant had the dominant tenement and the landlord, the servient.

In *London and Blenheim Estates Ltd* v. *Ladbroke Retail Parks Ltd* [1993] 4 All ER 157 the Court of Appeal held that it is not possible to create an easement without identifying the dominant land. In this case an option was claimed for an easement to park cars on unspecified land owned by the grantor but, by the time the option was exercised, the land had been sold to someone else; the claim to an easement here could not succeed.

[handwritten left margin: have to identify benefitted land.]

[handwritten bottom: was no dominant land (it was sold) because there]

Accommodating the dominant tenement

Just as in the pre-1996 law of leases where the covenant has to 'touch and concern' the land (see 5.7 above), the test is whether the claimed easement benefits the land itself and not merely the land-owner. Whether the easement touched and concerned (or 'accommodated' or benefited) the dominant tenement was a difficult question in *Re Ellenborough Park*. Earlier cases were divided on whether the right to use a garden could accommodate land, but Evershed MR concluded that it is 'primarily a question of fact'. In a case like this one, the dominant tenements did benefit from the garden use; it might have been different if the dominant tenements had not been family homes. *IMPT   held to be personal mgnt-*

A claim failed on this point in *Hill v. Tupper* (1863) 2 H & C 121 where the owners of the Basingstoke Canal leased part of a canal bank to Hill, granting him the sole right to hire out pleasure boats. A local publican then also rented out boats and Hill tried to stop him. It was held that, while a general right to put boats on the canal could benefit Hill's land, the exclusive right to hire out boats did not; it was a personal right only and could not be an easement. The courts have also had to consider claims arising from a new use of land, tower blocks of flats. It was held that the right to throw rubbish down rubbish chutes, for example, is capable of accommodating the dominant tenement (*Liverpool City Council v. Irwin* [1977] AC 239).

This requirement seems to have been adopted under the influence of Roman law during the last century, and Sturley (96 LQR (1980) 557) argues that the authority is very weak. He claims that allowing easements in gross (that is, easements which are not attached to benefiting land), such as the right to land a helicopter on distant land, would not now unduly burden titles but could encourage maximum utilisation of land. *encourages utilisation of land*

Different ownership or occupation

A person cannot have rights against herself. If both tenements come into the hands of one person, the easement is ended ('extinguished by unity of seisin'), but it might one day come back to life (see 7.5 below).

Capable of being the subject of a grant

The requirement that the easement must be capable of being the subject of a grant is not altogether clear. It seems to mean that the nature and extent of the easement must be capable of being described reasonably precisely, and that it must not amount to a claim to the whole of the servient tenement so that an owner is actually excluded from her own land. (The tenant in Miller's case succeeded because he would only have been using the lavatory some of the time.) In *Re Ellenborough Park* the deed was sufficiently precise about the house owners' rights to use the garden, and these rights did not amount to an indefinite right to wander all over the Park, but merely to use it as a garden: to walk on paths, sit about or have picnics, for example. This use did not exclude the owner.

In *Copeland* v. *Greenhalf* [1952] Ch 488 on the other hand, the defendant was a wheelwright who had for many years used a strip of the plaintiff's land alongside a road for storing and mending vehicles. He claimed an easement acquired by long use but failed, because it amounted to a claim over the whole of the land; this is more like a claim for adverse possession. Car parking is capable of being an easement, for it can accomodate the dominant tenement, but it depends on the precise nature of the claim; such a claim could have been an easement in the *London and Blenheim Estates* case (above and see Bridge [1994] CLJ 229).

This rule also requires that there was once someone capable of granting the right (a limited company, for example, might not have the legal power to do so). Also, there must be someone capable of receiving the grant, that is, the owner of the alleged dominant tenement must be a legal person (see 7.8 below).

Types of easement

The cases mentioned so far give a fairly good idea of the sort of things which can amount to easements. Other well-known easements include the right to light; this is normally restricted to enough light coming through a specific window for the 'comfortable' use of the premises. There are also easements for the use of naturally running water and for the support of a building (for example, semi-detached houses have mutual easements of support).

All the easements referred to thus far have been capable of being enjoyed without the owner of the servient tenement having to take any positive action, but the 'spurious easement of fencing' is an exception. In such a case, the owner of the servient tenement must keep her boundary fences in repair. Some judges have said that new claims which demand positive action from the servient owner will not be recognised as easements, but this might be unduly restrictive. In *Liverpool City Council* v. *Irwin* [1977] (above), tenants in a tower block stopped paying rent because the common parts of the block were in such a bad condition. They had no written tenancy agreement, only a list of rules, and the House of Lords implied into the tenancies easements to use the passages, lifts and rubbish chutes. On the facts of this case they held that the lessor was not in breach of duty to repair, but suggested that where, for example, there was an easement of way along a passage with no natural light, there might be a duty to maintain reasonable lighting since without it the easement would be unusable.

The courts have also said that easements which have a negative effect will not be permitted. An example of a 'negative easement' is a claim that a neighbour may not demolish her house because this would expose a house on the alleged dominant tenement to the wind and rain. This claim was held not to be an easement in *Phipps* v. *Pears* [1965] 1 QB 76 because it would 'unduly restrict the enjoyment' of the servient land.

Restrictive covenants probably offer more appropriate solutions to this kind of need, but the solution might also be found in the law of tort. In *Bradburn* v. *Lindsay* [1982] 2 All ER 408 the defendant, owner of one of a pair of semi-detached houses, allowed dry rot to spread so that her house had to be demolished. As a result the party wall shared by the plaintiff's house was damaged by the weather. Since there was no easement of support, and there cannot be a general easement of protection against the weather, the plaintiff relied on the tort of negligence, and won. Statute has also stepped in: s.29 Public Health Act 1961 provides that a local authority can order the weatherproofing of a building exposed by the demolition of an adjoining building.

A more detailed list of easements can be found in Cheshire (1994) p. 525. In the future, a right to plug into a neighbour's computer network might be recognised as an easement; the list is not closed.

7.3 Profits

The rules about profits are fairly similar to those about easements, but, as already stated, a profit can be either 'appurtenant' (benefiting a dominant tenement) or exist 'in gross' (without a dominant tenement). Thus, a person can own a profit to graze a goat on someone else's meadow, even though she owns no land which can benefit.

Where a profit is attached to land, it must accommodate the dominant tenement, just like an easement. In *Bailey* v. *Stephens* (1862) 12 CB NS 91, the owner of a field claimed a profit appurtenant to take wood from a neighbouring copse. It was held that this was not valid because it did not benefit the field. (It might have been different if the alleged dominant tenement were a house and the wood used as firewood.)

Again, as in the law of easements, the right has to be sufficiently definite and must not amount to a claim to the whole of the servient tenement.

Profits can be held by a group of people: for example, rights to take firewood from, or graze cattle on, common land; these are often called rights of common and are shared with other commoners and with the owner of the common. A profit can also be 'sole' (also called, very confusingly, 'several'): only one person can take the thing, and the owner of the servient tenement is excluded from it.

There are profits of piscary (fish), turbary (turf), estovers (wood) and pasture (grazing); some of them are still economically very important.

7.4   Legal and Equitable Easements and Profits

There can be both legal and equitable easements and profits:

A LEGAL EASEMENT OR PROFIT MUST BE:
1   **FOR THE PROPER LENGTH OF TIME,**
    AND
2   **CREATED BY DEED (OR BY LONG USE)**

An easement or profit can be legal provided it is to last for ever (like a fee simple absolute) or for a period of time with a fixed beginning and end (like a lease: s.1(2) (a) LPA). If the easement is for an indefinite but limited time, such as 'until I sell my house' or 'for your life', it *cannot* be legal (see 5.3 above). However, even if the easement or profit is 'for ever', or 'for two years, starting next Monday', it still may only be equitable, because – like any other interest in land – these interests must be created with the proper formalities or by long use (see 7.5 below).

As usual, it is important to know whether an easement or profit is legal or equitable, because a legal interest binds the world but an equitable one may be less secure if the servient tenement changes hands (see 9.3 below, for unregistered land; 10.5 for registered land and the recent case of *Thatcher* v. *Douglas* 146 NLJ (1996) 282).

7.5   Acquisition of Easements and Profits

There are a number of ways of acquiring a legal easement or profit. The obvious way is to create one in a deed, but other methods of creation are based on behaving as if one had such a right, together with a – usually mythical – deed. Legal easements and profits can also be directly created by usage (compare adverse possession in 3.1 above).

It is important to be aware that the owner of the dominant tenement only has the right to do what the easement permits. So, for example, in *London and Suburban Land and Building Co (Holdings) Ltd* v. *Carey* (1991) 62 P & CR 480 the owner of the dominant tenement had the express right to use an access road across the servient land to get to her warehouse, but this did not give her the right to stop her vehicles on the access road to load and unload them.

Easements

Figure 7.2 shows the various ways in which an easement can be acquired. ('Grant' is where the seller gives a right over a part of her land to a person buying another part of it. 'Reservation' is where she reserves for herself a right over a part of her land which she is selling.)

There is an awful lot of law about the acquisition of easements. Judges do not use categories consistently, so in practice categories overlap (especially easements of necessity and intended easements). Additionally, some of the cases could just as easily be explained by reference to the ancient principle that a woman cannot derogate from her grant (see 5.6 above). Therefore only the bare outlines of the rules are given here. The main thing is to understand the variety of ways in which these interests can be created and acquired, so that you can recognise the circumstances in which one might arise, either to take advantage of it or to avoid it.

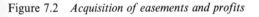

Figure 7.2 *Acquisition of easements and profits*

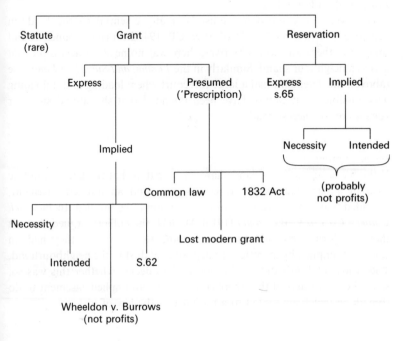

Court Order

A special easement may be created by court order under the Access to Neighbouring Land Act 1992. In certain circumstances specified in the Act, a land-owner may go to court to obtain the right to enter a neighbour's land to carry out essential repairs to her own property (and see 56 Conv (1992) 225).

Express grant

If Imran, the owner of a block of flats, sells a fourth-floor flat to Paula, he will probably expressly grant her an easement over the hall and staircase. If she does not have a deed in her favour, she will be merely an equitable owner of the flat and of the easement (see *Walsh* v. *Lonsdale* (1882) 21 Ch D 9, at 2.3 above).

Grant implied by necessity

Where land is (at the time of the sale) completely unusable without an easement, one will be implied into the conveyance. In the example given above, Paula's flat would be useless without a right to use the stairs so an easement to this effect would be implied, by necessity, into the lease. An easement can only be implied if the alleged servient land is owned by a party to the conveyance, as shown in *MRA Engineering Ltd* v. *Trimster Co Ltd* (1988) 56 P & CR 1.

However, the claimed use must be really essential to the land: in *Manjang* v. *Drammeh* (1991) 61 P & CR 194 the Privy Council found that, since there was access by river, there was no need for access on foot across a neighbour's land. Similarly in the *London and Suburban Land* case (above), the defendant had a large forecourt where loading and unloading was possible, so it cannot have been intended that she should stop her vehicles on the access road.

Intended grant

If the buyer and seller of land share an intention that the land should be used in a particular way, the courts may find an implied easement, provided that this is necessary for the intention to be fulfilled. In *Pwllbach Colliery Co Ltd* v. *Woodman* [1915] AC 634, the colliery argued that, as their landlord knew that they were going to mine coal, they had an easement, implied by intention, to deposit coal dust in the neighbourhood. The House of Lords did not in fact need to decide whether this was so, since the Lords agreed that there could not be an implied easement to do something which amounted to a nuisance in the law of tort.

The rule in Wheeldon v. Burrows (1878) 12 Ch D 31

Thesiger J stated the rule in this case twice, but unfortunately not consistently. The basic principle is that, where a person sells a part of her land, the buyer gets the benefit of any rights over that land which the seller was enjoying at the time of the sale. (These rights are not, before the sale, easements, because there cannot be an easement if one person owns both dominant and servient tenements; they are referred to at the stage before sale as 'quasi-easements'.) The rule also applies if the owner of the land sells two or more parts simultaneously to different people; the buyer of the 'quasi-dominant tenement' will get the benefit, and the buyer of the 'quasi-servient', the burden.

WHEELDON v. BURROWS

1   **THE QUASI-EASEMENT WAS USED, AT THE TIME OF THE GRANT, BY THE OWNER OF THE WHOLE FOR THE BENEFIT OF THE PART SOLD, AND**

2   **THE USE WAS 'CONTINUOUS AND APPARENT' AND/ OR 'NECESSARY FOR THE REASONABLE ENJOYMENT' OF THE LAND**

It is essential, if the rule is to apply, that both dominant and servient were owned by one person at the date of the conveyance. 'Continuous' means 'reasonably permanent', and 'apparent' means 'reasonably discoverable'. It is not known whether Thesiger J meant either or both of the conditions in 2 to be fulfilled; in most cases, of course, if the quasi-easement (for example, a right of way) satisfies one test, it will also satisfy the other.

In *Millman* v. *Ellis* [1996] 71 P & CR the Court of Appeal held that Millman had successfully proved an easement under this rule. He had bought a large house from Ellis and part of Ellis' remaining land, and claimed the right to use the driveway which Ellis had always used to get to the house and which was safer than using the main road. In *Wheeler* v. *JJ Saunders Ltd* [1995] 2 All ER 697, however, Wheeler had bought part of a farm and claimed to be able to pass through a gap in a wall southwards to get to a road. It was held that this access was not 'necessary for the reasonable enjoyment of the house' because there was another equally suitable access in the east.

Easements implied by s.62 LPA

S.62 LPA is a 'word-saving provision' which transfers with land, when it is sold, all benefits which are attached to the land (see 2.7 above). It can be excluded by the express intention of the parties. The section may only operate where the dominant and servient tenements are in separate ownership or occupation. This was stated by a minority in the House of Lords in *Sovmots Investments Ltd* v. *Secretary of State for the Environment* [1979] AC 144. The case concerned a controversial compulsory purchase order made by a London borough; the order was invalid unless s.62 applied to create an easement of way along hallways in the building. It was held that s.62 did not apply to a compulsory purchase order and, further, the section could not be invoked because the building was wholly owned and occupied by Sovmots at the time of the 'conveyance'. The order was therefore invalid. This decision has been criticised (for example, by Jackson (1978) pp. 100–3). If it is correct, then s.62 only applies where *Wheeldon* v. *Burrows* does not.

Goldberg v. *Edwards* [1950] Ch 247 illustrates the potential of s.62. Here, a tenant was using a passage in a house under a licence and then, when a new lease was granted, the licence became an easement because s.62 implied it into the deed. It was an 'advantage . . . appertaining to the land' and, when it was thus implied, it grew into a legal easement and could not be revoked by the landlord. (In any problem about a person who lives in land owned by another and has permission to do something extra, and who then receives a grant, the answer will probably involve s.62.)

Prescription

Use for many years of a right which is capable of being an easement can actually create a legal easement; this is called 'prescription', and the rules are extraordinarily obscure. Prescription may arise if an easement has been used openly, as of right, without permission and continuously, by one fee simple owner against another. There are three forms, common law, 'lost

Table 7.1   *Comparison of* Wheeldon *v.* Burrows *and s.62 LPA*

Wheeldon v. Burrows	S. 62
Applies in will, deed or contract but only to easements	Applies in deed only, but to easements and profits
Both tenements in the same ownership or occupation	Tenements in separate ownership or occupation
Easement was used by grantor for the benefit of the part granted, continuously and apparently and/or it is reasonably necessary	Easement appertained, etc., to the dominant tenement

modern grant' and statutory, under the Prescription Act 1832. The periods of use required vary according to the method of prescription claimed and the type of easement (see Megarry and Wade (1984) pp. 869–92). Thirty years have now passed since the Law Commission recommended the abolition, or, at least, simplification, of prescription law, but no new statute is as yet proposed: it would not do to rush such things.

Reservation

When a seller reserves an easement for herself in a conveyance, the courts always interpret it in as limited a way as they can, because of the rule against derogation from grant (see above). It is none the less possible expressly to reserve an easement, or to reserve one by necessity or common intention, although this is hard to prove.

Profits

Profits can be acquired in most of the same ways as easements. However, because a profit cannot be 'continuous and apparent', *Wheeldon* v. *Burrows* probably cannot apply. In addition, the periods for prescription under the Act are longer for profits.

7.6 Remedies for Infringement of Easements and Profits

The remedies available to the aggrieved owner of an easement or profit are 'abatement' and 'action'. Abatement means that the owner of the easement or profit can go onto the servient tenement and, for example, break a padlock on a gate. However, the courts are wary of abatement and the do-it-yourselfer must choose the least mischievous method and refrain from unnecessary damage.

The owner of the easement or profit may claim an injunction and/or damages and/or a declaration against the owner of the servient land. She can also take action against third parties who interfere with her right, so the owner of a profit of piscary could win damages from a factory upstream which polluted the river and killed the trout.

7.7 The Ending of Easements and Profits

Easements and profits may be ended by: (1) statute; (2) an act of the parties: (a) release, (b) abandonment, or (c) unity of seisin.

Statute

In the bad old days, Acts of Enclosure often extinguished such rights, especially profits in common. Today they can also be ended under the Commons Registration Act 1965; the right to keep a pig on common land, and to collect firewood is no longer a matter of life and death for most people, and the Act seems to be less concerned with registering such interests than with allowing owners of common land to destroy them.

There is no provision equivalent to s.84 LPA which allows the Lands Tribunal to discharge or modify a restrictive covenant (see 8.4 below), but under the Town and Country Planning Act 1971, local authorities, in the course of development, may end easements and profits.

Act of the parties

Release
An easement of profit can be released explicitly by deed. An agreement to release – without a deed – may be enforceable in equity.

Abandonment
If the owner of the easement or profit abandons the right, she cannot later resurrect it. However, abandonment is hard for the owner of the servient tenement to prove, for there must be a clear intention to abandon. This can be implied from the circumstances, but rarely is. In *Benn* v. *Hardinge* (1992) 66 P & CR 246 the Court of Appeal held that 175 years of non-use did not, in itself, indicate the necessary intention to abandon. *Moore* v. *Rawson* (1824) 3 B & C 332 held that, even where the windows which benefit from an easement of light are blocked up for years, this only amounts to abandonment if there was no intention to replace the windows (and see Davis [1995] Conv. 291.)

Unity of seisin
As stated in 7.2 above, a person cannot have an easement or profit against herself, so an easement ends if one person owns both tenements; of course it might be resuscitated under the rule in *Wheeldon* v. *Burrows.*

7.8   Other Rights Over Another's Land

There are a number of other interests in land which most people take for granted. They look a bit like easements or profits, but are classified differently by lawyers.

Public rights

These are rights which can be used by anyone, such as the right to fish between high- and low-water marks. The most familiar are rights of way, which include roads as well as footpaths, but the 'right' to use a road is now more like a licence, since it can be denied at the discretion of a policewoman (see Public Order Act 1986).

Natural rights

These rights exist automatically and arise out of the nature of land. All land has a natural right of support from neighbouring land, so you may not dig a large hole in your garden if your neighbour's land consequently collapses. There is also a right to water flowing naturally in a definite channel.

There are no automatic rights to light and air, so if such rights are to exist they must amount to easements, unless the tort of nuisance can provide a remedy.

Customary rights

Sometimes a group of people – for example, the residents of a particular village – have a right which looks like an easement, but it is not because 'the inhabitants of a village' are not a legal person.

Licences

See Chapter 13.

7.9   Comment

This chapter has indicated the wide variety of 'interests in land' which can exist within the categories of easements and profits and shows how land law can adapt to changing land use, such as tower blocks of flats. 'Modern circumstances' perhaps however require that the law of easements should be reformed. For example, there is strong argument that easements should be capable of existing in gross: public utilities such as gas and water providers have had to gain statutory rights to the land of others because such rights could not have been easements while the companies do not own neighbouring land which could be accomodated by the easements (although the effect of these special statutory rules may come under new pressure as the service providers move into private hands). In addition, the law of contract (in relation to profits) and tort (especially nuisance) has had to provide for other situations where the law of easements fails satisfactorily to resolve neighbours' conflicts.

Summary

1 To be an easement, a claim over another person's land must fulfil the four requirements; there must be dominant and servient tenement, accommodation of the dominant tenement, different ownership or occupation, and it must be capable of being the subject of a grant.
2 Easements include a wide variety of rights but, in order for a new one to be recognised, it must fit the general character of easements.
3 Profits are rights to take something from another person's land; they may or may not be appurtenant, and may be in common or sole.
4 A legal profit or easement must be equivalent to an interest in fee simple or to a lease, and must be created, expressly or impliedly by deed or long use; all other profits and easements are equitable.
5 Easements and profits may be acquired by court order, or expressly or impliedly, or by grant or reservation. They may also be acquired by prescription.
6 Remedies for infringement of an easement or profit are abatement or action.
7 Easements and profits may be ended by statute, release, abandonment or unity of seisin.
8 Easements and profits must be distinguished from other claims, such as natural, customary or public rights, and from licences.

Exercises

1 How would you define an easement? In what ways is it different from a profit?
2 What is the importance of dominant and servient tenements in the law of easements and profits?
3 Is there an easement to provide protection against the weather? Should there be?
4 What is necessary in order for an easement or a profit to be held to have been abandoned?
5 In 1975 Megan sold half her farm to Jeff, but she continued to keep her tractors in one of the barns. In 1985 she leased one of her remaining fields to Jeff, by deed, for 20 years, giving him permission to use a short cut to the field across her land 'for as long as he needs to'; he had in fact already been using the field and short cut for several weeks. Last year Jeff agreed in writing with Megan that the children attending her nursery school could play on his smallest field.

Megan has just died and her heir, Sam, wants to know if any of these arrangements will affect him.

8 Covenants in Freehold Land

8.1 Introduction

This chapter concerns promises made between freeholders in relation to the use of land. While the law of easements is concerned with one land-owner's use of another's land, this chapter is about one land-owner's direct control over what another does with his own land. Unlike nuisance law, it is concerned with contractual relationships, but – unlike leasehold covenants – here there is no privity of estate.

~ It had long been possible for the *benefit* of any promise to be transferred with land without a leasehold relationship, but in the mid-nineteenth century the courts of equity for the first time allowed the *burden* of certain covenants to be attached to land so that they affected anyone who owned the land. The only burdens which equity enforced were those of covenants which were 'restrictive': that is, which prevented the owner from doing something. Even today, restrictive covenants can only be equitable interests; they therefore suffer limitations because of the doctrine of notice and the discretionary remedies. These new equitable rules were derived from the law of leases and easements, for the courts inevitably adopted the established policy test of 'touch and concern'/ 'accommodate'. This is because, as already demonstrated, the rules of freehold covenants, leases and easements are all concerned with finding a balance between protecting third party interests in land and ensuring easy conveyancing.

Tulk v. *Moxhay* (1848) 41 ER 1143 is the first case in which a court enforced a covenant on freehold land. The owner of part of Leicester Square in London was selling the freehold and the buyer promised to:

'keep and maintain the said parcel of ground and square garden, and the iron railing around the same in its present form and in sufficient and proper repair, as a square garden and pleasure ground, in an open state and uncovered with any buildings, in a neat and ornamental order and shall not nor will not take down nor permit to be taken down or defaced at any time . . . the equestrian statue now standing in the centre of the said garden.'

The land changed hands several times and a later owner decided to build on the garden, although he had known about the covenant before he had bought the land and had paid less because of it. In a dramatic decision by the Court of Chancery, the original covenantee (that is, the person to whom the promise was made) successfully enforced the covenant against the later owner.

In succeeeding decisions, equity provided a cheap and effective planning law a hundred years before the state seriously took on the control of land use, and many urban areas have their present shape and character because of covenants imposed by careful developers. Nowadays the public restrictions on the use of land, for example, planning law and building regulations, are normally of greater significance, but covenants are still imposed and enforced because they allow for a more detailed control than public planning law is capable of providing.

Covenants are now capable of being 'discharged or modified' by statute, since public policy requires that, for example, a covenant which has been rendered obsolete because of a change in the neighbourhood should no longer be enforceable. This jurisdiction is briefly reviewed at the end of the chapter, but first it is necessary to explain the rules about covenants 'running with the land'.

The basic pattern is simple: there are two sets of rules, legal and equitable, and each set is divided into rules for the benefit and for the burden. The legal and equitable rules in regard to the benefit are similar but not identical; the sets of rules for the burden are quite different. Equity also provides a third set of rules, for 'schemes of development'. These sets of rules are the result of case-law and are therefore open to argument – and are expressed differently in each textbook. The present statement is as simple and accurate as possible, and there is a summary at the end of the chapter for reference (and see Figure 8.5).

The first thing to do when approaching a problem in this area of land law is to identify who might have the benefit of a covenant and who might have the burden, that is, who might be able to enforce it and who might be bound by it. The easiest way to do this is by using diagrams, and a technique is explained in 8.2 below.

Land law texts rarely deal with the *content* of these covenants, but this can cause problems in practice. A covenant which is too vague will not be enforced, and neither will one which is against public policy (for example, because it is racist).

8.2 The Running of Covenants

The use of diagrams

To take a typical story in this area of land law: Eve was the fee simple owner of Paradise House and in 1980 she sold a part of her garden to Adosh who promised her that he would not build on the land. Eve moved to the seaside for her health and sold her remaining land to Mike. Adosh took early retirement and sold his land to Claire who has obtained planning permission for a block of flats on the land. Advise Mike.

In order to find an answer, it is necessary to establish the relationships of the plaintiff and the defendant to the promise which has been or may be broken. The promise is usually represented by a vertical line with the benefiting person (the covenantee, Eve in this case) at the top and the burdened person (covenantor, Adosh) at the bottom. As with leases, sales of the land are usually shown by horizontal lines as in Figure 8.1.

Claire is clearly planning to breach the promise made by Adosh, her predecessor. The question is, 'Can Mike prevent Claire building the flats?' For lawyers this becomes two questions, 'Has the burden of the covenant passed to Claire? Has the benefit passed to Mike?' In order to find the answers, some of the rules in the next section must be applied. (An answer is given in *Applying the Rules*, p. 123 and see Figure 8.5, p. 125.)

The legal rules

The burden at law
As indicated earlier, the common law did not allow the burden of a covenant to be attached to land so as to bind buyers (unless there was privity of estate: see 5.7 above). The position remains the same today: the burden of any freehold covenant cannot run at law. The reason for this was a cautious decision in 1885, made on the basis that it could not be

---

Figure 8.1

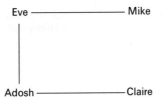

done because it never had been (*Austerberry* v. *Corporation of Oldham* (1885) 29 Ch D 750).

The benefit at law

In answering the question, 'Can the plaintiff sue at law?' ('Has the benefit passed to the plaintiff at law?'), two separate rules must be examined: the first provides for the express transfer of the benefit of a contract, and the second for the automatic running (implied transfer) of a benefit when the land is sold.

First, anyone can expressly transfer the benefit of any contract to which he is a party except a purely personal one: thus, under s.136 LPA, the benefit of a promise relating to the use of land can be sold. The benefit will be enforceable at law by the buyer, provided that the assignment is in writing and express notice in writing was given to the covenantor.

Second, the law provides rules allowing the automatic implied transmission of the benefit of a promise at law if (a) it benefits the land; and (b) the covenantee had a legal estate in the land when the promise was made; and (c) the plaintiff now has a legal estate in that land; and (d) the benefit was intended to pass. For the covenant to benefit the land, it must be shown that the promise affects the land itself rather than its owner and (and see 'touch and concern' and 'accomodate', above 5.7 and 7.2). For all covenants made since 1925, by s. 78 LPA the benefit of a promise which 'relates to' (that is, touches and concerns) land is deemed to be made not only with the covenantee but also with all his successors in title. The section means that since 1926 anyone who owns a legal estate in land automatically has the benefit of any covenant which touches and concerns it.

The basic rule can be traced back to 1368, but the modern statement is found in *Smith and Snipes Hall Farm* v. *River Douglas Catchment Board* [1949] 2 KB 500. In 1938 the Board promised Ellen Smith that it would maintain the banks of the Eller Brook adjoining her land in Lancashire. She sold the land to John Smith (the first defendant) and he leased it to Snipes Hall Farm (see Figure 8.2).

Figure 8.2   *Smith and Snipes v. River Douglas Catchment Board*

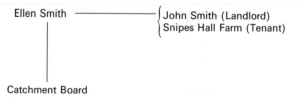

When the river flooded the fields because of the Board's failure to carry out proper maintenance, John Smith and the farm tried to recover their losses from the Board on the ground that the benefit of the promise had automatically passed to them when they bought the land. It was held that (1) the covenant did benefit their land; (2) it had been made with a legal owner of the land; (3) the present plaintiffs were both legal owners; and (4) the covenant had been intended to run by s.78. Both plaintiffs could therefore claim damages for the Board's breach of covenant. The tenant farmer succeeded only because of s.78 LPA (above) which enables any legal owner – freeholder or leaseholder – to enjoy the benefit of a covenant relating to land.

The equitable rules

There are three sets of equitable rules on covenants: for the burden, for the benefit and for 'schemes of development' (special arrangements concerning both benefit and burden).

The running of the burden in equity

Tulk v. *Moxhay* (8.1 above) was an apparently straightforward decision; if the court had failed to enforce the promise, Lord Cottenham believed that 'it would be impossible for an owner of land to sell part of it without incurring the risk of rendering what he retains worthless'. This is strictly true, but a land-owner who wanted to maintain control over a part of his land after he had sold it could always create a long lease with the appropriate covenants, and these would be enforceable against subsequent assignees of the lease.

Later in the nineteenth century, the judges seem to have thought that the depressed land market required minimal restrictions on land use in order to encourage purchasers, so they introduced increasingly complex and technical requirements. Today the burden of a covenant runs in equity if (1) it is restrictive, and (2) it benefits land once owned by the covenantee and now owned by the plaintiff, and (3) it was intended to run. Further, because this is merely an equitable interest, (4) the notice or registration rules must be complied with and (5) the plaintiff must have clean hands. (The doctrine of notice and the registration rules are set out in Chapters 9 and 10.) In more detail:

1 *The covenant must be restrictive* Whether a covenant is 'restrictive', or negative, is a question of 'substance not form'; what matters is the reality not the appearance. The covenant in *Tulk* v. *Moxhay* (to 'maintain the land uncovered with buildings') although positive in form is negative in substance because the covenantor can comply by

doing nothing (that is, without spending money). It is easily enforced by an injunction; if the court were to try to enforce positive covenants such as the promise to maintain the statue, it would have to order specific performance and then supervise the continuing observance.

The rule that the burden of restrictive covenants only can be enforced was recently restated by the House of Lords in *Rhone* v. *Stephens* [1994] 2 All ER 65 (and see [1994] Conv 477). The case concerned a promise to mend a roof – the whole roof belonged to the main house, but part of it was essential to the adjoining cottage owned by the plaintiff. The original buyer of the cottage had a promise from the owners of the house that they would maintain the roof, but a subsequent owner of the cottage found that it could not be enforced against a new owner of the house because it was a positive covenant: the burden could not pass.

Lord Templeman reviewed all the authorities and concluded that the rule of restrictive covenants is a rule of property: an owner of land cannot exercise a right which has never been transferred to him. Equity follows the law, and:

> 'Equity cannot compel an owner to comply with a positive covenant entered into by his predecessors in title without flatly contradicting the common law rule that a person cannot be made liable upon a contract unless he was a party to it. Enforcement of a positive covenant lies in contract; a positive covenant compels an owner to exercise his rights. Enforcement of a negative covenant lies in property; a negative covenant deprives the owner of a right over property.' (at p. 69)

Further, any judicial alteration of the rule now would cause chaos for land-owners. (The case might be partially solved by the possibility of a court order under the Access to Neighbouring Land Act 1992 allowing the owner of the cottage to go onto the defendant's property to carry out essential maintenance, although he would have to pay for this himself; see above 7.5.)

2   *The covenant must benefit the plaintiff's land once owned by the covenantee*   The plaintiff's land must be 'benefited' ('accommodated') by the covenant and it must be identifiable. The person trying to enforce the covenant need not own a legal estate and need not have bought the whole of the covenantee's land, so long as the part owned is capable of benefiting from the promise. In *London County Council* v. *Allen* [1914] 3 KB 642, Mr Allen promised the Council that he would not build on a strip of land needed for the continuation of a road. The

land was conveyed to Mrs Allen and she mortgaged it to another (see Figure 8.3). It was held, with great regret, that the plaintiff authority could not enforce the covenant because it had sold the benefiting land. Statutes now provide that local authorities and certain other bodies, such as the National Trust, are exempt from this rule.

3 *The covenant must be intended to run*   Since 1925 this has been implied by s.79 LPA (similar, but not identical, to s.78, which concerns the *benefit* of land).

The running of the benefit in equity

Equity also developed its own rules about running the benefit; these rules are based on the legal rules but are slightly more complicated. They were radically simplified by the decision of the Court of Appeal in *Federated Homes Ltd* v. *Mill Lodge Properties Ltd* (1980) 1 WLR 594 (and see P. N. Todd 49 Conv (1985) 177). The facts of the case were relatively simple. M Ltd owned a huge estate which was divided into three large plots, blue, green and red. They sold the blue to Mill Lodge Properties who promised, for the benefit of the green and red land, that they would not build more than 300 houses. Both the green and the red land then came into the hands of Federated Homes. There was an unbroken chain of express assignments of the benefit of Mill Lodge's promise with the green land, but not with the red (see Figure 8.4).

Federated Homes successfully claimed an injunction for breach of the covenant when Mill Lodge began building 32 houses more than was allowed. The defendant's arguments centred on technical details of the planning permission, but this was decided in the plaintiff's favour. It then became clear that, as owners of the *green* land with an unbroken chain of express assignments, Federated Homes had the benefit of the covenant and could enforce it against Mill Lodge. However, the judge at first instance went further and said that, under s.62 LPA (by which a conveyance of land transfers all rights which benefit it, see 2.7 and 7.5 above), Federated Homes could also enforce the covenant as owners of the *red* land.

Figure 8.3   *LCC v. Allen*

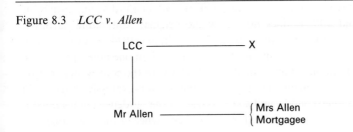

Figure 8.4   *Federated Homes v. Mill Lodge*

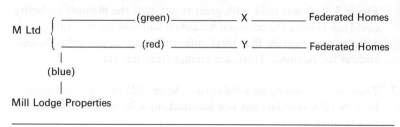

The Court of Appeal agreed with the judge on the planning issue and the green land, but took a different view on the red land. Rather than s.62 they chose to use s.78 LPA to pass the benefit of the covenant to the plaintiff. Until then, it had been thought that the section was merely a 'wordsaving' provision but Brightman LJ rejected this interpretation as it seemed to him to 'fly in the face of the wording'.

The widest interpretation of *Federated Homes* is that the benefit of any covenant made since 1925 automatically runs in equity if it touches and concerns the land, but this represents the radical obliteration of a century of case law about the annexation or assignment of freehold covenants. Annexation and assignment cases (briefly outlined at the end of this section) had been lovingly analysed by generations of academics and the Court of Appeal's decision left many commentators open-mouthed. However, the decision has not been challenged, so the present rule for the benefit in equity seems to be that it probably passes if (a) the covenant benefits the land, and (b) either s.78 applies so that the benefit is deemed to have been intended to run, or there is annexation, or assignment (express or implied).

There are a number of complications with *Federated Homes*' simplification of the law. For example, the operation of s.78 is probably limited to covenants made since 1925. In addition, it may only apply to the running of the benefit of *restrictive* covenants because of the wording of the section. It might also be limited to cases such as *Federated Homes* itself, where the burden did not have to run.

One difficulty with s.78 is that, unlike the other word-saving provisions in s.62 and s.79, it does not allow the original contracting parties to express a contrary intention. In *Roake* v. *Chadha* [1984] 3 WLR 40 there was a 50-year-old covenant not to build more than one house per plot on land in a London suburb, and a further clause in the conveyance that the benefit of the covenant would not pass unless it was expressly assigned. All the land changed hands, and a later owner of the burdened land wanted to build another house in his garden. The then owner of the benefiting land sued for an injunction; he argued that, although there was no express assignment of the benefit, this was unnecessary because of s.78 and *Federated Homes*.

Judge Paul Baker QC found himself in a difficult position, for the Court of Appeal in *Federated Homes* had not considered the possibility of a contrary intention. He held that the *Federated Homes* decision on s.78 did bind him, but he interpreted it so as to give effect to the intention of the original covenantor and covenantee in this case:

> 'The true position as I see it is that even where a covenant is deemed to be made with successors in title as s.78 requires, one still has to construe the covenant as a whole to see whether the benefit of the covenant is annexed.' (p. 46)

Thus, despite *Federated Homes,* the benefit of the covenant had not passed to the plaintiff.

The old concepts of annexation and assignment were created in nineteenth-century cases. 'Annexation' can be illustrated by *Rogers* v. *Hosegood* [1900] 2 Ch 388. Here the Duke of Bedford had bought a plot of land in Kensington and promised not to build more than one house. The deed stated that this was:

> 'with intent that the covenants might so far as possible bind the premises . . . and might enure to the benefit of the [sellers] . . . their heirs and assigns and others claiming under them to all or any of their land adjoining or near to the said premises.'

The Duke's land passed to Hosegood who decided to build a large block of flats but Rogers, an owner of adjoining land, wanted to prevent the development. The burden of the covenant had definitely passed to Hosegood, so the question was whether Rogers had the benefit. It was held that the benefit had been annexed to his land by the words of the deed: anyone who owned that land could enforce the covenant.

Whether or not the benefit has been annexed depends solely on whether the kind of wording in *Rogers'* case can be found in the original conveyance. If it cannot, the only alternative is to find a chain of assignments; there was such a chain of express assignments for the green land in *Federated Homes*. If there is no complete express chain, the old rules stated that there could yet be an implied assignment of the benefit of the covenant. In *Newton Abbot Cooperative Society* v. *Williamson and Treadgold Ltd* [1952] Ch 286 there was such an implied assignment: the magic words which would have annexed the benefit to the land were missing and there was no express assignment, but the heir of the covenantee automatically received the benefit implied by operation of law – and he could then assign it expressly.

If the covenant does not touch and concern the land, or if s.78, annexation and assignment all fail, then the benefit of the covenant does not run to the plaintiff. The covenant may, however, be enforceable by someone else.

Schemes of development

A scheme of development (or 'building scheme') is another creation of equity. If the conditions for a scheme are fulfilled, then the benefits and burdens of restrictive covenants run automatically to *all* owners in the area, thus greatly simplifying the question of whether one owner can stop another breaching a covenant.

There is a scheme of development if there is a defined area of land and all the original purchasers of plots within the area knew that the covenants imposed on them all were intended to be mutually enforceable. As Stamp J said in 1970, it is a kind of 'local law involving reciprocal rights and obligations' (*Re Dolphin's Conveyance* [1970] Ch 654). (A recent building scheme case is explained in relation to obsolete covenants, see 8.4 below.)

The first known scheme was created in 1767 and upheld in 1866. A large number were created in the nineteenth century and upheld by the courts, but after 1889 a change set in and the number of schemes successfully established began to fall. Strict rules were laid down in the judgment in *Elliston* v. *Reacher* [1908] 2 Ch 374, which later judges treated as if it were part of a statute. Four conditions had to be satisfied: there had to be (1) one seller, (2) plots laid out in advance, (3) mutual restrictions established for mutual benefit, and (4) knowledge by the purchasers of the intended mutual enforceability.

Between 1908 and the 1960s only two schemes were successfully enforced in reported cases but then the climate appears to have changed. In *Re Dolphin's Conveyance* (above) there was neither a common vendor nor plots laid out in advance, but the local authority in Birmingham was nevertheless prevented from developing the site because it was held that a building scheme had been created. Stamp J said that *Elliston* v. *Reacher* was only part of a wider rule; here, a scheme arose because of the existence of 'the common interest and the common intention actually expressed in the conveyances themselves'. In every case it is a question of fact as to what actually were the intentions of the original seller and buyers.

There are often problems in the older cases in finding sufficient numbers of the original documents, and often the original owners are beyond recall as well. Building schemes are still, however, a useful method for a modern developer to create and preserve small landscaped estates.

(The proposed 'commonhold' may offer an alternative scheme to developers: see 5.11 above.)

Applying the rules

A return to the problem of Claire and Mike (see p. 115) may make the application of all these rules clearer. The question was whether Mike had the benefit and Claire the burden of the promise, made by Adosh to Eve, that there should be no building on the land. (Obviously no building scheme can exist here.)

A glance at the summary of the rules relating to the benefit and the burden (Table 8.1 in the Summary) shows that the strictest requirement relates to the running of the burden. This is therefore always the place to start in a problem of this kind, since otherwise you may go to all the trouble of tracing the benefit and then find that the burden does not run anyway.

To decide whether the *burden* has passed with the land from Adosh to Claire, it is necessary to apply the equitable rules, for the burden cannot run at law: (a) the covenant is negative in substance, (b) it does benefit the land of the original convenantee (Eve) now owned by Mike, and (c) by s.79, it is deemed to have been intended to run (there is no evidence of a contrary intention). The final answer regarding the burden depends on whether the covenant was properly protected by registration (see 9.3 and 10.6 below).

The next stage is to test whether the *benefit* has passed with the land from Eve to Mike. Here a, fundamental principle emerges. It is not permitted to mix legal and equitable rules: *burden and benefit must run in the 'same medium'*. (In practice this means that if the burdened land has changed hands, so that it is necessary to trace the burden, which can only be done in equity, then the equitable rules must also be used for the benefit.) The covenant here does touch and concern the land, so by *Federated Homes* the benefit probably passes in equity. Therefore – subject to registration – Mike will probably obtain an injunction against Claire.

It is possible for the benefit to pass to the plaintiff but not the burden to the defendant, and vice versa. The original covenantor will always be liable in contract law (unless a contrary intention is expressed in the contract), but the remedy against him can only be damages if he no longer owns burdened land.

As a final point here, in *Hall* v. *Ewin* (1887) 37 Ch D 74 a head landlord of a London house sued his subtenant for breach of a covenant in the head lease not to commit a nuisance. (The sub-subtenant was keeping lions in the garden – as one does.) There was no privity of estate, so the burden could pass to him by the equitable rules on restrictive covenants. However, the landlord did not win his injunction; for this, he should have sued the person in possession, the sub-subtenant.

8.3   The Use of S.56 LPA

S.56 LPA 1925 may be relevant whenever the person claiming the benefit (or his predecessor in title) owned land nearby at the time the covenant was made. It is a legal extension of privity of contract and provides:

> 'A person may take. . . the benefit of any . . . covenant . . . over or respecting land . . . although he may not be named as a party to the conveyance or other instrument.'

It is a way of giving the benefit of a covenant to someone other than the people who are named in a deed. S.56 can be relevant to the problems in this chapter, but it is not strictly concerned with the running of benefit or burden because it makes a person a party to the deed, makes him a covenantee. The section applies if the person alleged to have the benefit of the covenant was identifiable in the covenant agreement, and was in existence at the date of the covenant. The reason for these rules is that it would be unfair if the covenantor were effectively making his promise to everyone in the district; he needs to be able to identify, on the day he made the promise, the land-owner(s) who might be able to take action against him.

The rules were established in *Re Ecclesiastical Commissioners for England's Conveyance* [1936] Ch 430. In that case, the court had to decide whether a grand house by Hampstead Heath in London was subject to a restrictive covenant (in an application under s.84(2) LPA). The issue was whether neighbouring land-owners had the right to enforce it and this depended on whether the original neighbours, who had owned the neighbouring land at the time of the covenant, could enforce it through s.56. It was held that a clause in the conveyance which stated that the original covenantor made the promise:

> 'also as a separate covenant with . . . owners for the time being of land adjoining or adjacent to the said land hereby conveyed'

was enough for s.56. The neighbours were identifiable in the agreement and in existence at its date. Their successors in title were able to claim the benefit from them by the usual rules for the running of the benefit, so they could enforce the covenant.

Figure 8.5 *Can a covenant be enforced?*

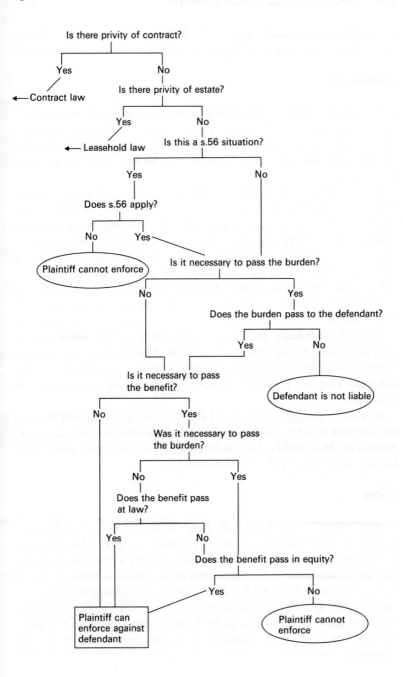

8.4   Discharge and Modification

Covenants are automatically ended ('discharged') in two ways: by the common law, and by statute. Statute also allows covenants to be modified.

Common law

First, if the burdened and benefiting lands are owned by the same person, the covenant cannot be enforced: a person cannot contract with himself. However, if the covenant is part of a building scheme, life after death is possible: the covenants revive if the plots come into separate ownership again later.

Second, if the covenant has been abandoned the courts will not enforce it. This was argued in *Chatsworth Estates* v. *Fewell* [1931] 1 Ch 224. There was a covenant on a house in a seaside resort restricting its use to private dwelling only. Thirty years later, the then owner started taking paying guests. The plaintiffs warned him of the breach and asked whether he wished to apply to have the covenant modified or discharged under s.84 LPA (below) but he did nothing. When taken to court for the breach, he argued that they had waived breaches by others in the neighbourhood and had delayed enforcement against him, and that therefore they had abandoned the benefit. He lost on both counts and the plaintiffs won their injunction. Abandonment is a question of fact in every case; here the plaintiff could not be expected to have to peep regularly through the defendant's keyhole to see how he was using the land in order to maintain their rights.

In *Shaw* v. *Applegate* [1977] 1 WLR 970 a café owner in another resort was allowed to keep his amusement arcade, contrary to the covenant, because of the plaintiff's delay in enforcing it. An injunction was refused but the plaintiff was still entitled to damages.

Statute

Several statutes authorise the discharge of a covenant; a well-known example is s.127 Town and Country Planning Act 1971 which allows a local authority to carry out a development against a covenant, provided they pay compensation. The most important provision, however, is s.84 LPA, as amended by s.28 LPA 1969. The power to discharge or modify covenants is important because the very existence of the power encourages people to agree to waive covenants. In many cases which do not go to litigation, it is merely a question of the developer 'buying off' the covenants.

A statutory power to end freehold covenants was deemed necessary in 1925 because restrictions on land use could 'enclose individual premises and often whole streets and neighbourhoods in a legal straitjacket' (Polden 49 MLR (1986) 195). There was no discussion of s.84 in Parliament, although it allows the state to destroy private property (the right to enforce the covenant), often without compensation. This issue has been tested before the European Commission of Human Rights. The applicant lost her case there, on the particular facts, but it seems unlikely that any other application, even on different facts, would succeed because of the public interest element (see Dawson 50 Conv (1986) 124).

Applications under the section are made to the Lands Tribunal, a body which spends much of its time determining land valuations for the purposes of rating and compulsory purchase. Appeal on a point of law can be made to the Court of Appeal. Under s.84 the Tribunal has power to modify or discharge any restrictive covenant and some covenants in long leases. There is provision for compensation to be paid in certain cases.

S.84 itself, as amended, is horrendous. Briefly, a covenant may be discharged or modified if:

---

1   IT SHOULD BE DEEMED OBSOLETE; OR
2   IT IMPEDES SOME REASONABLE USE OF THE LAND,
    PROVIDED MONEY IS SUFFICIENT COMPENSATION
    AND *EITHER* (a) 'IT PROVIDES NO PRACTICAL
    BENEFITS OF SUBSTANTIAL VALUE OR ADVANTAGE'
    OR (b) IT IS CONTRARY TO THE PUBLIC INTEREST; OR
3   THE PARTIES AGREE; OR
4   THIS WILL NOT INJURE ANYONE ENTITLED TO THE
    BENEFIT.

The Tribunal must have regard to any planning permissions or local plans but these are not decisive. There are innumerable cases on s.84 and each 'turns on its own facts'; five examples are briefly explained here.

Re Bass Ltd's Application (1973) 26 P & CR 156 concerned an application to use land, restricted to housing, as a lorry park; the owner of the burdened land already had planning permission, and the objectors to the covenant's discharge (owners of the benefit) already suffered from serious traffic noise. The adjudicator found, from a visit to the site, that, although living close to heavy lorries was far from pleasant, the restrictive covenant still conferred a substantial advantage on the objectors in preventing any increase in the number of lorries, and the application therefore failed. (This case is useful in that it lists the questions which must be asked in an application under s.84.)

In *Keith* v. *Texaco Ltd* (1977) 34 P & CR 249 the arrival of the oil industry in Scotland rendered obsolete a covenant which had been made only six years before. As a result, the land-owner was not restricted to building only one house, as the covenant required, but could sell the land for the building of 20 houses; it might be said that he had also struck oil. No compensation was payable because the covenantee had not sold at less than the then market value.

Re Forestmere Properties Ltd's Application (1980) 41 P & CR 390 concerned an application by the company, the lessee of a 999-year lease, to demolish a cinema in order to build a block of flats. (Unusually, therefore, the covenant was therefore a positive, leasehold covenant.) The landlords, trustees of an elegant garden suburb, refused to waive the covenant because they did not like the plans for the flats, but they were ready to consider alternatives. It was held that, although the cinema might be obsolete, the covenant was not as it had value to the trustees in ensuring that they maintained control over the appearance of the site. Money would not be an adequate compensation for loss of this control, so the application also failed under the second head.

In *Re Bromor Properties Ltd's Application* (1995) 70 P & CR 569 the plaintiff owned a house which was held to be part of a building scheme, under the *Elliston* v. *Reacher* rules (above). A covenant in the scheme prevented him using the land to provide access for a new development of houses on his other land nearby. He applied for discharge of the covenant, but the Lands Tribunal held that the very existence of a building scheme made it less likely that a covenant would be discharged, and in this case he failed because the covenant still secured 'practical benefits of substantial advantage' to other land-owners within the scheme. (Costs of nearly £800 000 were awarded against the would-be developer.)

Finally, in *Re Hounslow and Ealing LBC's Application* (1996) 71 P & CR 100 a London park was subject to a covenant for use only as a public park or sports ground, and the buildings could only be used in connection with this. The boroughs wanted to use part of the land as a commercial wholesale nursery, and part of a building for training gardeners. The covenant had already been partly modified, and the further modification was allowed because no one objected and because the new arrangements would be financially to the benefit of the park: it was therefore in the public interest to modify the covenant.

It can be seen, even from this brief review, that the Lands Tribunal has a challenging role. Many different interests are involved in these cases:

developers, nearby land-owners intent on preserving the *status quo*, 'expert' planners, the general policy that contracts be respected, the wider public interest in land use, and the views of particular political parties (such as the Conservative government's policy of reducing planning restrictions during the 1980s and 1990s). These difficult issues are part of the background of all planning law, private and public.

8.5 Comment

Restrictive covenants are part of the private law of planning, but are just one of several legal strategies to control use of land by others. Alternative ways are: long leases, which may be enlarged to a freehold with the covenants remaining enforceable; conditional fee simples subject to a right of re-entry (see 4.2); and the mutality principle (as in *Ives (ER) Investment Ltd* v. *High* [1967] 2 QB 379: see 9.3 below). All these also can provide means to avoid the rule that the burden of positive covenants cannot pass, as may the proposed new commonhold estate (see 5.11 above) if it becomes law. However, all such arrangements require careful planning: *Rhone* v. *Stephens* illustrates the problems which may arise if the buyer of land fails to consider fully the implications of the non-enforceability of a positive covenant.

Reform of covenants in freehold land has been considered several times over the last 25 years. The Law Commission Report No. 127 (1984) proposed a new and simple law to govern the running of benefit and burden *at law* of both restrictive and positive covenants through the creation of new legal interests in land, 'Neighour Obligations', and a new kind of building scheme in 'Development Obligations'. These new legal interests would continue to resemble easements in that enforcement would depend on the plaintiff owning nearby land capable of benefiting from the obligation. This proposal was supplemented by a Report in 1991 (Law Commission No. 201) which recommended that a restrictive covenant should cease to be enforceable after 80 years unless the owner of the benefit could show it was not obsolete. Any of these old covenants, if accepted, would become part of the new structure of interests.

Both proposed reforms are linked also to commonhold as part of a more effective and simpler regime of controlling land use and maintaining its value in a modern urban society. Given the complexity of present planning rules, a coherent scheme can only be welcomed. However, the difficult decisions about land use will remain, often providing evidence of the usually concealed political and economic forces affecting land law.

Summary

1   There are separate sets of rules to pass the benefit of a covenant at law, and to pass both the benefit and the burden of a covenant in equity. Equity also provides for building schemes which create a mutually enforceable local law (see Table 8.1).
2   S.56 allows a person not named in a deed to be a party to it if he was referred to in the deed and identifiable at that time.
3   Covenants (except those in building schemes) may be ended at common law if the benefiting and burdened land come into the same hands or if the benefit is abandoned.
4   S.84 LPA provides a machinery for the discharge or modification of restrictive covenants which have outlived their useful life; each case is decided on its own facts.

Exercises

1   To what extent do the equitable rules supplement the legal rules about covenants in freehold land?
2   Why is *Federated Homes* a problem?
3   What are the advantages of proving a building scheme in an action for enforcing a restrictive covenant?
4   How and why is the operation of s.56 limited?
5   In 1930 Karen sold part of her large garden in the Chequers Estate to Barry who built 'The Palace' on it. In 1945 she sold another part of her garden to Phil who promised her that he would not build more than one house on the land and that he would erect and maintain a fence around the land. The promise was stated to be made 'also with owners for the time being of adjoining land, formerly part of the Chequers Estate'.
    In 1980 a council estate was built in the fields neighbouring the estate. Karen died and her executors sold her remaining land to Yehudi. Rita has bought Phil's land and plans to build a block of flats with an open, unfenced garden.
    Who can enforce the covenants, and who is bound by them? What remedies are available to the parties?

Table 8.1 Summary of the rules relating to freehold covenants

Burden		Benefit	
Law	Not possible	1	It benefits the land
		2	Covenantee had a legal estate in the benefiting land
		3	Plaintiff has a legal estate in the benefiting land
		4	It was intended to run (s.78)
Equity	1 It is restrictive	1	It benefits the land
	2 It benefited land owned by covenantee, now owned by plaintiff	2	Either (i) s.78 applies, or (ii) annexation or assignment.
	3 It was intended to run (s.79)		
	4 It was protected by notice or registration		
	5 The plaintiff will not be denied an equitable remedy		

(Note also building schemes)

Transferring Land

9   Conflicting Interests in Unregistered Land

9.1   Introduction

This chapter describes what happens to interests when land which is not yet registered is sold. Chapter 2 was concerned with the normal methods of buying and selling land, but here the issue is not *how* to transfer an interest; rather, the question is what happens when there is a conflict between the new owner of land and the owner of another, pre-existing interest in the land, such as a lease or an easement. Although all land must now be registered on sale it is still necessary to understand the rules about unregistered land: some land will still be unregistered even when present law students retire.

As in other areas of land law, the rules are easier to grasp if they are seen as answers to real questions. For example, suppose that Mr and Mrs B are about to complete their purchase of a house and have just found out about Jean who lives in the attic and has paid the mortgage instalments for the past five years. In addition their new neighbour, Lloyd, tells them that they cannot alter the outside of their house. They want to know whether they can get rid of Jean, and whether they can install a bay window at the front of the house. Their question is, 'Do these people own interests which will affect us?'. At the same time, Jean and Lloyd (who claims to own the benefit of the restrictive covenant) would each ask: 'Will the Bs be able to defeat my interest?' (The same questions arise in relation to a buyer of any interest in land, such as a mortgagee or a lessee: see 2.1 above.)

In order to answer such questions, it is necessary to be able (1) to identify all the interests which can exist in land, and (2) to decide whether they are legal or equitable; a glance at the summaries of the preceding chapters may therefore be useful from time to time.

When the land is unregistered there are three sets of rules to be applied in turn: the register of land charges, overreaching and the doctrine of notice:

- *The register of land charges* (see 9.3 below) is a list of burdens on unregistered land.

- *Overreaching* (see 9.4 below) simplifies the buying of land which is subject to a trust, so that a buyer need not worry about beneficiaries: if the buyer pays the purchase price to two trustees, any beneficial interests are automatically detached from the land and attached to the money.
- *The doctrine of notice* was explained in 1.5 above (and see 9.5 below).

Finally, there is also the important register of local land charges. Burdens on land entered into this register by local authorities bind the buyers of both registered and unregistered land. Details may be found in 10.5 below.

9.2   The General Framework

The basic picture

Before the great flood of the 1925 legislation, the basic rules were (briefly) as set out in the box below. (The most important words to concentrate on are *legal* and *equitable*.) Understanding these old rules is essential to grasping the present law because the 1925 changes were a refinement, not a replacement. Briefly:

PRE-1925 RULES

1   **A buyer of a legal interest was bound by all pre-existing legal and equitable interests *except*:**
   (i)   **trust interests which were overreached, and**
   (ii) **equitable interests of which the buyer for value did not have notice, provided she acted in good faith.**
2   **A buyer of an equitable interest was bound by all pre-existing legal and equitable interests.**

Legal interests would normally be discovered during the enquiries made before purchase but if, for example, a buyer later found a legal mortgage she would be bound by it. (Of course, the seller would be liable in damages if she failed to deliver the unburdened land she had promised.)

   In practice, a buyer of the legal estate normally would have notice of an equitable interest either from the deeds (for example, a restrictive covenant might be found in an earlier conveyance of the land) or from an inspection of the land itself. Buyers had to act with caution because the courts would hold that they had 'constructive notice' of anything a prudent buyer would have discovered.

The basic picture in unregistered land after 1925

POST-1925 RULES

A buyer in good faith and for value of a legal interest is bound by:

1 **any pre-existing legal interest, except an unregistered puisne mortgage (see below), and**
2 **any interest which must be registered under the Land Charges Act, and is properly registered, and**
3 **any other interest which has not been overreached, and of which the buyer has notice, actual, imputed or constructive.**

(The rules relating to a buyer of an equitable interest remain unchanged.)

After 1925, therefore, the basic scheme in unregistered land was changed by the establishment of a set of registers. Registering interests in these registers is intended to protect both the buyer and the holder of the interest (see 9.3 below). Thus, registering an interest in the appropriate register is deemed to be 'actual notice' of the charge, so that it binds the buyer, while failure to register usually means that the charge is void, and does not bind her. There are five separate registers kept under the Land Charges Act 1972 (LCA) which replaced the 1925 Act. (There is also the separate register of local land charges, which will bind any buyer of land (see 10.5 below).

The registers kept under the LCA are:

1 *Land Charges:* a fairly random list of (eleven) burdens on land, divided into 'classes' A to F.
2 *Pending land actions:* including petitions in bankruptcy and any unresolved court actions relating to land.
3 *Writs and Orders:* any court judgments affecting land.
4 *Deeds of arrangement:* documents which give control over a debtor's property to, for example, a trustee.
5 *Annuities:* now obsolete.

The first, the Land Charges Register (see 9.3 below), is the most important of the five. The interests which can be registered there are, in theory, those which are otherwise difficult for the buyer of land to discover; equally, it would be hard to protect them by notice. These registrable interests are mostly equitable and are often described as 'commercial' rather than 'family' interests. ('Family' interests are in theory dealt with since 1925 by overreaching.)

Alongside the five charges registers and overreaching (see 9.4 below), the doctrine of notice resolves any remaining problems (see 9.5 below).

9.3　The Land Charges Register

The registrable charges

Under s.2 LCA, the following eleven interests are registrable in the Land Charges Register held by the Chief Land Registrar:

Class A　*charges created by a person applying under a statute.*

Class B　*charges created by a statute, not by a person's application*: for example a charge on land created under the Legal Aid Act 1974.

Class C　(i) *a puisne mortgage:* a *legal* mortgage where the borrower did not deposit the title deeds with the lender; it is therefore frequently not a first mortgage.
　　　　(ii) *a limited owner's charge:* this arises where an owner's interest is limited by a trust: if she pays a tax bill herself instead of mortgaging the land to pay it, she owns this equitable interest.
　　　　(iii) *a general equitable charge*: this seems to cover, for example, an equitable mortgage of a legal estate without deposit of title deeds, and certain annuities.
　　　　(iv) *an estate contract:* a contract to transfer a legal interest in land (see below).

Class D　(i) *an Inland Revenue Charge:* a charge on land arises automatically if the tax due on an estate at death is not paid.
　　　　(ii) *a restrictive covenant* created since 1925, excluding leasehold covenants.
　　　　(iii) *an equitable easement* created since 1925 (see below).

Class E annuities: now obsolete.

Class F a spouse's right of occupation in the matrimonial home (see below).

Further details of difficult classes

Estate contract

> 'An estate contract is a contract by an estate owner . . . to have a legal estate conveyed to him to convey or create a legal estate, including . . . valid option of purchase, a right of pre-emption or any other like right.' (s.2(4)(iv) LCA)

As shown in Chapter 2.3, a buyer of land (whether of a fee simple or a lease or some other interest) is normally recognised as having some *equitable* interest in the land as soon as there is a contract: this right is an estate contract. Most solicitors do not bother to register estate contracts because the contracts are nearly always successfully completed. If, however, completion is delayed, or if the buyer is suspicious of the seller, then the charge will be registered.

An option to purchase arises for example where Maria agrees that Jason can buy her land at a certain price, if *he* decides he wants to. A right of pre-emption, on the other hand, is where Maria agrees that Jason can buy her land if he wants to, but only if *she* decides to sell it. An option to purchase is an estate contract and must be registered, but a right of pre-emption only needs to be registered if the owner decides to sell.

An equitable lease ought to have been registered as an estate contract in *Hollington Bros Ltd* v. *Rhodes* [1951] 2 All ER 578 but it was not registered and it was therefore held void against the buyer of the freehold reversion – even though he had known about it from the start and had paid less in consequence.

A tenant's option to renew a lease, or to buy the freehold, is a registrable interest within this Class; this is so even if it is contained within a legal lease and was known about by all parties (*Phillips* v. *Mobil Oil Co Ltd* [1989] 1 WLR 888).

Equitable easement
This is:

> 'an easement, right or privilege over or affecting land . . . being merely an equitable interest.' (s.2(4)(iii) LCA)

Unfortunately, this definition is not as simple as it appears. An equitable easement is the sort of informal, neighbourly arrangement which no one would think of seeing a solicitor about, so it is unlikely to be registered but to declare it void seems unjust. Exactly this kind of problem arose in *Ives (ER) Investment Ltd* v. *High* [1967] 2 QB 379. A block of flats was being built on a bomb-site and it was discovered that the foundations trespassed on the next-door plot. The owner of that plot agreed, unfortunately not by deed, that he would allow the foundations to remain there if he could use a drive over the flat-builders' land. This arrangement is clearly an equitable easement but it was never registered.

Both plots of land changed hands and the new owners of the flats decided they wanted to stop their neighbour's use of their drive. They argued that the right was an equitable easement and was void for non-registration. The Court of Appeal decided that the LCA 'was not the end of the matter'. There were rights arising from the mutuality principle and from estoppel (see 2.6 above) and these were not affected by the failure to register. The neighbour was therefore allowed to continue to use the drive so long as the foundations of the flats remained on his land. Mutuality is an ancient principle: a person cannot reject a burden, the neighbour using the drive, so long as she wants to enjoy a related benefit, the trespass of the foundations.

The case was recently followed in registered land in *Thatcher* v. *Douglas* 146 NLJ (1996) 282 (see 10.5 below). However, it may be contrasted with *Lloyds Bank plc* v. *Carrick* (1996) 140 NLJ 402 where estoppel did not protect an unregistered estate contract (see 10.5 below).

Ives v. *High* represents one of the very few examples of courts finding a way around the LCA in order to arrive at a just result. In most cases, the principle may be expressed as '*Register or be damned!*'

Spouse's right of occupation

S.1 Matrimonial Homes Act 1983, replacing a 1967 Act, gives a married person a statutory right to occupy the matrimonial home, provided she is not a legal owner of it. This right of occupation is available to both husband and wife and, if registered, it binds everyone except a trustee in bankruptcy (see also 10.6 below). The charge was created in an attempt to solve some of the problems which can arise when one spouse (typically, the husband) is the sole legal owner of the home. Under the pre-1967 law he could sell it and run off whenever he liked, and the deserted spouse could not protect herself and their children in advance. In theory the Class F charge is a simple, cheap and efficient solution – except that many wives do not discover the possibility until it is too late. It is also of no use to people living together who are not married. Even where it has been registered, there is no guarantee that the wife will win against a buyer of the land: see *Kashmir Kaur* v. *Gill* [1988] 2 All ER 288, 10.6 below.)

The mechanics of the register

Registering a charge

Registering an interest is a simple matter. The owner of it fills in a short form giving her own details, the nature of the charge and the name of the owner of the land which is subject to the charge (the estate owner). All charges are registered against the name of the land-owner and not against the land itself, although a name-based register like this causes all kinds of problems, not least because people who fill in forms make typing errors; apparently, the register contains charges registered against people with first names like Nacny, Brain and Farnk.

If the wrong name is given on the charge registration form, the registration may well be ineffective. In an extraordinary case where both the registration and the search were against (different) incorrect names, the attempt at registration was held to be valid against a mortgagee, who had taken two years after his discovery of the mistake to take action (*Oak Cooperative Building Society* v. *Blackburn* [1968] Ch 730).

It is of course possible to register ineffective charges on the register, because registration alone does not make the charge valid; it may also be necessary, for example, to ensure that the benefit and burden of a restrictive covenant have run with the land. The Registrar has the power to remove invalid charges (to 'vacate the register'). In fact, many charges in the register are a waste of space; for example, all the estate contracts which have been completed and the puisne mortgages which have been redeemed. The Registrar thus tends to increase rather than reduce the apparent 'blots' on title.

Searching for a charge

To search for a charge it is simply necessary to fill in a form giving the names of the people who have owned the land. Anyone can search the Register but it is usual – and safer – to have an official search. The staff at the Registry search against the estate owners' names as requested and send back a form giving details of any charges they discover. In practice, these are often already known to the buyer from the investigations before exchange of contracts (see 2.2 above).

The official certificate of search is conclusive (s.10 LCA); if it fails to give details of a charge, the charge (although registered) is void. However, the charge-owner will receive compensation for the negligence of the registry. The official certificate also gives the person who required the search 15 working days' protection from having any charges registered (s.11 LCA). Thus, once the official search has been made, the buyer is safe providing the sale is completed within the 15 days.

It is of course possible that a charge was registered, say in 1930, against the name of the then estate owner, but today's buyer of the land may never discover her name because it is hidden 'behind the root of the title' (the document establishing the seller's title over a minimum of the last 15 years: see Chapter 3.2). The buyer is deemed to have notice of the registered charge and to be bound by it although no amount of prudence could have uncovered it. In these circumstances, the buyer can claim compensation (s.25 LPA 1969).

As time passes, more and more charges lie behind the root of title. Wade described this problem as a 'Frankenstein's monster' which grows more dangerous and harder to kill as the years pass ((1956) Camb L Jo 216).

The effect of registering a charge

S.198 LPA is clear that:

'The registration of any instrument or matter under the provisions of the Land Charges Act . . . shall be deemed to constitute actual notice . . . to all persons and for all purposes connected with the land affected.'

The system thus creates a new way of giving notice of an interest to a buyer of land: registration of a charge binds everyone because registration is 'actual notice'. There is, however, a change from the pre-1925 rule that a prudent buyer could protect herself, for now the buyer (because of Frankenstein's monster) has 'actual notice' whether or not she could ever have found the charge in the register. The only exception to the rule that registration is actual notice is where the official search certificate omits to mention a charge (see *The mechanics of the register*, above). It is therefore effectively the official certificate of search which counts as notice, not the Register.

The effect of failing to register a charge

As shown in *Hollington Bros Ltd* v. *Rhodes* [1951] (9.3 above), an unregistered estate contract did not bind the buyer: it was void. However, the rules of voidness are in fact more detailed:

UNREGISTERED LAND CHARGES: s.4 LCA

Classes A, B, C(i), C(ii), C(iii) and F	are void against	anyone who gives 'value' for any interest
Classes C(iv), D(i), D(ii) and (iii)	are void against	anyone who gives 'money or money's worth' for a legal interest

---

Charges in the first group are therefore void for non-registration against anyone who buys any interest in the land, legal or equitable. 'Value' means 'money, money's worth or marriage'.

The second group of charges is only void for non-registration against a person who buys a *legal* interest and who has paid *money or money's worth* for it; 'money's worth' means exactly what it says, that is anything which is worth money, such as other land or company shares. Where someone is only buying an equitable interest, or is getting married as consideration, an unregistered charge in this group is *not* void as far as she is concerned. Whether or not she is bound depends not on the LCA but on the pre-1925 law (see 9.2 above).

It is only when the burdened land changes hands that a charge may become void. Between the original parties, the charge is obviously enforceable and damages for breach of contract may still be available even if a charge is void against a later buyer of the land. Anyone who gets land by squatting or as a gift will also be bound by all interests in the land, whether or not registered, because she is not a buyer.

S.4 LCA is given even more force by s.199 LPA which provides that an unregistered charge is void even if the buyer did actually know about the charge:

'A purchaser shall not be prejudicially affected by notice of . . . any instrument or matter capable of registration under the provisions of the LCA. . . which is void or not enforceable against him under that Act. . . by reason of non-registration thereof.'

This ruthless section has been interpreted by some ruthless judges, as in the *Hollington Bros* case (above) where express notice in writing of an unregistered estate contract (an option to renew a lease) was held to be irrelevant. This was taken even further in *Midland Bank Trust Co Ltd* v.

Green [1981] AC 513. A father and son made an estate contract for the sale of a farm belonging to the father but which the son was managing and occupying with his family. The Class C(iv) charge was not registered; neither was the contract completed. Later the father changed his mind about his son and discovered that, if he sold the legal estate in the land to 'a purchaser for money or money's worth', the son's estate contract would be void. He did just that; the purchaser was his wife, mother of the owner of the unregistered charge, and she knew about the father's scheme and paid far less than the value of the land. One after another, those concerned in the conflict died and the executors had to sort out who had owned what, and who was now entitled to it.

The House of Lords (reversing the Court of Appeal) held that the unregistered charge was void against the mother. She was the purchaser of the legal estate for money and that was all that was needed:

> 'The case is plain: the Act is clear and definite. Intended as it was to provide a simple and understandable system for the protection of title to land, it should not be read down or glossed; to do so would destroy the usefulness of the Act.' (Lord Wilberforce, p. 32)

The result is not what the creators of the 1925 legislation intended (and conflicts with the position in registered land, see 10.5 below). They wanted to retain the old principle of constructive notice so that, where a charge owner actually lived on the land, she should not lose her interest if she failed to register it. This rule is contained in s.14 in Part I of the LPA but unfortunately it was wrongly placed there; it should have been moved to the 1925 LCA when that Act was carved out of the original 1922 Act (see 1.2 above). As s.14's effect is limited to 'This part of the Act', it cannot affect either s.199 LPA or the LCA.

Recently, in *Lloyds Bank plc* v. *Carrick* (1996) 140 NLJ 402, an estate contract was void for non-registration and the Court of Appeal had to decide whether the promise could nevertheless be enforced through a constructive trust (see 11.5 below) or proprietary estoppel (2.6 above). The buyer of the land had paid the whole price, and had moved in, but had simply not completed the contract. If the trust argument worked, then the rights of the claimant against the bank would have depended on the doctrine of notice (payment had been made to only one trustee so there was no overreaching); since she was in occupation of the land, the bank would have been deemed to have constructive notice of her rights. However, the appeal court held that she had rights against the seller under the estate contract, but no rights in estoppel against the bank which had made no promises to her, and:

'It cannot be unconscionable for the Bank to rely on the non-registration of the contract. I do not see how it could be right to confer on Mrs Carrick indirectly and by means of a proprietary estoppel binding on the Bank that which Parliament prevented her from obtaining directly by the contract it has declared to be void.' (Morritt LJ)

The ruthless simplicity of these cases, where the buyer either knew or could easily have discovered the interest of the occupier of land, is the sort of thing that makes people cynical about lawyers and their justice. In registered land, the opposite result will be reached in such a case because of s.70(1)(g) LRA 1925 (see 10.5 below).

9.4   Overreaching

It was intended by the framers of the 1925 scheme that trust interests should all be capable of being overreached. This was supposed to solve the problems of family members and the buyers of their land. S.2 LPA states:

'A conveyance to a purchaser of a legal estate in land shall overreach any equitable interest or power affecting that estate, whether or not he has notice thereof.'

Provided the buyer of any interest in land pays two trustees or a trust corporation, such as a bank, beneficial interests are kept behind the 'curtain' of overreaching, a curtain which the buyer need not lift. The beneficiaries still have rights but these are automatically detached from the land and attached to the purchase price in the hands of the trustees (see Chapter 11 for the roles of trustees and beneficiaries in the new 'trusts of land').

Overreaching applies to any interest under a trust of land, and to a sale by a mortgagee or a personal representative or under a court order. None of the LCA interests, such as equitable charges, restrictive covenants and estate contracts, can be overreached.

Overreaching beneficiaries' interests simply by paying two trustees is very convenient for buyers; in theory, the beneficiaries are happy too because they are entitled to (their share of) the proceeds in the safe hands of their trustees (certainly safer than in the hands of a single trustee who might be tempted to run off with the cash). However, it is only convenient for beneficiaries if they agree that the money is as good as the land. Frequently it is not, since their share of the proceeds is not enough to buy a new home. For this reason, a better metaphor than 'behind the curtain' might be 'under the carpet'.

9.5   The Doctrine of Notice

If an interest cannot be registered because it does not fit in the categories set out in the LCA, the next step is to decide whether the interest can be overreached. If it cannot be (or if it has not been) overreached, then any conflict between the interests of buyers and owners of pre-existing interests must be resolved by the pre-1925 rules (see 9.2 above). The same is true for a buyer of land who is not the kind of buyer against whom an unregistered charge is void under the LCA (see 9.3 above).

Conflict between the buyer of a *legal* interest in land and the owner of some pre-existing *equitable* interest in it must be resolved by the doctrine of notice. A buyer in good faith of a legal estate for value ('equity's darling') is only bound by equitable interests of which she had notice, actual, imputed or constructive (see 1.5 above). Constructive notice means that a buyer is deemed to have notice of the rights of anyone living there (or receiving rent from the person living there). Therefore, all buyers must carefully inspect the land to discover who is there and what rights they may have.

In *Kingsnorth Finance Co Ltd* v. *Tizard* [1986] 1 WLR 783, a husband was sole legal owner but his wife shared the equitable interest in their home. The marriage deteriorated and she spent most of her nights away from home, unless he was away on business, but she looked after the house, cooked the children's meals and kept most of her belongings there. He then mortgaged the house and went to America with the money, leaving Mrs Tizard and the finance company to fight it out. Judge Finlay QC held that the mortgagee had constructive notice of her rights because she was, on the facts, 'in occupation'. The bank's agent knew that the legal owner, the husband, was married, although he had described himself as single on the mortgage application form, and so the agent ought to have made more enquiries about the wife:

> 'the plaintiffs had, or are to be taken to have had [through their agent], information which should have alerted them to the fact that the full facts were not in their possession and that they should make further inspections or inquiries; they did not do so and in these circumstances I find that they are fixed with notice of the equitable interest of Mrs Tizard.' (p. 794)

What a prudent buyer ought to do depends on the facts of each case. There is no need to open drawers and wardrobes to see what clothes are there, but in suspicious circumstances an unannounced visit should probably be made. In a case like this, further enquiries should have been pursued and the wife should have been interviewed.

The broad view taken of 'occupation' in this case applies to all cases of constructive notice. In the *Tizard* case it was probably the right decision, although the wife's 'occupation' there was probably borderline. Of course, if the finance company had paid two trustees, Mrs Tizard's interest would have been overreached and she would have had to leave the house. Also, if she had an estate contract that her husband would sell the house to her as part of a divorce settlement, she would also have lost (*Carrick*, above).

The case of *Equity and Law Home Loans Ltd* v. *Prestidge* [1992] 1 WLR 137 (see 10.5 below) suggests further limitations where the buyer is a mortgagee. The final decision in a case like *Tizard* will probably now depend on the operation of ss.14–15 Trusts of Land and Appointment of Trustees Act 1996, see 11.8 below.

Table 9.1 shows some of the important cases where the doctrine has been applied, but it must be stressed that, since any interest in unregistered land which is not governed by the rules of land charge registration and has not been overreached is subject to the doctrine of notice, this is an open-ended category. Note also that all pre-1926 restrictive covenants and equitable easements are subject to the doctrine of notice, as well as class C(iv) and Class D charges against a purchaser for marriage.

9.6 Comment

Interests in unregistered land are governed by an assortment of rules. The LCA represents a small part of the system but its complexity usually absorbs more time than its importance deserves. The major problem must

Table 9.1   Doctrine of notice in unregistered land

Case	Type of interest	Result
Kingsnorth Finance v. *Tizard* (above)	Equitable interest behind a trust	Notice; wife won (but compare *Prestidge* (see 10.5)
Ives v. *High* (above)	Equitable easement, mutual rights, estoppel	Notice; drive-user won
Binions v. *Evans* [1972] Ch 359	Contractual licence	Notice; little old lady won
Shiloh Spinners Ltd v. *Harding* [1973] AC 691	Equitable lessor's right of re-entry	Notice; lessor won

be the immoral way in which buyers can destroy unregistered interests even though they knew, or ought to have known, about them before buying the land, contrary to the aim of the 1925 draftsmen. It is also unjust and unjustifiable since it is relatively easy for a buyer to inspect land and discover an occupant, and to enforce a rule protecting occupiers would not necessarily lead to injustice through uncertainty.

Other problems with the LCA are the narrow definitions of the registrable interests, the illogical difference between the provisions for voidness, the nature of the name-based register and the way in which the system tends to clog titles rather than to clear them. These have led to much criticism. Various reforms have been suggested; but the final answer seems to be that of the 1956 Report on Land Charges (Cmnd 9825). The Committee confessed that 'to rectify the machinery is a task beyond the wit of man' (Wade (1956) Camb L Jo 216). However, the importance of the actual custom and practice of conveyancers is shown by the fact that, 'the note on which to end is that, fortunately, none of these deficiencies seem to matter in real life.' (Wade, above p. 234)

The difficulties are such that lawyers have given up, in the expectation that when all the land in the country has been registered the Land Charges Register can be given a quick and efficient burial, preferably in an unmarked pauper's grave. However, the hope that registration of title will solve all the problems of buyers and sellers of land is over-optimistic, as will be seen in the next chapter which continues the story of tensions between the rights of beneficiaries and of buyers of the land (often a building society lending money on the security of a mortgage) where title to land is registered.

Summary

1   A buyer of any interest in unregistered land is automatically bound by (nearly) all existing *legal* interests in the land.
2   Eleven 'commercial' interests must be registered in the Land Charges Registry if they are to bind a buyer of the burdened land.
3   If interests which are registrable under the Land Charges Act have not been properly registered against the correct name of the estate owner, or do not appear on the official search certificate, they do not bind the buyer even if she actually knew about them.
4   Much of land charges registration law is complex, illogical and unfair, but probably impossible to reform.
5   'Family' (trust) interests are not registrable but can be overreached by a buyer who pays two trustees.
6   If an equitable interest is not registrable and has not been overreached, the rights of a buyer of a *legal* interest in the land depend on the doctrine

of notice; the buyer of an *equitable* interest is probably bound by any existing equitable interests.

Exercises

1 When does equity's darling appear on the scene in unregistered land?
2 Against whom is an unregistered land charge void?
3 Did the House of Lords come to the right decision in *Midland Bank Trust Co v. Green?*
4 Hilary is the sole legal owner of a four-storey house which is subject to a restrictive covenant that it should be used as a private dwelling house only. She lives on the first floor and her aged mother, Lucy (who contributed a quarter of the cost of the house when it was bought), occupies the ground floor.

   Hilary is a compulsive gambler on the Stock Exchange and recently lost a good deal of money. She met Emma at the hairdresser's and in the course of a chat they agreed that Emma, who had recently divorced her husband, should rent the basement of Hilary's house for three years. Emma moved in and has paid rent regularly. Hilary then accepted £2000 from Clive, a colleague, as a deposit on a ten-year lease of the top floor of her house. Nothing was put in writing for tax reasons.

   Six weeks later Hilary decided to emigrate. Clive has discovered that she has made an agreement in writing to sell the whole house to Dee.

   Clive, Lucy and Emma seek your advice.

---

10   Registered Title

10.1   Introduction

The concept of a register of land ownership was popularised in the nineteenth century by a non-lawyer, Robert Torrens. Working in a deeds registry in South Australia, he was shocked by the complication of traditional conveyancing, especially when large areas of land were simply the subject of government grants to settlers in places where there were no lawyers. His idea, which worked efficiently in Australia, spread through the common law world. In England, at the start of this century, Lloyd George's radical Liberal government attempted to introduce such a register; this vision included a 'new Domesday', a register of land owner-ship as a first step towards a tax on land owning.

The actual reforms of 1925 were only a pale shadow of Lloyd George's scheme. Nevertheless registration of title to land was adopted, along the lines of the register of company share ownership, so that the title deeds would not need to be investigated each time the land was transferred: the permanent register would replace the accumulating title deeds. The Conservative government, which introduced land registration, claimed it would be a solution to the depressed land market, providing a cheap and easy conveyancing which would encourage sales and result in an improve-ment of the land.

The plan in 1925 was that the system of registration would gradually be extended across England and Wales, district by district. Registration thus crept across the country by successive Orders in Council and, since 1 December 1990, _all_ freehold land and legal leases over 21 years must be registered on sale (or, in the case of such leases, on creation).

Michael Joseph has argued that the main effect of the reforms has been the security of the solicitors' profession (_The Great Conveyancing Fraud_, 1989). It is probably true that the increase of land ownership has had very little to do with the legal structure of land transfer for registration, by itself, cannot even guarantee simple conveyancing, let alone speed, cheap-ness or public confidence.

The main statute in this country is the Land Registration Act 1925 (LRA), as amended by the Land Registration Acts of 1986 and 1988. There are many sections and many further Rules, made under s.144 LRA.

Land law courses – and this text – explain the bare outline of the system but not the intricate details of its working.

In theory, there are three essential elements of title registration, known as Mirror, Curtain and Guarantee. The register of owners is supposed to *mirror* the actual structure of rights in the land itself. The *curtain* principle refers simply to overreaching, the mechanism by which land subject to beneficial interests can safely be bought (see 9.4 above). Finally, the state *guarantees* the titles on the register, a state insurance scheme.

It is very important to remember that:

1 Land registration is concerned with the registration of *ownership*, not merely with some rights in land;
2 The Land Registry has *no* connection with the Land Charges Registry which is only concerned with interests in unregistered land.

Some people are at first confused by these two different concepts of registration. It is worth referring regularly to the summaries of this chapter and the last, and to Table 10.1.

As with unregistered land, however, the main issue for land lawyers is the potential conflict between buyers of land and the owners of pre-existing interests in the land. It is still necessary to be able to identify interests and determine whether they are legal or equitable, but there are also new categories of interests and a new vocabulary to learn. Figure 10.1 on p. 153 offers an alternative view of the system.

Table 10.1 Comparison of unregistered and registered land

	Unregistered land	Registered land
Evidence of title	Title deeds	Land Register/Land Certificate
Types of interest	Legal/equitable	Legal/equitable; title/overriding/minor
Discovery of third-party interests	Deeds, LC register, notice (including land inspection for constructive notice)	Register, land inspection for overriding interests
Protection for buyers	LCA, overreaching, prudence (constructive notice)	Register as mirror (notices, etc., of minor interests), overreaching, inquiry, indemnity

10.2   The Register

The divisions of the register

The mirror of the title, the Register, is on computer at thirteen District Land Registries. There are now about 13 million titles on the register, accounting for about 85 per cent of the total land area. The register is divided into three sections:

> **PROPERTY REGISTER**
> **PROPRIETORSHIP REGISTER**
> **CHARGES REGISTER**

There is also a pending applications register and, like unregistered land, registered land is also subject to the Local Land Charges Registers (see 10.5 below).

The property register

This part of the register gives the good news about the title: it describes the title to the land, (freehold or leasehold) and any benefits attached to it (such as the benefit of an easement). One plot of land may have several registered titles for example, the freehold and one or more long leases; each has its own number and entry in the Register. The address is given and reference is made to a plan on which the land is outlined in red; unlike the Land Charges Register, the Land Register is a 'land', not a 'name' register.

The proprietorship register

This gives the nature of the title under the registration system; there are several kinds (see 10.4 below). It states the name and address of the owner, who must now be called 'the registered proprietor'. In problem questions therefore, any reference to 'fee simple owner' suggests the land is not yet registered, while a 'registered proprietor' means that it is registered; similarly, a reference to title deeds means the land is unregistered, because a registered proprietor has a Land Certificate, his copy of the entry on the Register.

Figure 10.1 *The effect of third party interests in registered land*

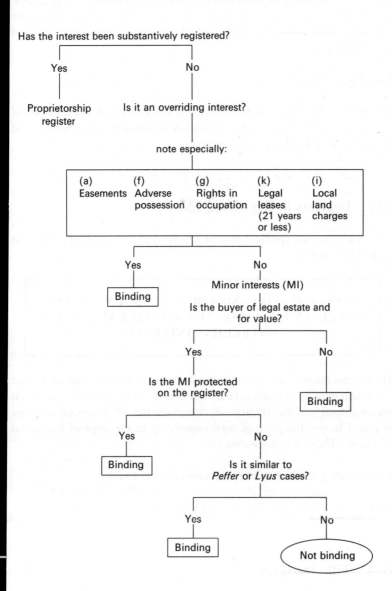

Note: This figure concerns interests after land has been registered; on first registration, different rules apply in some instances.

The Proprietorship Register also contains any 'inhibitions', 'restrictions' and 'cautions' to which the land is subject. These quaint terms are references to methods of protecting third party interests in registered land (see 10.6 below).

The charges register

This part of the register contains the bad news about the title: details of burdens on the land, such as the interests which in unregistered land would appear in the Land Charges Register.

10.3　Interests in Registered Land

The basic rule, in a conflict between a buyer and the owner of an interest in the land, is that:

IN REGISTERED LAND A BUYER IS BOUND BY ANY INTEREST WHICH IS ON THE REGISTER AND BY ANY OVERRIDING INTEREST

The normal range of interests – freeholds, leases, easements and all the rest – can still exist in registered land, but a new set of categories has been superimposed on the traditional structure: the 1925 legislators were prepared to pay the price of legal complexity in the hope of functional simplicity. These new categories are:

- *Title interests*, which can be substantively registered;
- *Overriding interests*, which bind everyone (listed in s.70(1) LRA);
- *Minor interests*: everything else; they bind only if entered on the register.

10.4　Title Interests

Registrable title

These are the interests which can have their own number and certificate. Normally, this means legal freeholds, and leases with more than 21 years to run (s. 123 LRA as amended by s.2 Land Registration Act 1986). Any of the legal interests in s.1 LPA can be substantively registered; mortgages are usually registered as Registered Charges (see 10.7 below). Each title registered over one piece of land is noted on the Property Register of the other titles to that land.

Types of title

In unregistered land, some titles are in practice not as secure as others: for example, a title obtained by adverse possession, because there are no title deeds to prove it. In registered land the register is supposed to reflect the actual state of the title to land, so it is necessary to classify the titles to show how strong they are. There is provision for second-rate titles to be improved ('cured') and this was simplified by s.1 Land Registration Act 1986. All registered titles are potentially subject to being corrected by the Registrar ('rectification', see 10.8 below).

A registered title may be any of the following:

TITLES IN REGISTERED LAND	
FREEHOLD: ABSOLUTE POSSESSORY QUALIFIED	LEASEHOLD: ABSOLUTE POSSESSORY QUALIFIED GOOD- LEASEHOLD

'Absolute' freehold or leasehold title is the best: the registered proprietor with absolute title has a better right than anyone else to the land. Absolute title is only subject to overriding interests and to any minor interests which are on the Register; if the registered proprietor is a trustee, his rights are also subject to the trust or, if a lessee, to the covenants in the lease.

'Possessory' titles are very rare indeed; they are granted by the Registrar when the alleged owner's title is based only on possession, not on title deeds. The Registrar guarantees the title only as far as dealings after first registration are concerned; no promises are made concerning the right of the first registered proprietor to the land.

'Qualified' titles are almost unheard of; they are granted only if there is some specific reservation about the title. 'Good leasehold' title is as valuable as absolute leasehold title except that, because the freehold has not yet been registered, the Registrar does not guarantee the right of the freeholder to have granted the lease.

10.5   Overriding Interests

Overriding interests in general

Any of the interests on the list in s.70(1) LRA will *override* the buyer's interests, whether or not he knew, ought to have known, or even could have known, about it. Overriding interests therefore have the same effect as *legal* interests in unregistered land – they bind the world – although some of them may be based on equitable interests. The overriding interest must normally be in existence at the moment that the buyer's interest is registered. However, for s.70(1)(g), a claimant must be in 'actual occupation' at the moment the buyer's contract is *completed* (see below).

The greater the number of interests which are given overriding status, the less the Land Register acts as an accurate mirror of the title since these interests are binding even though they do not appear on the register. Unfortunately, the list in s.70 is long and somewhat confused; only a brief version is given here:

OVERRIDING INTERESTS

(a)   natural rights, easements and profits (see below);
(b)   ancient rights of tenure;
(c)   liability to repair a chancel;
(d)   liability to repair a sea wall;
(e)   payments connected with tithes;
(f)   rights of adverse possessors (see below);
(g)   rights of people in occupation (see below);
(h)   rights to which titles (except absolute titles) may be subject;
(i)   local land charges (see below);
(j)   fishing and sporting rights;
(k)   legal leases for 21 years or less (*amended by s.4 LRA 1986*) (see below);
(l)   certain mining rights.

Easements and profits

S.70(1)(a) refers to easements and profits, and also to 'easements not being equitable easements required to be protected on the register' and it was assumed that it covered only legal easements. However, in *Celsteel Ltd* v. *Alton House Holdings Ltd* (1) [1985] 1 WLR 204 an easement was part of a lease of a garage; the lease was equitable and therefore the easement was also equitable. It was held that s.70(1)(a) included equitable easements which are 'openly enjoyed and exercised' and which, because of some other rule, did not need to be entered on the register for protection. The 'some other rule' in the case was Rule 258 of the Land Registration Rules; it provides that rights enjoyed with land are overriding interests, so long as they are attached to land (the dominant tenement) and adversely affect registered land (the servient tenement). Thus the equitable easement ranked as an overriding interest: it was binding although it did not appear on the Register.

The case was followed in *Thatcher* v. *Douglas* (1996) 146 NLH 282 where an equitable easement (created orally in 1966 but supported by part performance) was also held to bind a buyer of registered land. The easement was the right to use a slipway for launching boats. (The defendant's case was probably not helped by his accusing the trial judge of corruption and threatening him with grievous bodily harm.)

These cases mean that, in registered land, an equitable easement binds a buyer of land even though it would not if the land were unregistered. Therefore, although the registration system was supposed just to provide a cheap means of conveyancing, it can actually lead to a different result in a conflict of interests; it can change the relative value of interests in land. This creates a potentially large blank spot in the theoretical Mirror of the land register (and see 10.9 below for proposed reform).

Adverse possession

S.70(1)(f) ensures that a person can gain title to registered land through squatting (see Chapter 3), for 'rights acquired or in course of being acquired under the Limitation Acts' are overriding interests. An example is *Chowood Ltd* v. *Lyall* [1930] 2 Ch 156 where Mrs Lyall was sued for trespass by the company, the first registered proprietor of the land. She successfully argued that she had title to the land by adverse possession and that the company should never have been registered as proprietor. The register was rectified so that she became the registered proprietor (see 10.8 below).

Rights of occupiers

S.70(1)(g) tends to expand to fill all the space available in students' minds. It is certainly the one on which most academic attention is focused because of the serious problems which arise here, but it must be remembered that the 'right of a person in actual occupation' protected in this subsection is only *one* of the overriding interests.

A claimant must prove three things:

1   a right 'subsisting in reference to land, and
2   the owner of the right was in 'actual occupation' (or in receipt of rents and profits), and
3   no enquiry was made of the person.

This is clearly similar to constructive notice in unregistered land. The three conditions must be proved to have been in existence at the moment the sale, mortgage and so on is completed.

Only certain interests are rights which 'subsist in reference to land' in order to satisfy s.70(1)(g). For example, an interest under the old strict settlement will not do (LRA s.3(xv)(b); now see s.1 Trusts of Land and Appointment of Trustees Act 1996, Chapter 11 below), and nor will a spouse's statutory right of occupation of the matrimonial home (s.2) Matrimonial Homes Act 1983) or a licence to occupy land, but estate contracts and equitable interests under trusts will be enough.

Whether or not a person is 'in actual occupation' is a question of fact in every case. Someone may be in occupation even though he does not sleep in the house every night, as in the unregistered land case of *Kingsnorth Finance Co. Ltd* v. *Tizard* [1986] 1 WLR 783 (see 9.5 above). On the other hand, merely leaving a few possessions in the house or parking a car occasionally on a strip of land will not do. As yet there are no cases on 'receipt of rent and profits'.

There is no overriding interest if the person in occupation fails to disclose his interest when asked by the prospective buyer of the land. (It is *not* enough for the buyer to make inquiries of the registered proprietor.) It may be difficult to find out who is in actual occupation if the seller is trying to conceal it and, also, the owners of lesser interests may not realise the significance of the question from a stranger. It has recently been held when a person is buying land and is granting a mortgage on the land, then a mortgagee is protected by the inquiries made by the buyer: in *UCB Bank plc* v. *Beasley and France* [1995] July 26 an occupier of a seaside café had an unpaid vendor's lien (a right to stay on land until the price is paid, which is sufficient right for s. 70 (1)(g)). However, she had told the buyer (unfortunately for her, a rogue) that there was no overriding interest, and this was held to protect also the buyer's mortgagee.

No cases have yet been decided in regard to the level of enquiry that must be made, or about whether a buyer should be entitled to rely on the answer of an occupant who suffers from, for example, senile dementia or deafness.

Cases on s.70(1)(g)

These rules are best illustrated by a few of the cases; four are explained here and the section ends with a comment on them.

Williams & Glyn's Bank Ltd v. *Boland* [1981] AC 487

The wife had an equitable interest in the family home but she had not protected it as a minor interest. Her husband, the sole registered proprietor, mortgaged the house to the bank but there was no overreaching of her interest as the bank did not pay two trustees. When he could not repay the loan, the bank wanted to sell the house. Mrs Boland argued that she had an equitable interest, was in actual occupation of the house and the bank had not made any enquiries of her. The House of Lords decided that she had an overriding interest under s.70(1)(g).

City of London Building Society v. *Flegg* [1988] AC 54

The House of Lords had to decide between two beneficiaries (the parents of the two registered proprietors) and the mortgagee. The parents had a beneficial interest in the house, they were in actual occupation, and no enquiry had been made of them, but the mortgagee won. The parents had argued (successfully in the Court of Appeal) that they had a right 'subsisting in reference to land' for s.70(1)(g) when the mortgage was registered and that they therefore had an overriding interest. The basis of their claim under s.70(1)(g) was their right to occupy the land under the trust. The House of Lords held that, from the moment that the mortgagee overreached the beneficial interests by paying two trustees, the beneficiaries did not have a right to occupy the land but merely a right (under the rules of the old trust for sale) to share in the proceeds of sale. (On the new trust of land which replaces the trust for sale, and the new beneficial right to occupy, see Chapter 11.)

Lord Templeman said:

'The right of the respondents to be and remain in actual occupation of Bleak House ceased when [their] interests were overreached by the legal charge . . . There must be a combination of an interest which justifies continuing occupation plus actual occupation to constitute an overriding interest. Actual occupation is not an interest in itself.' (p. 1272)

The difference between this case and *Boland* is that here there was payment to two trustees, and therefore overreaching succeeded, whereas in *Boland* payment was made to only one trustee, so there was no overreaching. The moral for beneficiaries is that, if *two* people hold the legal title, the beneficiaries must protect themselves by entering their interest on the register as a minor interest. If there is only *one* legal owner, the beneficiary is safe so long as he remains in actual occupation and, if asked, tells enquirers about his rights. Conversely, a buyer of registered land paying two trustees is safe from any beneficial owners, but, if he pays only one, his rights are subject to what Lord Templeman referred to as 'the waywardness of actual occupation'.

Ashburn Anstalt v. *Arnold* [1989] Ch 1

Arnold enjoyed a rent-free 'licence' over a shop, subject to 3-months' notice by the freeholder if he were going to develop the land. The freeholder promised that, if such notice were given, Arnold would be offered a 21-year lease (at a market rent) of a shop in the new development. Ashburn Anstalt bought the freehold and tried to get Arnold out. The Court of Appeal held that the arrangement was a (legal) lease, not a licence (but now see *Prudential Assurance Co Ltd* v. *London Residuary Body* (1992), 5.3 above) and the new landlord was therefore bound. However, if this had been only a licence, Fox LJ held that a 'mere contractual licence would not be binding on a purchaser of land even though he had notice of the licence' (p. 15), because it is not 'an interest subsisting in reference to land' for s.70(1)(g). If such a licence affected the conscience of the buyer, then a constructive trust might be imposed (see 11.4 below) and this would be sufficient for (g), but that would not have been appropriate on the facts of this case.

Abbey National Building Society v. *Cann and Another* [1990] 1 All ER 1085

A son bought a house in his own name, partly with his mother's money, for his mother to live in. She knew that he was raising a small amount by mortgage and, according to the earlier decision in *Paddington Building Society* v. *Mendelsohn* (1985) 50 P & CR 244, she would not be able to deny priority to the lender for that small mortgage. However, he actually borrowed a much larger amount. Her belongings were moved into the house 25 minutes before completion of the purchase (and execution of the mortgage). The House of Lords held that she did not have an overriding interest under (g) and she was therefore bound by the building society's mortgage (even though it was for a larger sum than she had known).

The Lords also answered other questions raised by the case. First, they held that the moment to test for s.70(1)(g) was at the moment of execution of the mortgage. (This followed the Court of Appeal decision in *Lloyds*

Bank plc v. *Rosset* [1991] 1 AC 107; see below, 11.5.) It is difficult to fit this within the provisions of the LRA but:

'it produces a result which is just, convenient and certain, as opposed to one which is capable of leading to manifest injustice and uncertainty.' (Lord Oliver at p. 1100)

Second, the Lords unanimously held that she was not sufficiently in occupation at the time. Lord Oliver affirmed that 'actual occupation' is a question of fact, but it does 'involve some degree of permanence and continuity'. Moving furniture and so on into the house were, he said, 'acts of a preparatory character' which could not be 'occupation'.

Third, her beneficial interest under the resulting trust took effect a split second *after* the mortgage so that she did not have, at the moment of the mortgage's execution, an 'interest in land':

'The reality is that the purchaser of land who relies on a building society or bank loan for the completion of his purchase never in fact acquires anything but an equity of redemption, for the land is, from the very inception, charged with the amount of the loan without which it could never have been transferred at all and it was never intended that it should be transferred.' (Lord Oliver at p. 1100)

Comment

A beneficiary will now only be able to claim the protection of s.70(1)(g) if:

1   the land was bought before the mortgage was granted; and
2   he was in 'permanent and continuous' occupation before the mortgage; and
3   no enquiry was made of him; and
4   there was only one registered proprietor; and
5   he had no knowledge of any mortgage.

Boland's case represented the high point of protection for beneficial owner-occupiers in registered land, and decisions since 1981 show a gradual withdrawal from it. The result of the case was that mortgagees began – properly – to ensure that there were no resident beneficiaries with rights. Anyone who was going to live in the house was required to agree that the mortgage would take priority over their interest, if any, and this meant that occupying beneficiaries would not be caught out by a secret mortgage or sale by their trustee.

It was the House of Lords' decision in *Flegg* which began the process of reducing the protection of equitable owners in occupation against mortgagees. As Swadling remarked:

> 'One wonders what has happened to the demands of social justice which justified their Lordships' decision in 1981 over such a brief period of time.' ((1988) Conv 451, p. 452)

This process culminates in *Cann*. An unregistered land case since then suggests that there may yet be some further reduction of the beneficiary's protection. In *Equity and Law Home Loans Ltd* v. *Prestidge* [1992] 1 WLR 137 a sole trustee borrowed £30 000 on a mortgage, with the knowledge of his equitable co-owner. He later, without her knowledge, took out a new mortgage of more than £40 000, with which he paid off the first mortgage and then ran away. Was she bound by this later mortgage?

In unregistered land, the issue should have been whether the mortgagee had (constructive) notice of her rights (the old equivalent of s.70(1)(g)). Although earlier cases indicate that he would have had constructive notice because of her occupation, and that on the facts of this case, the mortgagee did have actual notice, the issue was not referred to in the judgment. The Court of Appeal held that, since she would have had a windfall (freedom from liability for the first mortgage) had she defeated the later mortgagee, she was bound by the later mortgage to the extent of the first loan.

This analysis fails to take account of existing law, and the fact that the mortgagee knew of her position and failed to protect itself by informing her of her trustee's schemes. However, if the decision is translated into registered land, it would mean that an additional condition is to be added to the summary above:

6   the mortgage was not taken out to repay an earlier loan; if so, the resident beneficiary will still be liable to the extent of the earlier loan.

However, this will not work if the mortgage was a forgery (see 10.8 below). The only hope for the Mrs Canns of the future lies in the Law Commission, which appears not to share the judges' desire to ensure that a financial institution will always win against an equitable co-owner (see 10.9 below).

Local land charges

S.70(1)(i) ensures that a buyer of registered land is bound by the 'public' interests protected by the Local Land Charges Act 1975. These include a 'charge' which a local authority can impose for an unpaid debt under public health or highways statutes, and local authority covenants on land (excluding ordinary restrictive covenants).

Unlike other interests which have to be registered in order to be protected, local land charges bind the whole world whether or not they have been registered, and whether or not they appear on the official certificate of search (s.10 Local Land Charges Act 1975). Anyone who suffers damage as a result is entitled to compensation.

Legal leases

By s.70(1)(k) (as amended by s.4 LRA 1986) any legal lease for 21 years or less is an overriding interest. A legal lease for a longer period must be registered as a title interest. An equitable lease may be protected under s.70(1)(g) if the lessee is in occupation (*Webb* v. *Pollmount* [1966] Ch 584).

10.6 Minor Interests

Minor interests in general

According to the scheme of registered title, anything which is not capable of substantive registration, and which is not an overriding interest within the list in s.70, is a minor interest: minor interests are 'everything else'. This category therefore includes, for example, restrictive covenants, equitable leases and beneficial interests under trusts (s.3(xv) LRA).

In practice, some interests may be capable of being either overriding or minor. For example, the owner of an equitable lease who is in occupation will have an overriding interest under s.70(1)(g) and will be safe against a buyer of the land; if he chooses to enter the estate contract on the register, it will be even better protected against the buyer as a minor interest. Similarly, a beneficiary under a trust of land may be protected under (g) if he is in actual occupation of the land and no enquiry is made of him, provided there is only one trustee.

If a minor interest is not also an overriding interest and if it has not been protected by entry on the Register, it is void against a purchaser of the legal estate for value (s.20 and s.59(6) LRA). Therefore, a buyer of an equitable interest only, or someone who receives land as a gift, may be bound by minor interests even though they have not been protected by entry on the register. Where there is a conflict between different minor interests, they are ranked in order of their creation (not in order of registration). Therefore, an unprotected minor interest may nevertheless bind a subsequent minor interest.

Two cases have suggested that the doctrine of notice might be reintroduced, despite the clear wording of s.59(6):

> 'a purchaser acquiring title under a registered disposition, shall not be concerned with any . . . matter, or claim (not being an overriding interest . . .) which is not protected by a caution or other entry on the register, whether he has or has not notice thereof, express, implied or constructive.'

The first case was *Peffer* v. *Rigg* [1977] 1 WLR 285. Mr Peffer and Mr Rigg married two sisters, and bought a house for their joint mother-in-law to live in. Mr Rigg was the sole registered proprietor and Mr Peffer had an equitable interest, but he did not enter it on the Register. The Riggs divorced, and as part of the divorce settlement Mrs Rigg paid her husband £1 for the house and became the registered proprietor. Had she defeated Mr Peffer's unprotected minor interest? It was held that she had not: first, she was not a purchaser 'for value', and second, she had actual notice of the trust and it would be unconscionable for her to hold the land free of Mr Peffer's interests. Graham J decided that she held the land on trust for Mr Peffer.

The second case is *Lyus* v. *Prowsa Developments Ltd* [1982] 1 WLR 1044. Lyus had an estate contract – an option to purchase – on a plot in a housing development. The builder went bankrupt, and the mortgagee sold the land to Prowsa. The first sale was expressly subject to the option, although it did not have to be as the estate contract was not an overriding interest (Lyus was not 'in actual occupation') and it had not been entered on the register. Prowsa sold the land on to another, subject to the estate contract 'so far as, if at all, it might be enforceable'. Dillon J found the question whether the buyer was bound one 'of considerable difficulty' but imposed a trust because it would be a fraud if the buyer were able to ignore the term in the conveyance. Despite the wording of s.59(6), Lyus could enforce his unprotected minor interest: the buyer was bound, effectively because of the special terms of the agreement.

It is interesting to compare these cases with decisions in unregistered land such as *Midland Bank Trust Co Ltd* v. *Green* [1981] AC 513 and *Lloyds Bank plc* v. *Carrick* [1996] 146 NLJ 405 (see 9.3 above). Although many people would say that justice was done in *Peffer* and *Lyus*, they create another, potentially large, blank spot on the magic mirror of the register. It is hard to say how far they will be followed in the future (see the Law Commission' suggestions at 10.9 below).

The protection of minor interests

The owner of a minor interest should protect it by entering one of the following:

1 Notice (s.49) – on the Charges Register;
2 Caution (s.52) }
3 Inhibition (s.57) } on the Proprietorship Register.
4 Restriction (s.58) }

A Notice is designed to protect the sort of interests which are registrable in unregistered land under the LCA, estate contracts and restrictive covenants for example. The rules require that the Notice must also be entered on the Land Certificate which usually means that the registered proprietor must agree to it, but this can be a difficulty in practice. The Notice appears on the Charges Register and binds everyone. Uniquely however, entry of a Notice does not automatically protect the spouse's right of occupation; here, the court must take all the circumstances of the case into account in a dispute between the spouse and a buyer of the land. In *Kashmir Kaur* v. *Gill* [1988] 2 All ER 288, a blind purchaser defeated a wife even though she had entered her statutory right of occupation on the register.

If for some reason a Notice cannot be entered – for example, the registered proprietor does not consent – a Caution may be entered on the Proprietorship Register. The Cautioner is entitled to be warned by the Registrar if there is any proposed dealing with the land; he gets fourteen days in which to take action. The registered proprietor may 'warn off' a cautioner, who then must defend his claim. There is also a Caution against first registration, where the cautioner is entitled to notice of the owner's intention to register the land for the first time.

An Inhibition is placed on the Proprietorship Register by order of the court or the Registrar and forbids any dealing with the land. It is therefore a serious matter, used often in bankruptcy. A Restriction is usually entered (in the Proprietorship Register) by the registered proprietor to protect the beneficiaries under a trust.

10.7 The Mechanics of Registered Land

Registration of title

As already mentioned, registration has been extended across the country gradually by successive Orders in Council. S.123 LRA (as amended by

LRA 1986) declares that, where an unregistered title to land should be registered, then:

'every conveyance . . . [of the land] shall. . . on the expiration of two months from the date thereof. . . become void so far as regards the grant or conveyance of the legal estate in the freehold or leasehold land comprised in the conveyance, grant or assignment . . . unless the grantee (that is to say the person who is entitled to be registered as proprietor of the freehold or leasehold land) or his successor in title or assign has in the meantime applied to be registered as proprietor of such land.'

Thus, if the first registration rules are not complied with, only equitable titles ultimately pass. The same punishment is imposed once title has been registered; by s.19 LRA the registered proprietor can only sell his legal interest if the disposition goes through the register. Once title has been registered, it therefore stays registered. An intending buyer of any interest in the land must check the title with the Registry.

Title is first registered, and later dealings are recorded, by filling in the appropriate form and sending it with the fee to the District Land Registry. The fee payable depends on the value of the property. On first registration the Registrar checks the title as if he were buying it and decides whether the title is good enough for 'absolute title', or only something less. Any benefits he discovers will be entered on the register, as will any burdens, like restrictive covenants found in the Land Charges Register; once the land has been registered, however, anything in that register becomes totally irrelevant. Any other details, such as the title number of the freehold reversion of a lease, will also be noted in order to ensure that the register really does mirror the title to the land.

If a mistake is made by Registry staff, there are provisions for compensation: the state indemnity (see 10.8 below). The prospective buyer must also check the Local Land Charges Registry (10.5 above) and will – if he is buying from a single registered proprietor – prowl around the property to see who is occupying it.

Mortgages in registered land

A legal mortgage of registered land may be created by long lease or charge (see 6.3 above) but the charge is more usual. The chargee receives a Charge Certificate and the Land Certificate remains in the Registry until the charge is redeemed. Priority between legal charges is determined according to the date of registration.

Equitable mortgages may also be created (see 6.2 above).

10.8 Rectification of the Register and Indemnity

Rectification

The registered proprietor 'is deemed to have vested in him . . . the legal estate' (s.69 LRA) but this statutory title can be stripped from him because of the wide provision for correcting the register. However careful the Registrar at first registration, and however cautious a buyer checking the Register, a registered proprietor might find he has in fact bought nothing.

S.82 LRA provides (briefly) that the register may be rectified:

1 because of a court order that a person is entitled to any interest in the land, or
2 because of a court order due to an entry, omission, default or delay by the Registry, or
3 where all concerned consent, or
4 where there was fraud, or
5 if two or more people are wrongly registered as proprietors, or
6 if a mortgagee is mistakenly registered as proprietor, or
7 if a person is registered as legal owner but would not have been so in unregistered land, or
8 where it is just because of a serious omission or mistake in the register. The case of *Norwich and Peterborough Building Society* v. *Steed* [1993] Ch 116 established that there is no general discretion to rectify; even this final ground for rectification is limited to cases of serious omission or mistake.

This list may be frighteningly long to a registered proprietor with absolute title who thought his position was guaranteed. However, by (s.82(3)) a proprietor *in possession* can only lose his absolute title where:

(a) he contributed to the error, or
(b) it would be unjust not to rectify, or
(c) rectification will give effect to an overriding interest.

In *Re Chowood's Registered Land* [1933] 1 Ch 574 (and see 10.5 above) the register was rectified against a proprietor with absolute title, in possession, to give effect to an overriding interest: adverse possession under s.70(1)(f). In *Re Sea View Gardens* [1967] 1 WLR 134 a strip of land had been sold first to A and later, by mistake, to B and B became the first registered proprietor. (In unregistered land, B could not have become legal owner because, once the land had been sold to A, the seller had nothing to sell to B.) It was held that the register should be rectified to register A as the proprietor, but only if he could prove that he had not delayed while B spent money on the land.

In *London Borough of Hounslow* v. *Hare* (1992) 24 HLR 9 Knox J had to decide whether to rectify the register against a registered proprietor in possession; she had bought the freehold reversion of her lease from the council under right to buy provisions, but in fact the provisions were wrongly applied in the case and the sale was outside the council's powers and therefore void. He held that, since she had been a tenant for years before buying the freehold, her situation was 'not to be measured purely in financial terms'; an inemnity would not compensate her for her loss, and therefore he refused the rectification; the council were entitled to compensation.

Indemnity

S.83 LRA provides for this essential part of title registration, state compensation for loss. A person is entitled to compensation if a document is lost by the Registry, or there is an error in an official search. He is also entitled if he 'suffers loss by reason of':

1   any rectification, or
2   an error or omission in the register but the register is not rectified, or
3   forgery, where the register is rectified.

Sadly for Chowood above, the company did not 'suffer loss by reason of' the rectification. This was because, when it had bought the land, it was already subject to the overriding interest; the later rectification did not cause the loss but was merely a recognition of the existing position.

Anyone hoping for an indemnity must take care: s.83(5) provides that there will be no compensation if the loser caused, or substantially contributed to, the loss by fraud or lack of proper care.

Forgery

In unregistered land, a forged deed has no effect at all, so a buyer with a forged title deed owns nothing; his remedy is against the fraudulent seller, who may also be guilty of deception. In *Penn* v. *Bristol and West Building Society* [1995] 2 FLR 938 a husband and his friend forged the wife's signature on a conveyance to the friend of unregistered land in order to gain a mortgage by deception from the society, and then applied for registration of the friend as first registered proprietor. The Court of Appeal held that the forged deed, a nullity, could pass no interest which could be registered: the sale and mortgage were both void so the Register was rectified. Further, the careless solicitors who should have been alerted by the odd circumstances of the case were liable in negligence to the wife and to the building society.

Once the title is registered, the registered proprietor is the guaranteed legal owner and rights in any dispute depend on the rectification and indemnity jurisdiction. A forged transfer resulting in the 'wrong' person being the registered proprietor raises fundamental questions about the Mirror and Indemnity principles of registered land. In *Steed's* case (above) it had been claimed (in *Argyle Building Society* v. *Hammond* (1985) 49 P & CR 148) that the transfer had been forged, and in such a case there might have been justification to rectify in favour of the 'real' owner, Mr Steed, under s.82(1)(d) or (g). However, it was held that the transfer was not a forgery; it was merely voidable and had not been avoided when the transfer and mortgage were made so there was no rectification and hence no indemnity available here.

10.9 Comment

There have been a number of recent Reports from the Law Commission concerning registered land. In the Third Report (No. 158, 1987) the Commission proposed that there should be only five overriding interests (legal easements and profits; adverse possession; legal leases for 21 years or less; rights of a person in actual occupation; customary rights). However, an indemnity should in future be available where the register is rectified because of an overriding interest. In addition, the Commission recommended that rectification against a registered proprietor in occupation should be further restricted. Finally, only a buyer in good faith and for value should take free of minor interests which have not been entered on the register; however, 'bad faith' would mean more than mere knowledge of the competing interest.

In 1988 a bill was published to incorporate a number of changes to the registered land system (Law Commission Fourth Report, No. 173). However, it appears that a less extensive reform may take place; the 1995 Report of the Working Group (Law Commission No. 235) recommended greater caution, and proposed merely amendment to s. 123 regarding first registration and the broadening of the indemnity provision (above).

In 1989 the Law Commission (No. 188) recommended that there should be no overreaching without the resident equitable co-owner's consent. Part of the recommendations in this Report were made law in the Trusts of Land and Appointment of Trustees Act 1996 (see 11.2 below), but not this part; if it were implemented, *Flegg* would no longer be good law.

Registration of title to land is uniformly considered A Good Thing but it is nonetheless valuable to consider its failings and limitations. Only then is it possible to decide whether, as is usually assumed, registration of title really is of benefit to all buyers and sellers of land. For example, it is clear that title registration does not automatically solve the conflicts of interests seen in this and the preceding chapter; for example, the extent to which occupiers should be protected. This is, at least partly, because the land registration system was modelled on the register of company shares, but land is not like shares. Land can be enjoyed in more ways than as a right to an income, and people have different needs in relation to it.

At least some of the difficulties are caused by the fact that the Land Register was introduced simply to replace repetitive examinations of the title deeds but this limited aim has now been confused with the wish to make the register a perfect mirror of the title, for some expectations currently seem to be that all that any buyer (or mortgagee) should have to do is to check the register (and see Pottage (1995) 15 OJLS 371). The danger is that, as registered title expands, 'simple conveyancing' becomes the rationale of all land law, at the expense of the other and equally important land law principle, security of occupation.

In any event, although registered conveyancing is much more convenient for the conveyancers, it appears that the system is neither quicker nor cheaper than traditional conveyancing. Costs are roughly equal for both systems and are about twice the rate of conveyancers in the United States, where there is little title registration. There are also complaints about the cost of the Land Registry and its delays despite its annual profits.

Summary

1   Registration of title to land is designed to provide a simple and efficient form of conveyancing, by providing a guaranteed mirror of most rights in the land and promising state compensation for loss.
2   The register is divided into three sections: property, proprietorship and charges. Each part of the register contains specific information about the land, the title and the burdens on the land.
3   Interests in registered land are also divided into three groups: title interests, overriding interests and minor interests.
4   Legal freeholds and leases over 21 years are substantively registrable; title to them may be absolute, possessory or qualified, or good leasehold.
5   Overriding interests are listed in s.70, and include interests such as easements, leases and adverse possession rights, as well as 'the rights of people in actual occupation of land'. Overriding interests override any buyer of an interest in registered land.

6 Minor interests are 'everything else'; they are (normally) only binding on a purchaser in good faith if they are entered on the register by the appropriate method: notice, caution, inhibition or restriction.

7 The register may be rectified, even against a registered proprietor in possession. The state provides compensation where anyone suffers loss by reason of rectification, but this does not include a proprietor who has effectively bought nothing because of a pre-existing overriding interest.

8 Problems which were apparent in unregistered land remain as problems in registered land.

Exercises

1 What goes where on the Land Register?
2 Which interests can be given a certificate and a number?
3 What are overriding interests and what is their importance?
4 When are minor interests binding?
5 Why do the provisions for rectification and indemnity detract from the basic principles of title registration?
6 Jake was the registered proprietor with absolute title of 'Albatross Cottage'. He agreed by deed to sell it to Agnes, aged 80, for £30 000 and she paid the price and moved in, but failed to complete the transaction at the Land Registry because she did not believe in lawyers. Soon afterwards, Jake brought Maria to see the cottage. She liked it so much that she offered him £35 000 for it. Jake agreed to sell it to her. She met Agnes briefly in the kitchen, and asked her what she was doing there. Agnes replied that she was just having a cup of tea.

Maria paid Jake the price and became the first registered proprietor. Jake gave her the keys and she moved in when Agnes was in Majorca for a month. Agnes has now returned and seeks rectification of the register against Maria. Who will win?

Would your answer be different if Jake and his sister Josephine were joint registered proprietors?

Part IV

Trusts of Land

11 Trusts of Land

11.1 Introduction

Much of this book has been concerned with dividing up the enjoyment of land: for example, between a tenant (entitled to possession) and a landlady (entitled to the rent), or between an owner of land who is entitled to occupy the whole and her neighbour who is allowed to use a path over it. Sharing the enjoyment of land between several people through the mechanism of the trust is also by now familiar from case law.

The basic principle of the trust is that there is a division between the legal and equitable ('beneficial') ownership of the land; in its simplest form, a trustee holds the legal title for the benefit of the beneficiary. However, it is fairly common in trusts of land for a trustee also to be beneficiary at the same time. (A beneficiary is sometimes referred to as *cestui que trust* (pronounced 'setty key trust'.) At this point it is useful to note that there can be no more than *four* legal owners (that is, trustees) of land (s.34(2) Trustee Act 1925).

In all trusts, it is essential to be aware of the various rights at law and in equity and to keep them separate, as in the examples in Table 11.1.

Table 11.1 Examples of legal and equitable ownership

	Law	Equity
Abbey National Building Society v. *Cann* (1990)	Son	Son and mother
Williams & Glyn's Bank Ltd v. *Boland* (1981)	Husband	Husband and wife
City of London Building Society v. *Flegg* (1988)	Mr and Mrs Maxwell-Brown	Mr and Mrs Maxwell-Brown and Mr and Mrs Flegg

The detailed rules concerning people who currently share the enjoyment of land through a trust are covered in the law of co-ownership in Chapter 12. A full understanding of trusts of land is only possible when the law in both chapters has been studied.

As shown in the many trusts cases already discussed, the trust is the form of land-sharing usually appropriate to families, and modern developments in this area of law are largely the result of the growth in land-ownership by ordinary families (including families where the adults concerned are not married). If a family breaks up, the people involved need to sort out who owns what; the costs of this may be enormous for, as well as providing the family home, the real and symbolic focus of family life, land may be one of the most valuable assets owned by any family member.

In this area, the courts often have to analyse open-textured and informal family arrangements within the formal structure of trust law; as a result, some of the case law here is very interesting but not straightforward. The topic is made more challenging because the basic rules are part of wider equitable principles. Further, because many cases in this chapter lie on the boundary between land law and family law, there can be an unseen conflict of values; crudely, land law is concerned with 'justice through certainty', while family law is more interested in 'justice in the individual case'. Where the demands of 'certainty' and 'individual justice' diverge, there is bound to be some confusion.

There used to be two kinds of trusts of land: the strict settlement and the trust for sale. The strict settlement was used by the aristocracy to keep land in the family through the generations, while the trust for sale developed as a means of holding land as a temporary investment. The Trusts of Land and Appointment of Trustees Act 1996 (TLATA) abolishes them both for the future from 1 January 1997, and replaces them with the simple 'trust of land'. While this new law provides a radical and simple conceptual basis for trusts of land, much of the old law of trusts remains in place – including the creation of trusts and co-ownership. The rules about overreaching by buyers of trust land are also little directly changed.

11.2   The Old Law of Trusts of Land

The strict settlement

Strict settlements were the traditional family arrangements of the aristocracy where the aim was to keep the land 'in the family'. Complicated inheritance rules were created within the family, and these sometimes restricted improvements of the land and prevented sale over many generations. Successive reforms were made over centuries to prevent long-lasting settlements (the 'rules against perpetuities') and to free the land from too many restrictions. In 1925, the Settled Land Act provided an elaborate and expensive legal mechanism to govern these trusts; under this the 'tenant for life' (the current beneficial owner of the land) became a trustee of the settlement and could deal fairly freely with the land.

S.2 of the TLATA 1996 states that (with very limited exceptions) strict settlements may no longer be created. Such trusts of land were already virtually obsolete because of punitive tax laws, but a strict settlement could still be created by accident, for example in a home-made will, or when a child inherited land, and so the whole regime had become largely an expensive trap for the uninformed, or for careless solicitors. (For further details of the old cumbersome and technical rules of strict settlements see Cheshire (1994) Chapter 9.)

The trust for sale

Until 1997, where there was a trust of land it *had* to be either a strict settlement or a trust for sale. It was a strict settlement if there were consecutive beneficial interests, unless it called itself a trust for sale. Any trust with concurrent beneficial interests had to be a trust for sale, so the trust for sale included not only family land (for example, where cohabitees shared the land on trust for sale) but also land held commercially (for example, by a firm of solicitors).

The trust for sale was imposed on many family arrangements by the LPA 1925, but unfortunately the concept never quite matched the reality and it was for this reason that the TLATA has replaced it with the 'trust of land'. The essence of the problem was that, under a trust for sale, the land was deemed to have been bought as an investment so there was an 'immediate and binding duty' to sell it although in reality of course the land had been bought for occupation, and sale was merely a possibility in the future. The trustees' *duty* of sale meant that if one trustee wanted a sale, the land had to be sold. S.30 LPA gave the court a discretion about ordering sale, and a long line of case law resulted from the tension between the duty to sell – when one family member wanted to turn the land into money – and the rest of the family's need to stay in their home. Conflicts between one family member who wants the land sold and the other who wants to keep it will of course still arise, (and the TLATA provides a statutory replacement for the old law, see 11.8 below).

A further problem with the duty to sell was that, because of the equitable principle that '*equity looks on that as done which ought to be done*', the courts pretended that the land was *converted* into money so the beneficiaries behind a trust for sale did not have an interest in land, but merely in money (the 'proceeds of sale'). This is the 'doctrine of conversion'. However, a number of cases showed that, although the beneficiaries in theory were only interested in the proceeds of sale, in practice they might still be recognised as having some interest in the land itself. A famous case here is *Bull* v. *Bull* [1955] 1 QB 234 (and see 11.7 below); a son, who was the sole trustee of the trust for sale and a joint beneficiary under it, wanted to evict his mother (the other beneficiary) but it was held that she had a right to occupy the land. Cases such as *Boland* [1981] and *Flegg* [1988] (see 10.5 above) were also concerned with the actual nature of the beneficiary's interest under s.70(1)(g) LRA and their right, if any, to occupy the trust land.

In the end of course, because the imposition of the trust for sale with its accompanying doctrine of conversion was simply inappropriate to the reality of family land owning, there could be no solution to the problem. As well as replacing the old trust for sale with the new 'trust of land', s.3 TLATA abolishes the doctrine of conversion for all trusts, except a trust for sale created by a will where the testator died before the Act came into effect.

There was a further problem with the strict settlement/trust for sale scheme, and this was that the bare trust (where 'A holds on trust for B', and B is a capable adult) was left outside, and the overreaching rules did not apply.

11.3   The New Law of Trusts of Land

The TLATA 1996 (and see Hopkins (1996) Conv. 411) was the result of the Law Commission's proposals (No. 181, 1989):

> 'We consider that the present dual system of trusts for sale and strict settlements is unnecessarily complex, ill-suited to the conditions of modern property ownership, and liable to give rise to unforeseen conveyancing complications.' (p. iv)

As already stated, the Act sweeps away old statute and case law, and Part I of the Act imposes on all trusts of land a new simple system. S.2 prevents the creation of any new strict settlements, or adding land to an existing strict settlement; s.4 provides that express trusts for sale become 'trusts of land', and s.5 (with Schedule 2) amends existing rules in ss.32–6 LPA which imposed the trust for sale onto concurrently shared trust land. The Act replaces certain sections of the LPA (including s.26, on consulting beneficiaries, and s.30, on disputes between owners of trust land) and also makes transitional provisions for existing trusts: most existing trusts for sale will be subject to most aspects of the new regime.

As will be seen (below 11.6), the trustees of a 'trust of land' have no duty of sale but a power either to sell or to retain the land; in addition, some beneficiaries now have a statutory right to occupy the trust land (see below 11.7). The relationship between beneficiaries and trustees is somewhat altered too, for example in respect of consultation, and some beneficiaries gain limited powers over the appointment of trustees. In order to make dealing with the land simple, buyers of trust land continue to be given special protection (see below 11.8).

As recommended by the Law Commission in 1989 (see 10.9 above), the bare trust is now brought within the general scheme of trusts of land, and is subject to overreaching provisions (s.1 TLATA).

11.4   Creation of Trusts of Land

A trust of land may be created expressly or impliedly; implied trusts may be created by the parties' actions or by statute (see Figure 11.1).

An express trust *inter vivos* (between living people) occurs whenever land is conveyed on trust to two or more people: formerly, this would normally have been 'on trust for sale', but all such trusts are now merely 'trusts of land' with power to sell or retain the land. Trusts of land by will are frequent – for example, when one spouse dies and leaves all her property to the other, or to her children. Although the strict settlement, invented to keep land unsold, has now been abolished, the new 'trust of land' may be expressly created with a provision that the land may not be sold without the consent(s) of certain people (for example, the widow of the trust's creator) (s. 8(2) TLATA). This ensures that the purpose of

---

Figure 11.1   *The creation of trusts of land*

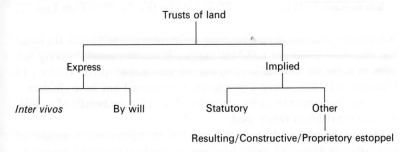

keeping the land in the family may still be achieved, at least for some period of time.

In 1925 statutory trusts for sale were imposed in a number of different circumstances. These included:

1   where a land owner died intestate (without having made a will): s.33(1) Administration of Estates Act 1925;
2   where land was shared by two or more people at the same time (unless there was a strict settlement) (ss.34–6 LPA);

A full list can be found in Cheshire (1994) pp. 208–9). All of them, whenever created, are now merely 'trusts of land' (ss.4–5 and Schedule 2 TLATA 1996).

11.5   Trusts Implied by Intention and/or Conduct

Equity recognises an implied trust relationship between people in a number of different circumstances, and this area of the law is untouched by the TLATA. The problem for the courts arises typically when a couple live together and share household costs (in the broadest sense) as part of a joint venture, but only one of them is the registered proprietor (or legal owner, in unregistered land). If the relationship breaks down the question is: has the other person any equitable interest in her home? Is she a beneficiary under a trust of land? (The question arises rather more dramatically if the trustee mortgages the land or goes bankrupt.)

As Clarke remarked:

'In an ideal world, those who intend to own property or a share in it would do three things: they would agree what they intended to do; they would then record their intentions; and they would take legal advice to ensure that what they wanted had been achieved in a manner which the law recognises. However . . . life is not like that.' ((1992) Fam Law 72)

Where the parties are married and the marriage comes to an end, the judge has discretion under the s.37 Matrimonial Proceedings and Property Act 1970 to make an order allocating real or personal property. Under s.15 Children Act 1989, where a couple are not married but have children a court also has power to order a transfer of land for the benefit of a child, but this provision is rarely used.

Most of the cases under consideration here therefore concern unmarried home-sharers where the courts have power only to state what is owned by whom, not to re-allocate property rights. The sort of arrangement which cause particular problems are those where the land already belonged to one partner when the other moved in; the couple would probably not be joint registered proprietors, but they may well have an understanding that the 'non-owner' will contribute to the mortgage repayments, or in some other way to their shared lives on the land. When they try to extricate themselves from their complex financial and emotional relationships, the judges have to decide what are their property rights from their whole relationship, including the traces of old bank accounts and half-remembered conversations.

Resulting and constructive trusts

Lawyers have three main tools of analysis for these kinds of problem: constructive trusts, resulting trusts, and proprietary estoppel. (Proprietary estoppel was discussed in 2.6 above, and is only referred to in passing here.) There are very many decided cases here: in one of the most recent, *Drake* v. *Whipp* [1996] 1 FLR 826, Peter Gibson LJ referred to the 'usual lengthy litany of authorities', and added, '. . . as is notorious, it is not easy to reconcile every judicial utterance in this well-travelled area of law' (at p. 827).

A *resulting trust* is a trust which 'results' from an agreement by the parties together with a significant contribution to the purchase price of the land at the time of the acquisition; a typical example is *Flegg* [1988] (see 10.5 above).

Proprietary estoppel arises when one person acts to their detriment in reliance on a promise knowingly made by an owner of land that she will convey an interest in the land. The remedy awarded might well be that the interest of the victim is protected by a constructive trust, as in *Re Basham* [1986] (see 2.6 above). However, if there is also a contract to transfer the land, and if this has not been registered as an estate contract and, if the land is unregistered, or if the land is registered and the person is not living there, then estoppel may not be able to protect her: see *Lloyds Bank plc* v. *Carrick* (1996) 140 NLJ 402, see 9.3 and 10.5 above.)

Constructive trusts are potentially much wider than either of the foregoing. They do not necessarily depend on a voluntary relationship created by the parties, where equity demands that promises are honoured, but rely on a more fundamental moral principle. They can be imposed by the courts whenever people find themselves in a situation where one would naturally trust the other because of the underlying social consensus on what is 'fair'. A constructive trust may therefore be imposed whenever a person would otherwise get 'a manifest and unfair advantage'. Examples include: when someone would otherwise benefit from a fraudulent act or a crime, or where a trustee has acted in breach of trust, or where there is unjust enrichment.

During the late 1960s and 1970s, Lord Denning MR used the constructive trust as a means of achieving a fair solution to family disputes over land, and the constructive trust is used in this way both in America and in Australia. However, over the last 20 years in Britain, the constructive trust has been more limited. The current House of Lords authority is *Lloyds Bank plc* v. *Rosset* [1991] 1 AC 107. Mr Rosset bought a semi-derelict farmhouse with money from a Swiss trust fund; the trustees insisted that his name only should appear as the registered proprietor. For six months, Mrs Rosset did all the work of supervising the renovation and decorated the house. Did she have an equitable interest under an informal trust? If so, would it enable her to claim an overriding interest under s.70(1)(g) LRA (see 10.5 above) so as to defeat a mortgage taken out by Mr Rosset without her knowledge? The House of Lords held that she had not shown that she had gained an interest, and therefore the bank won (see Ferguson (1993) 109 LQR 114).

Lord Bridge said that an equitable interest could only arise if there were a *common intention*. This could be shown by either:

1   *an express agreement plus some act by the claimant.* This will give rise to rights, according to Lord Bridge, under a constructive trust or proprietary estoppel; or,
2   *an act by the claimant from which the court may* infer a common *intention,* giving rise to an interest under a constructive trust. It is likely that the only act which will be adequate is the direct contribution of money (such as the repayment of a mortgage).

Although many pre-*Rosset* cases may no longer be good law, some may indicate how disputes might be judged today. For example, Lord Bridge approved the earlier Court of Appeal decision in *Grant v. Edwards* [1986] 2 All ER 426 where, a man and a woman lived together for about ten years and had two children. He was the sole registered proprietor, but there was evidence of an agreement as to their 'common intention' in that he had lied to her initially about why he could not put her name on the Land Certificate, and they had shared equally some money left over from an insurance claim when the house had partly burnt down. In addition, she acted to her detriment in reliance on this intention by paying all the household bills.

'In a case such as the present, where there has been no written declaration or agreement, nor any direct provision by the plaintiff of part of the purchase price so as to give rise to a resulting trust in her favour, she must establish a common intention between her and the defendant, acted on by her, that she should have a beneficial interest in the property . . . In my judgment [she must prove] conduct on which [she] could not reasonably be expected to embark unless she was to have an interest in the house.' (Nourse LJ at pp. 431–3)

Clearly this case might also fit under Lord Bridge's second category. If the woman had not made her contribution, the man would not have been able to repay the mortgage. Her indirect financial contribution might be evidence from which the court could exceptionally infer the common intention (although of course his lie actually shows that in reality the intention was *not* 'common' to them both).

An older case, *Burns* v. *Burns* [1984] Ch 317, reinforces Lord Bridge's view that a claimant is unlikely to succeed under the second category unless there is 'the solid tug of money'. A man and a woman lived together for 19 years in a house which belonged legally to the man. She brought up their children, kept house and, when the children were older, she had a job and contributed to the house-keeping and various household items such as a washing machine. She also decorated inside the house. Her claim to a beneficial interest failed:

'What is needed, I think, is evidence of a payment or payments by the plaintiff which it can be inferred was referable to the acquisition of the house . . . the mere fact that the parties live together and do the ordinary domestic tasks is, in my view, no indication at all that they thereby intended to alter the existing property rights of either of them.' (Fox LJ at pp. 252, 254)

A similar result was reached in *Thomas* v. *Fuller-Brown* [1988] 1 FLR 237 where a man claimed an interest in his girlfriend's home. He had done significant repair work, but it was held that their agreement was that this would be in exchange for free board and lodging.

More recently, in *Hammond* v. *Mitchell* [1992] 1 WLR 1127 (and see [1994] Fem LS 83) a man and woman lived together for 12 years in a bungalow registered in his name. He had promised that she was equally the owner of the property but said that he could not put her name on the register for tax reasons. There were also several businesses, and a house in Spain and she claimed a half share in all of these. The full flavour of the dispute can only be gained from reading the report: in the end Waite J, in some despair at the detailed and conflicting evidence and the 19 days of the trial, finally awarded her a half-share in the bungalow.

There was evidence of a promise that the land was half hers, and there was also her involvement in the businesses, their sharing of whatever money they had and her agreement to risk any interest she might have in the bungalow as security for a bank loan for business purposes. All these taken together showed a common agreement plus an act to her detriment. She therefore satisfied the first *Rosset* category. However, Waite J commented:

'The primary emphasis accorded by the law in cases of this kind to express discussions between the parties . . . means that the tenderest exchanges of a common law courtship may assume an unforeseen significance many years later when they are brought under equity's microscope and subjected to an analysis under which many thousands of pounds of value may be liable to turn on fine questions as to whether the relevant words were spoken in earnest or in dalliance.' (at p. 1139).

Most recently, in *Drake v. Whipp* (above), Mr Drake and Mrs Whipp lived together for six years and then split up; she claimed an interest in the house they had converted together, held in the sole name of Mr Drake. She had contributed 40 per cent of the purchase price and the Court of Appeal unanimously held that this could have given her rights under a resulting trust: she had said in evidence:

'I thought it was joint, otherwise I wouldn't have put my money into it. He said he would put my name on it in about a month's time. I trusted him completely.' (at p. 829)

Subsequently, they both contributed to the costs and to the labour of renovating the house. It was held that these subsequent contributions created a larger equitable share – under Lord Bridge's first category of constructive trust. (For the size of her share, see below.)

Recent cases illustrate two other aspects of the creation and enforcement of implied trusts. In *Tinsley v. Milligan* [1993] 3 WLR 126 the House of Lords had to decide on the relevance of the misconduct of the claimant. Here, the parties had expressly agreed that, although the property would be registered in the name of one cohabitee only, the other would contribute to the purchase. When the relationship broke up, she claimed her share, but the legal owner argued that the arrangement had been made in order to defraud the Department of Social Security: she claimed that therefore the plaintiff did not have 'clean hands'. The House disagreed: the claimant could establish her claim without relying on the illegality and therefore did not need to show her dirty hands. (In any event, of course, both parties knew the purpose of the arrangement, and neither had clean hands.)

Secondly, in the law of trusts, there is an old doctrine called the 'presumption of advancement': the courts used to presume that money given by a parent to her child for the purchase of land was a gift, and was not intended to acquire any interest in the land. In *McGrath* v. *Wallis* [1995] 2 FLR 114 the Court of Appeal followed the modern line that this presumption is rebuttable by even the slightest evidence. Here, where a father had provided money to help his son buy a house for them to live in together, there was evidence of a common intention (from an incomplete deed) that the land was to be held on trust for them both. Therefore, when the father died intestate, the son's sister successfully claimed a share of her father's interest in the land.

What share of the equitable interest?

Once an informal arrangement has been held to have created an equitable interest in the land, the next problem is to decide what share of the equity the successful claimant is entitled to. Any trustee or beneficiary can go to court (now under s.14(2)(b) TLATA) for a declaration of the 'nature or extent of a person's interest' in property (and see 11.8 below).

It would seem that in a resulting trust, the parties are entitled to a share of the equitable interest in proportion to their contribution to the price, but there is conflict in decided cases as to whether subsequent direct financial contributions can increase the share under a this kind of implied trust. However, if there is sufficient evidence of a resulting trust, then there will also be enough evidence for a constructive trust in which the shares will be valued according to what the parties intended.

In such cases, the court has to discover their intention from the whole story of their conduct, and often this will be that they intended to share in proportion to their respective contributions. *Passee* v. *Passee* [1988] 1 FLR 263 is a good example of the process: here, the court had to work painstakingly through all the mortgage payments over many years to find the answer. A man was the sole owner of a house in order to simplify the mortgage arrangements, but other members of his extended family contributed to the purchase and the mortgage repayments. His mother successfully claimed a share based on her contribution in proportion to the current value of the house, because:

'They intended, or are to be taken to have intended, that each would be entitled to a share to be determined when the property ceased to be theirs on the basis of what would be fair, having regard to the contributions which in total each had by then made'. (Nicholls LJ at pp. 270–1)

More recently in *Midland Bank plc* v. *Cooke* [1995] 4 All ER (and see [1996] CLJ 194) the wife contributed £550 to the original purchase (her share of a wedding present) and the trial judge held that this entitled her under a resulting trust to 6.74 per cent of the value of the house. However, the Court of Appeal held that once there was evidence of the common intention, then the judge has to:

'undertake a survey of the whole course of dealing between the parties relevant to their ownership and occupation of the property and their sharing of its burdens and advantages'. (Waite LJ at p. 574).

Here, in the absence of express agreement as to shares and the complexity of their financial and other arrangements, the court inferred an agreement that she should have an equal share:

'[The court] will take into consideration all conduct which throws light on the question what shares were intended. Only if that search proves inconclusive does the court fall back on the maxim that "equality is equity".'

(She also won against the bank, under the undue influence rule, see 6.3 above.)

In *Drake* v. *Whipp* (above) Peter Gibson LJ agreed that in constructive trusts the court can adopt 'a broad brush approach' to determining the shares. In the end of reviewing the whole story of their joint enterprise in that case, including her work on the land and her contribution to the housekeeping bills, he awarded her a one-third share. The trial judge had decided that this was a resulting trust and only awarded a 19.4 per cent share (although, as already mentioned, one line of cases does allow subsequent contributions to extend the equitable share under a resulting trust).

11.6 The Trustees

The trustees of a trust of land are the legal owners, or registered proprietors in registered land, and their rights and duties are subject to the general law of trusts and to the particular provisions (if any) of the trust in question (s.8). The powers of a trustee of a strict settlement or a trust for sale were largely contained in the SLA 1925, and the TLATA tidies up and extends these provisions. The most important change is that under the new 'trust of land', there is no longer any duty to sell the land (ss. 4–5); there is a power to sell and a power to postpone sale.

S.6(1) TLATA provides that the trustees 'have all the powers of an absolute owner': thus, they may sell, mortgage, lease or otherwise deal with the land. This extends their powers under the old rules of strict settlements and trusts for sale, but the trust may restrict these powers. In addition, the powers of trustees of charitable, ecclesiastical and public trusts continue to be limited in special ways. Trustees also have the power (subject to the terms of the trust) to buy land with trust money (s.6(3)). However, despite these apparently unlimited powers, it is still possible – as under the old law – to make dealings with the trust land subject to the consent of a particular person or persons (s.8(2)). Nevertheless, if the land is sold without this consent a buyer without actual notice will nevertheless get a good title (s.16(3) for unregistered land; the same principle also probably holds under the general rules of registered land). The new law also provides rules about the occupation of land by beneficiaries (see below 11.7).

Where the beneficiaries are of full age and capacity, the role of trustees may be limited. Thus, s.6(2) restates the old rule that if such beneficiaries 'are absolutely entitled to the land', the trustees can convey the land to them. Subject to the terms of the trust, the trustees may also have the power to divide up ('partition') the land for any purpose (subject to the provisions of the trust), but only if the beneficiaries are adult tenants in common, absolutely entitled, and they all consent (s.7). The trustees may also (again, subject to the terms of the trust) delegate their powers to these beneficiaries (s.9), as under the old law of strict settlements.

The new law also restates and extends to all trustees of trusts of land the duty to consult beneficiaries. (Under the old s.26(3) LPA this right merely concerned statutory trusts for sale of land.) S.11 TLATA provides that, subject to a contrary intention being expressed in the trust:

'The trustees of land shall in the exercise of any function relating to land subject to the trust –

(a) so far as practicable, consult the beneficiaries of full age and beneficially entitled to an interest in possession in the land, and
(b) shall so far as consistent with the general interest of the trust, give effect to the wishes of those beneficiaries, or (in case of dispute) of the majority (according to the value of their combined interests).'

This section will not normally apply to an express trust created before 1997 (s.11(2)(b)).

Normally, trustees are appointed in the trust deed, or, in the case of implied trusts, the trustee will be the person(s) to whom the land is transferred (the legal owner, or registered proprietor). Of course, trustees of the family home are usually also beneficiaries, but, as shown in Table

11.1 above, legal and equitable ownership do not necessarily mirror one another. If there is no trustee (for example, if land is conveyed to a child who by s.1(6) LPA 1925 cannot own land) the court can appoint trustees. The TLATA provides, for the first time, that if no one is appointed to nominate a trustee, beneficiaries of full age and capacity and absolutely entitled can do so and they can also direct retirement of a trustee (s19), or replace one who is mentally incapable (s.20).

11.7   The Beneficiaries

In the Act, a 'beneficiary' of a trust of land is defined as *anyone* who has an interest in the land (s.22(1)); therefore, the term presumably includes the trustees since they have legal interests in the trust land. The person who has (a share in) the equitable ownership is a 'beneficiary who is beneficially entitled'. However, here the word beneficiary will be used in its ordinary meaning of 'beneficial owner'.

As already stated, many trustees will also be beneficial owners and entitled to (share) the enjoyment of the land. The trustees, whether or not they are beneficiaries too, must abide by the general rules of trusteeship, and the particular provisions of the trust. If they fail to do so, or for example if they do not consult the beneficiaries as required by s.11 (above), the beneficiaries may sue them for breach of trust. However, when one family member is trustee for another and acts in breach of trust she usually does so because of a desperate financial position and by the time the (other) beneficiary discovers what has happened, the trustee is either bankrupt or otherwise not worth suing (see for example *Flegg* or *Cann* in 10.5 above).

The beneficiaries of a trust of land are generally entitled to whatever the trust provides for them. Their rights under a trust for sale depended on the original purposes of the trust; this again posed a conceptual problem for land lawyers, since under the doctrine of conversion the land was to be sold straight away: it was decidedly odd that the beneficiaries might have a right to live there. In addition to the powers given to beneficiaries of full age (as in s. 11, consultation, and ss. 19–20, appointment of trustees) the TLATA now provides a statutory right for beneficiaries to occupy the trust land.

S.12 states that a beneficiary is entitled to live in the house 'if the purposes of the trust include making the land available for his occupation' or if the land is available for such occupation. The reference in this statutory right of occupation to 'the purposes of the trust' restates the existing case law rule and can be illustrated by two old decisions. In one,

Barclay v. *Barclay* [1970] 2 QB 677, an old man left his bungalow to his five sons and daughter-in-law stating that he wanted the land to be sold and the proceeds divided up equally between them. Here, there was no right for one beneficiary to live in the bungalow. In *Bull* v. *Bull* on the other hand, the son and his mother had bought the house to live in together and she had a right to live there. (The solution to conflicts such as these are determined now by ss.14–15 TLATA, replacing s.30 LPA; see 11.8 below.)

S.13 TLATA gives the trustees new and clearer responsibilities in cases where beneficiaries are entitled to occupy the land, as is common in trusts of the family home where adults share beneficial interests. It provides that trustees may not 'unreasonably exclude' any beneficiary from the land (s.13(2)) and may impose on an occupying beneficiary 'reasonable conditions' (for example, to pay expenses relating to the land). In making such decisions., which will probably arise if the family breaks up, they have to take into account the intentions of the creator of the trust, the purposes of the trust and the circumstances and wishes of the beneficiaries. When a beneficiary has been 'reasonably excluded' from occupation, the trustees may require another who is occupying to pay compensation (s.14(6)). (The previous law had been more complex, probably giving a right of compensation only in limited circumstances.)

An example of several typical problems which may arise can be illustrated by the pre-TLATA case of *Chhokar* v. *Chhokar* [1984] FLR. Here, a husband was the sole registered proprietor of a house which was bought as a family home. He held on trust for sale for himself and Mrs Chhokar, as she had gained a beneficial interest under a resulting trust by her financial contribution. The marriage broke down and in order to get rid of her he sold the house to a Mr Parmar, who knew all the facts and paid a lower price in consequence.

Mrs Chhokar was in actual occupation when Mr Parmar bought the land, so she clearly had an overriding interest and could not be evicted; he therefore held the land as trustee for Mrs Chhokar and himself (having taken over Mr Chhokar's legal and equitable interests). As a beneficial owner of land bought for occupation, it looked as if he had some sort of right to occupy the flat (with her and her husband, who had by then moved back into the property). The court refused to order that all three should live together. They also refused to order her to pay rent as compensation to him in these circumstances because it would not have been fair: he had excluded himself from the land by his own behaviour.

Therefore, all Mr Parmar owned for the time being was the right to share in the price when the land was finally sold. (What he really wanted was immediate sale of the land but this depends on the court's discretion, now under s.14–15 TLATA, see below.)

11.8   Sale or Other Dealing with Trust Land

Protection for buyers of trust land

A buyer of land (including a mortgagee, and so on) subject to a trust can overreach the beneficial interests, as already explained (see 9.4 and 10.5 above). Provided she pays two trustees or a trust corporation, she 'shall not be concerned with the trusts' (s.27 LPA, unaffected by the new law).

Where the trust makes any sale subject to the consent of more than two people, s.10 TLATA provides that the purchaser only has to be sure that two have actually consented (as in the old s. 26 LPA on statutory trusts for sale). The section provides also that a parent or guardian can consent on behalf of a child (in subs.(3)). Further, as already mentioned, a buyer of trust land need not make sure that proper consultations have been carried out under ss. 6 or 11, or that consent to partition under s. 7 has been obtained. However, if she has actual notice of a breach of trust, the conveyance will be invalidated: the buyer will herself become a trustee.

Conflicts between owners of trust land

As already mentioned, if the provisions for consultation and the gaining of consents are not observed and the land is sold (or mortgaged, and so on) in breach of trust, aggrieved beneficiaries can in theory sue their trustees. However, since the land will probably by then already have been irrevocably sold or mortgaged and the trustees will probably not be worth suing, it is far better to prevent mis-dealing if possible by taking the trustees to court to decide whether the land should be sold.

The old s.30 LPA discretion and the cases which explained how the court would exercise this discretion is now replaced by ss.14–15 TLATA. These sections are also crucial when a purchaser has stepped into the shoes of a defaulting trustee and seeks possession and sale against a beneficiary whose rights were not overreached (as in *Chhokar*, above), and also where there has been undue influence in a mortgage. Further, if any of the co-owners at law or in equity are bankrupt (and this includes where mortgage instalments are not paid), the case must be heard under the provisions of the Insolvency Act 1986, not under TLATA. (Under the old law, the Insolvency Act only applied to married owners in relation to the family home.) There are separate provisions for the courts to deal with domestic violence between owners of land (and see Law Commission Report No. 207, 1992).

S.14(1) allows any trustee or beneficiary of a trust of land to apply to the court, and the court may make any order:

'(a) relating to the exercise by the trustees of any of their functions (including an order relieving them of any obligation to obtain the consent of, or to consult, any person in connection with the exercise of any of the functions) . . . as the court thinks fit.'

By s.14(3) it is not possible to apply under this section for the appointment or removal of trustees; there is provision for this under the Trustee Act s. 57.

S.15 TLATA replaces the cases which indicated how the court should exercise its discretion:

'(1) The matters to which the court is to have regard in determining an application for an order under s. 14 include –

(a) the intention of the person or persons (if any) who created the trust,
(b) the purposes for which the property subject to the trust is held,
(c) the welfare of any minor who occupies or might reasonably be expected to occupy any land subject to the trust as his home, and
(d) the interests of any secured creditor of any beneficiary.'

When the application concerns exclusion of occupation rights under s.13, the court also must have regard to 'the circumstances and wishes' of each of the beneficiaries who might have a right to occupy (s.15(2)). In other applications, the court must normally take into account the wishes of the majority of adult beneficiaries currently entitled to the equitable ownership.

Under the old s.30, the court asked two questions: (1) what was the underlying purpose of the trust for sale? and (2) has the purpose ended? These two questions had had to be invented because under the old trust for sale the duty to sell was 'immediate and binding', and any power to postpone sale could only be exercised if the trustees were unanimous. Thus, the only way to block the duty of sale if even one trustee wanted to sell was to make paramount the purpose of the trust.

The new Act spells out the considerations to be taken into account in deciding whether the land was to be sold; these are taken from cases on s.30, and these old cases are probably still relevant to show how the new sections will probably operate in future. An example is *Chhokar* (above), where the rogue who knowingly colluded with a husband to get rid of his wife failed to gain an order for sale under the old s.30, because the voice of the innocent wife ought to prevail over the voice of 'the scoundrel who sought unsuccessfully to destroy her interest'. Cumming-Bruce LJ said:

> 'the court does have regard to the underlying purpose of the trust and will not, unless there are unusual circumstances or some special consideration, order a sale if the effect thereof will be to prevent the beneficiaries or one of them from occupying the home as a matrimonial and/or family home . . . Where there are third party interests . . . the court has to consider the voice of each of the parties and give proper weight to what those voices say.' (p. 327)

Therefore, if the underlying purpose of the trust was to live in the house, and this purpose had not ended, then sale would not normally be ordered. In *Jones* v. *Challenger* [1961] 1 QB 176 the house had been bought by a husband and wife as a matrimonial home but the marriage broke down and the wife left. There were no children and the Court of Appeal held that the house should be sold because, 'with an end of the marriage, that purpose was dissolved and the primacy of the duty to sell was restored.' (Devlin LJ, p. 183). In *Barclay* v. *Barclay* [1970] (see 11.7 above) too, when a house was left to five people on an express trust for sale, the court ordered a sale. Here, the purpose of the trust was the sale of land, right from the start.

It is not easy to see what the effects of the new law might be. The courts' prioritising of the 'purpose of the trust' to prevent sale had to be developed because of the inappropriateness of the trust for sale for most 'family land'. However, under ss.14–15 TLATA the trust is to sell or retain the land, and the purpose of the trust is only one consideration among several to be taken into account by the court: in this way, the new law is similar to the provisions under bankruptcy. Intended merely as codification, the new law may have unexpected results: the abolition of the duty of sale, and the downgrading of the 'purpose of the trust', may yet have unforeseen results when balancing the interests of the various parties.

Bankruptcy

The major exception to the principle that occupying beneficiaries may be able to prevent a sale of trust land is where any party is bankrupt; s.15(4) provides that such a case must be considered not under s.14–15 but under s. 335A Insolvency Act 1986. Here again the court must make such order 'as it thinks just and reasonable' having regard to the interests of the parties, including the needs of any children. However, by subsection s.336(5), once a year has passed since the bankruptcy was declared, the court:

'shall assume, unless the circumstances of the case are exceptional, that the interests of the bankrupt's creditors outweigh all other considerations'.

In *Re Citro (Domenico) (a bankrupt)* [1990] 3 All ER 952 (a case under the old trust for sale of land and Insolvency Act) the Court of Appeal explained that 'exceptional circumstances' relates to the circumstances of the creditor, not of the bankrupt's family. The disruption of losing a home and changing schools is 'not uncommon', and therefore not exceptional; Nourse LJ described this in ironic Dickensian terms as 'merely the melancholy consequences of debt and improvidence with which every civilised society has to be familiar' (at p. 892). As Brown concluded (55 MLR (1992) 284 at p. 291):

'In the necessary balancing exercise between creditors as against bankrupts and their families, the former will always win in the end, and that end comes sooner rather than later.'

Where any party to the trust went bankrupt therefore, it would appear that the purpose of the trust had ended and the land had to be sold to pay the debts. Mrs *Chhokar* (above) was lucky that her husband only behaved badly towards her, and did not also go bankrupt.

However, the section was more fully explained in *Abbey National Building Society plc* v. *Moss* [1994] 1 FLR 307. Here, old Mrs Moss had transferred her house into the names of herself and her daughter, on the understanding that she, the old lady, would live in the house until she died. A few years later, the daughter forged her signature on a mortgage and then defaulted on the repayments. The building society claimed possession of the land. Clearly, the forged deed had no effect on the legal and equitable rights of Mrs Moss but the society had stepped into the shoes of the daughter and had become a trustee of the land, and it applied for, and at first instance won, an order of sale under the old s.30. (At that time, the Insolvency Act only applied to spouses and the matrimonial home.)

On appeal, the Court of Appeal held that this was effectively a trust under which any sale or other dealing was subject to the consent of Mrs Moss and it refused to dispense with her consent in these circumstances. Further, it held that the underlying purpose of the trust – her occupation – still subsisted. This case was not like that of *Citro*, where it was one of parties who were intended to occupy the land who had become bankrupt; here the daughter had had no right to occupy the land under the trust and her failure to pay the mortgage therefore did not end the trust. In deciding whose interest should be protected, the court also took into account the fact that the witnessing of the mortgage deed was oddly presented and this should have put the mortgagee on alert.

As in many other s.30 decisions, the judges in this case were concerned with trying to work out a fair result within the structure of the trust for sale, to find a way through the doctrine of conversion and the 'immediate and binding' duty of sale. There is some doubt as to whether the Court of Appeal should have dealt with the application as if it were a bankruptcy. If they were right to do so, such a case would now fall under the Insolvency Act and – once a year had passed – the decision whether or not to sell would depend on whether the court agreed that the case was "exceptional". Since cases like *Citro* have established that 'exceptional' relates only to the circumstances of the creditor, a court might well have to agree that the unhappiness of an old lady was an unexceptional, 'normal consequence' of civilised society. However, if the Court were wrong in *Moss*, and this should not be treated as bankruptcy, then it should fall under the new ss.14–15 jurisdiction.

Although under the Insolvency Act, the land is very likely to be sold after a year has passed, whatever the purpose of the trust, ss.14–15 TLATA do not contain the 'year' rule, so under the new Act cases are likely to continue to be decided, as *Chhokar*, on the basis of 'which voice in equity should be heard'.

11.9   Comment

The TLATA 1996 provides a coherent conceptual foundation for trusts of land. It extends and clarifies the roles of trustees and beneficiaries in relation especially to partition, consultation, rights of occupation and delegation, and gives beneficiaries limited powers in respect of the appointment of trustees. The new ss.14–15 discretion about sale of trust land largely continues the old s.30 LPA and its case law, but it is impossible to predict the effects of the new trust to sell or retain and the balancing of matters to be taken into consideration in deciding whether the land should be sold or retained. By extending the application of the Insolvency Act 1986 to any bankruptcy, the TLATA however may reduce the discretionary powers exercised under the old law, as in, for example, the case of *Moss*.

However satisfactory the new conceptual base might be to land lawyers, the real problems remain. How far should people acquire rights to land by working and living there – and how far should others be able to exploit their labour? And when should a trustee in bankruptcy have the power to evict innocent people with established rights of occupation?

The present law on the acquisition of interests under trusts is particularly unsatisfactory, even apart from the evidential difficulties outlined in *Hammond* v. *Mitchell*. It operates to discriminate against female cohabitees – the likeliest claimants – for two reasons. First, because Lord Bridge's two headings in *Rosset*, in their reliance on agreement and common intention, rely on a 'contractual' analysis which is often inappropriate when exploring family relationships based on trust. For legal judgement in this area to rest on a contract (a private law voluntarily created by two equally placed individuals) rather than on the wider communal understanding of the nature of a trust relationship is as inappropriate as was the old trust for sale applied to modern family land.

Second, while 'the ordinary domestic role' of a man is to earn money which would go towards the purchase of the house, the 'ordinary domestic role' of a woman is not wholly a financial one. A woman is more likely to be working harder – work outside the home, plus house-keeping and childcare – while earning less than a man, and in taking only money or its equivalent into account as an 'act referable to land', the judges have adopted a commercial definition of the 'contribution' necessary to gain an equitable interest which denies the realities of family life. It can be argued therefore that the contractual and commercial basis of trust interests simply does not go far enough, and many argue that the wider understanding of constructive trusts in other jurisdictions should be adopted (see for example Gray (1993) pp. 455–9).

Summary

1 Strict settlements developed as a way in which families could hold land through several generations; trusts for sale were created to hold land as a temporary investment. The TLATA abolishes both for the future, creating a new 'trust of land' with power to sell or retain the land.

2 Under the old trust for sale, equity regarded the beneficial interest as an interest in money, not in land, although this was sometimes ignored in order to protect occupiers of land; the TLATA abolishes this doctrine of conversion.

3 An interest under a trust of land may arise expressly, or by statute, or by a resulting or constructive trust or by proprietary estoppel. A resulting trust may arise if there was a contribution to the purchase; a constructive trust may arise if there was an express agreement or common intention to share the equitable interest and acts referable to land.

4 The parties' equitable shares in a resulting trust are decided according to their contributions; in a constructive trust, the parties will share according to their common intention, or if none can be inferred, equally.

5 Trustees of a trust of land have, subject to the trust, the powers of an absolute owner of land; this may include powers to transfer the land to

adult beneficiaries absolutely entitled; to partition the land; to delegate their powers to beneficiaries. They have duties to consult the beneficiaries and to make reasonable decisions in relation to beneficiaries occupying the land.

6   Beneficiaries have the right to be consulted, and may have the right to occupy or receive compensation.

7   Under a trust of land, any trustee or beneficiary can go to court for an order of sale or otherwise, and the court may make such order as it thinks fit; where a party is bankrupt, the land will probably be sold after a year.

Exercises

1   Why was the doctrine of conversion abolished?
2   When do beneficiaries have the right to occupy trust land?
3   What should you do in order to get an equitable interest in a house?
4   When does land subject to a trust have to be sold?
5   In 1978, Sheila and Ronnie decided to live together. They bought a flat, with only Ronnie's name on the conveyance, both contributing to the deposit and mortgage repayments and sharing a bank account for all their expenditure. They originally intended to have children, but then Sheila decided not to because of her career. However, in December 1986 Ronnie fell in love with Tracey. She moved into the flat with her baby from a previous relationship and Sheila moved out. Shortly afterwards, Ronnie died and since then Tracey has paid all the mortgage instalments because Ronnie had told her (falsely) that he had registered her as a joint proprietor.

Sheila is now bankrupt. Advise Tracey.

12 Co-ownership

12.1 Introduction

Concurrent co-ownership of trust land may arise in various ways, but the simplest example is where land is conveyed to a husband and wife who share both the legal and equitable title. (Trusts of land are common also in commercial situations, as the cases in this chapter show.) The 1925 LPA established the rule that all *legal* title had to be co-owned under a particular set of rules called 'joint tenancy', in order to make conveyancing easier, but in respect of the *equitable* title to land it is possible to be a co-owner either under the 'joint tenancy' rules or under the rules of 'tenancy in common'. In addition, an equitable joint tenancy can be changed into an equitable tenancy in common.

Under the LPA and TLATA a trust of land exists in every case where land is 'co-owned', for example by a husband and wife, or in a commercial partnership. This chapter explains the ways in which land is co-owned at law and in equity, the rules of joint tenancy and tenancy in common. None of the law in this chapter is directly affected by the TLATA. However, the cases covered in Chapter 11 now gain an extra dimension as the rules of joint tenancy and tenancy in common – which apply to most of them – are detailed.

12.2 Sharing Land

Before 1925, there were four methods of co-owning land, and any of them could exist either at law or in equity. Since then, only two survive: they are called 'joint tenancy' and 'tenancy in common'. As 'land' includes all interests in land, there can be a joint tenancy of a lease or a life interest, for example, as well as of a fee simple.

A joint tenancy can exist in law or in equity but, as mentioned above, since 1925 a tenancy in common can only exist in equity:

CO-OWNERSHIP SINCE 1925	
LAW **Joint tenancy**	*EQUITY* **Joint tenancy** **or** **Tenancy in common**

Joint tenancy

The basic principle of joint tenancy is that the owners – as far as outsiders are concerned – are regarded as one person; there is a 'thorough and intimate union', as Blackstone put it. They are united in every way possible:

1 unity of Possession (P);
2 unity of Interest (I);
3 unity of Title (T);
4 unity of Time (T).

All the joint tenants are entitled to *possess* the whole of the land. They each hold an identical *interest* – fee simple or life interest and so on – and they obtained it by the same document (*title*), and it was vested at the same *time*. Joint tenancy was claimed for example in *A. G. Securities* v. *Vaughan* [1988] 3 WLR 1205 (see 5.4 above) where the claimants of joint tenancy of a legal lease failed because they had arrived at different times and there was therefore no unity of title.

The rule of joint tenancy is that the joint tenants do not have shares in the land: each owns the *whole* of it. In addition, joint tenants enjoy the 'right of survivorship' (*ius accrescendi*). The joint tenants are 'all one person', and if one dies it is as if he had never existed: the survivors still own the whole of the land so there is nothing for the heirs of the dead joint tenant to inherit. The last survivor of joint tenants will own the whole land absolutely. The right of survivorship means that holding land on a joint tenancy tends to make conveyancing easier as time passes. This is why, since 1925, this is the only kind of co-ownership which is possible *at law* (S.34 LPA): legal owners must hold as joint tenants and the maximum number is four (s.34 Trustee Act 1925). They hold on trust (now, a 'trust of land' with power to sell or retain) for any number of equitable joint tenants or tenants in common, and a buyer need not bother about any beneficial interests provided he pays at least two trustees (see 11.8 above).

The risk involved in the right of survivorship may seem unfair, but in fact it is quite convenient that legal ownership of, for example, trust land, or of the land of a commercial partnership, should not be affected if one co-owner at law dies. In equity on the other hand, although joint tenancy is possible, the risks can be inconvenient; for this reason, equity 'leans against' this form of co-ownership.

Tenancy in common

Tenancy in common is often referred to as an 'undivided share': the land is in shares but they have not yet been divided up. Tenancy in common has only one of the four unities: the unity of possession. An example is *Grant v. Edwards* [1986] (11.5 above) where a co-habitee gained an interest under a constructive trust by contributing financially after her partner had become the owner of the house.

As stated above, the risk attached to the right of survivorship in joint tenancy was not liked by equity. When a tenant in common dies therefore, he can leave his 'undivided share' to anyone he pleases, but this means that there may be more and more tenants in common as they die and leave their shares to their descendants. However, as far as a buyer of land is concerned, the interests shared in equity are 'behind a curtain': he can overreach all the beneficial interests (whether joint tenancy or tenancy in common) by paying two trustees (see 9.4 above).

12.3   Creation of a Joint Tenancy or Tenancy in Common

At the start of the relationship

At law there are no problems, because a joint tenancy arises whenever a legal interest in land is currently shared, that is, whenever land is conveyed into the names of two or more people. The difficulties arise in equity, because here there may be either a joint tenancy or a tenancy in common; it is also possible for there to be – in equity – both joint tenants and tenants in common simultaneously sharing under the same trust of land (see below).

The starting-point to determine whether a person is a beneficial joint tenant or tenant in common is that *'equity follows the law'*, so there will be a joint tenancy in equity unless there is some special reasons for there not to be. Special reasons are:

1 a missing unity;
2 express creation;
3 implied creation;
4 presumed creation.

A missing unity   The unity of either time, title or interest is not present as in *Grant* v. *Edwards* [1986] (above). It is likely that anyone who gains a share of the beneficial ownership under a constructive trust will be a tenant in common because they will probably not gain title at the same time.

Implied creation   If there are 'words of severance' in the conveyance (words which show an intention that the owners should have shares), a tenancy in common will be implied. These words include 'equally', 'in equal shares', 'amongst' and 'share and share alike'. An example is *Barclay* v. *Barclay* [1970[(11.7 above) where land was left equally under an express trust in a will to the testator's five children.

Presumed creation   There are three circumstances in which equity presumes a tenancy in common, These are, (i) where there are unequal contributions to the purchase – as in *Bull* v. *Bull* (see 11.7 above) – or (ii) where the sharers are partners or run separate businesses, or (iii) where they are mortgagees. If a person gains an interest under a resulting trust (by contributing to the price at the time of purchase), he could possibly be a joint tenant in equity if he contributed equally; if it was an unequal contribution, he will be a tenant in common.

Recently the Privy Council has made clear that equity still prefers tenancy in common:

'It seems to their Lordships that, where premises are held by two persons as joint tenants at law for their several business purposes, it is improbable that they would intend to hold as joint tenants in equity . . . Such cases are not necessarily limited to purchasers who contribute unequally, to co-mortgagees and to partners. There are other circumstances in which equity may infer that the beneficial interest is intended to be held by the grantees as tenants in common. In the opinion of their Lordships, one such case is where the grantees hold the premises for their several individual purposes.' (Lord Brightman in *Malayan Credit Ltd* v. *Jack Chia-MPH Ltd* [1986] 1 All ER 711 (PC))

12.4 Changing an Equitable Joint Tenancy into a Tenancy in Common

In what follows, it must always be remembered that a *legal* joint tenancy cannot be severed because there cannot be a legal tenancy in common (s.36(2) LPA).

An equitable owner may be a joint tenant at the start and then, at any time before he dies, he can change it to a tenancy in common. This change is called 'severance', and when it occurs, he becomes a tenant in common with an equal share of the value of the property, whenever it comes to be sold. If an equitable joint tenant severs his interest, from that moment he no longer suffers – or gains from – the right of survivorship.

Anything which 'creates a distinction' between equitable joint tenants is a severance and, as equity leans against joint tenancy, the trend is to recognise severance whenever possible. The methods of severance are:

1 *Breaking the unity of interest* by acquiring another interest in the land: for example, if a joint tenant of a lease buys (or makes a contract to buy) the freehold reversion.
2 *Breaking the unities of title and time*: for example, by sale (a contract to sell will do), or by going bankrupt.
3 *Agreement* to sever.
4 *Course of dealing* ('mutual conduct') which shows an intention to sever.
5 *Notice of immediate severance* in writing (by s.36(2) LPA, but, because of the wording, probably only where the legal and equitable owners are identical).
6 *Murdering another joint tenant* for, if the right of survivorship operated here, the killer would be 'profiting from his own wrong'. (See also s.2 Forfeiture Act 1982.)

Whether or not severance has taken place always depends on the evidence. Each case 'depends on its own facts' so, before giving a detailed example of the operation of these rules, it is interesting to consider some cases.

Cases on severance

There are many cases on severance, some of which seem inconsistent or unjust. The following five cases indicate the kind of problems that can arise; in all, the trigger for the dispute was the death of one co-owner, and the question arose of whether there had been a severance of the equitable joint tenancy before the death

In *Burgess* v. *Rawnsley* [1975] Ch 429, Mr Honick and Mrs Rawnsley had met at a Scripture rally. After a few months of friendship, they bought the house in which Mr Honick lived, as joint tenants at law and in equity. He thought they were going to get married; she merely intended to live in the upper flat. After a year or so, they had discovered each other's error and they agreed orally that he should buy her share, but they did not finally agree a price and nothing more was done. Three years later Mr Honick died, and Mrs Rawnsley claimed the whole house by the right of survivorship. Mr Honick's heir argued successfully that their negotiations had amounted to a severance of the equitable joint tenancy, so Mrs Rawnsley failed. In the Court of Appeal Lord Denning MR said:

> 'It is sufficient if there is a course of dealing in which one party makes clear to the other that he desires that their shares should no longer be held jointly but be held in common . . . it is sufficient if both parties enter on a course of dealing which evinces an intention by both of them that their shares shall henceforth be held in common and not jointly.' (p. 439)

The other judges, however, based their decision on the fact that there had been an agreement to sell.

The 'course of dealing' argument failed in *Greenfield* v. *Greenfield* (1979) 38 P & CR 570. Two brothers were joint tenants in law and of a house; when they both married, they converted it into two maisonettes but shared the garden and some bills. When the elder brother died his widow remained, claiming that the division of the house showed an intention to sever the beneficial joint tenancy and that she had inherited her husband's tenancy in common. The court held that the widow had 'come nowhere near' proving that there was a course of dealing showing an intention to sever, so she got nothing.

The need for both or all parties to show an intention to sever by course of dealing has recently been stressed in *McDowell* v. *Hirschfield* [1992] 2 FLR 126 where a mistress unsuccessfully claimed that her lover (who was a joint tenant in law and equity with his wife) had severed his equitable joint tenancy in their negotiations about a possible divorce and division of the family assets. The court held that there was no evidence of an intention to sever before he died, and therefore his wife kept all the land as survivor of joint tenants.

There was also no severance in *Barton* v. *Morris* [1985] 1 WLR 1257. An unmarried couple bought a guest house which was conveyed to them as joint tenants in law and in equity, mostly with her money. For tax reasons, the house was described as a 'partnership asset'; this normally implies that a tenancy in common in equity had been created (see 12.3 above). However, when the woman died and her mother (her heir) claimed a share of the house, it was held that there had been no severance because the tax declaration was a mere formality. The man took everything as survivor of legal and equitable joint tenants.

Re 88 Berkeley Road [1971] 1 Ch 648 concerned the written notice of severance. Two women were legal and equitable joint tenants of a house. When the younger, Miss Eldridge, decided to get married, the older woman decided to sever the equitable joint tenancy. She sent a notice of severance by recorded delivery (according to the rules in the LPA) The notice stated:

'I hereby give you notice of my desire to sever the joint tenancy in equity of and in the property described in the schedule hereto now held by you and me as joint tenants both at law and in equity.'

However, when it was delivered to the house the sender signed the receipt for it herself. After the older tenant's death Miss Eldridge, now married, discovered the notice of severance. Plowman J decided that the notice was properly sent, even though it may never have been received by another joint tenant. The right of survivorship therefore did not operate here.

12.5 Applying the Rules

Problem questions on co-ownership require a step-by-step analysis of what happens to the legal and equitable ownership. This is most easily done initially in table form, as in Table 12.1. The answers usually do not require advanced maths, so if odd fractions appear something has probably gone wrong.

Imagine that a group of nine people (A–I) bought a 99-year lease of a house as joint tenants, each contributing equally to the purchase. The first four over eighteen years old would be the legal owners as joint tenants (JTs) holding on trust for all nine. In the absence of one of the special reasons for finding a tenancy in common (see 12.3 above) they would all be joint tenants in equity as well.

This kind of problem question usually then goes on to say that some of the survivors now want to sell and others want to stay put. This requires a discussion of the case-law under ss.14–15 TLATA (11. 8 above).

12.6 Comment

The concepts of joint tenancy and tenancy in common are the creation of the judges, and on the whole they work quite well. However, the rules about severance of an equitable joint tenancy – on which so much may depend – are often unjust. It has even been suggested that the equitable

Table 12.1 Applying the co-ownership rules

	Law	Equity
At the start	ABCD (JTs)	ABCDEFGH and I (JTs)

	Law	Equity
If A died	BCD (JTs)	BCDEFGH and I (JTs)

(The right of survivorship operates for both legal and equitable joint tenants.)

	Law	Equity
If B bought the freehold	BCD (JTs)	B (t-in-C $\frac{1}{8}$) CDEFGH and I (JTs $\frac{7}{8}$)

(B's acquisition breaks his unity of interest with the other joint tenants; this affects his equitable joint tenancy but nothing can sever a legal joint tenancy.)

	Law	Equity
If C sold his interest to X	BCD (JTs)	B X (ts-in-c $\frac{1}{8}$ each) DEFGH and I (JTs $\frac{3}{4}$)

(There can be no change in the legal position unless all the legal owners sign a deed, so C can deal only with his equitable interest; X is a tenant in common as there is no unity of title with the joint tenants.)

	Law	Equity
If D sold his interest to E	BCD (JTs)	BX (ts-in-c $\frac{1}{8}$ each) E t-in-c $\frac{1}{4}$ FGHI (JTs $\frac{1}{2}$)

(E no longer is in unity with the other joint tenants, so this is a severance in equity.)

If F divided off his part of the house	. . . No Change . . .

(As in *Greenfield* (see above) this is probably not enough to amount to a 'course of dealing'.)

If F gave written notice to G, H and I	. . . No Change . . .

(The wording of s.36(2) on a strict interpretation only allows severance by notice if the legal and equitable owners are the same people.)

	Law	Equity
If F killed G and H	BCD (JTs)	B, X, F (ts-in-c $\frac{1}{8}$ each) E t-in-c $\frac{1}{4}$ I t-in-c $\frac{3}{8}$

(F's act probably amounts to severance but anyway he cannot profit from his own wrong; I takes by right of survivorship. F is now an equitable tenant in common since there is no one for him to be a joint tenant with.)

joint tenancy should be abolished, in order to avoid 'much troublesome and expensive litigation' (M. P. Thompson 51 Conv (1987) 29, p. 35). Certainly, it is hard to see why any 'family' co-owner would choose to be a joint tenant in equity today.

Summary

1 Legal title to land may only be shared under a joint tenancy, and the maximum number of legal joint tenants is four. Joint tenants share the unities of possession, interest, title and time, and take the risk of the right of survivorship.
2 Equitable co-owners may be joint tenants or tenants in common, depending on whether there were words of severance or the general circumstances of the creation of the trust; tenants in common share the unity of possession.
3 Equitable joint tenants can sever their tenancy and become tenants in common.

Exercises

1 How do you know if co-owners are joint tenants or tenants in common when a trust of land is created?
2 In what circumstances is the right of survivorship a convenient conveyancing device?
3 When is a joint tenancy severed?
4 Five friends, Denise, Michael, Florence, Jacob and Ben, who had just graduated and found jobs bought a 99-year lease of a flat in London; they intended to share it while they established themselves in their new careers. They each contributed £3000 to the deposit and were equally liable for the mortgage repayments.

Denise decided to leave her job and become a New Age traveller; she sold her share of the house to her friend Amanda who has now taken over her mortgage liability.

Florence and Michael became lovers and had twin babies who lived with them in half the house which they separated from the other half. Michael is, however, now on trial for killing Florence.

Ben has gone bankrupt.

Discuss the rights of all the parties and explain what will now happen to the land.

Land Law, Past and Future

Part V

Land Law: Past and Future

13   Licences in Land

13.1   Introduction

Licences are permissions to be on someone else's land; a person with a licence is simply not a trespasser, unless or until she is asked to leave. They have already been mentioned, usually as second-rate solutions, as in 'Is this a lease/easement or merely a licence?' This chapter examines the present law about licences and investigates the extent to which they are 'merely personal rights' or have achieved the status of 'interests in land', that is, 'property'.

The essential features of an 'interest in land' are said to be that:

1   The equitable remedies (injunction and specific performance) are available so that the interest may be specifically enforced, and
2   the right can be sold to another person, and
3   the burden of the right passes with the land, so a new owner of the land is bound by it.

Since licences are connected with virtually all of the rights to land in this book, they serve as a useful basis for revision.

There are dozens of important decisions on licences. The best approach is to take a representative sample and analyse them in terms of the facts and the reasons given for the decision, and then a plausible answer can be given to any problem or essay question. The issues are made more complex because some of the cases were decided during Lord Denning MR's time in the Court of Appeal and it is hard to know whether they will be followed now.

Licences can cover a huge variety of activities; the word 'licensee' includes a fan at a pop-concert, a secretary in an office and a customer in a shop. It can also describe a student living in a hostel, a cohabitee sharing her lover's house and a person walking her dog in the park. Licences can be for a few minutes, or for life; they can be created within a family or a commercial setting. It is hardly surprising that there are several types of licence and that the rights and remedies of licensees differ widely.

Licences are usually divided into the following categories:

1   Bare licences
2   Mutual licences
3   Licences coupled with interests in land
4   Contractual licences
5   Estoppel licences

13.2   Bare Licences

A bare licence is a (usually, temporary) permission to be on land, such as a postwoman delivering letters or a visitor having a cup of coffee. Such a licence can lawfully be withdrawn ('revoked') whenever the land-owner (the licensor) wishes; the licensee must leave within a reasonable time or she becomes a trespasser and can be physically removed. This kind of licence cannot be transferred by one licensee to another, and neither can it bind a person who buys the land from the licensor.

13.3   Mutual Licences

Mutual licences arise where two land-owners each have a licence over the other's land, as in *Ives (ER) Investment Ltd* v. *High* [1967] 2 QB 379 (see 9.3 above). The owner of a block of flats had to continue to allow his neighbour (over whose land the foundations of the flats trespassed) to use the drive belonging to the flats. The owner of the flats could not take the benefit of the licence to trespass unless he also accepted the burden of the neighbour's licence to use the drive, so the neighbour could continue to use it until the flats were demolished.

This very special kind of right obviously cannot – unlike the bare licence – be revoked by one side. It can be transferred with the land and will bind people who buy the land, as it did in *Ives* v. *High*. This case concerned unregistered land but the same is probably true in registered land as well (see 10.5 above).

13.4   Licences Coupled with an Interest in Land

When a person owns a profit or easement (see Chapter 7), she may need to go onto someone else's land to exercise it. An example is a right to fish: the

owner of the right automatically has a licence to cross the servient
tenement to get to the river. The value of this kind of licence depends
on the nature of the interest in land. If it is connected with a legal easement
or profit it will bind the world and will pass to any owner of the dominant
tenement: if it is dependent on an equitable easement or profit there may
be problems in unregistered land because of the requirements of registration (see 9.3 and 10.5 above).

13.5 Contractual Licences

Definition

A contractual licence is created wherever a person has permission to be on
another's land as part of a contract between them. The fan at a pop-
concert and the student in a hostel are both contractual licensees, as may
be a cohabitee who pays a share of the rent. As with any contract, it
may be express or implied, or partly implied. Additionally, in a family
setting it can be hard to know whether a contractual relationship was
intended. In *Coombes* v. *Smith* [1986] 1 WLR 808 (and see 13.6 below) a
man and woman had a relationship for over nine years. He bought a
house in which she and their child lived and he promised her he would
always look after her. When the relationship ended she claimed a
contractual licence in the house, arguing that she had provided consideration by leaving her husband, having the child and looking after the house.
Parker QC said:

'On the evidence before me I am wholly unable to infer an enforceable
contract under which . . . the defendant became obliged to provide a
roof over her head for the rest of her life.' (p. 815)

Where the courts do recognise a contractual licence, the rights of the
licensee depend on the terms of the contract concerned:

'A licence created by a contract . . . creates a contractual right to do
certain things which otherwise would be a trespass. It seems to me that,
in considering the nature of such a licence and the mutual rights and
obligations which arise under it, the first thing to do is to construe the
contract according to ordinary principles.' (Lord Greene MR in the CA
decision, *Winter Garden Theatre (London) Ltd* v. *Millennium Produc-
tions Ltd* [1946] 1 All ER 678, p. 680)

It is often assumed that a contractual licence is worth less than a lease, and this may be true in regard to the licensee's security if the land is sold (see 10.5 above). However, it is not necessarily so in regard to other issues. For example, in *Wettern Electric Ltd* v. *Welsh Development Agency* [1983] 1 QB 797, there was a licence of a factory. The premises were very badly constructed and became so unsafe that the licensee company had to leave. It successfully sued for breach of an implied term that the premises would be fit for their purpose; this term could not be implied into a contract for a *lease*, not being one of the 'usual' covenants (see Chapter 5.6), but in a *licence* the ordinary rules of contract law applied:

> 'The sole purpose of the licence was to enable the plaintiffs to have accommodation in which to carry on and expand their business . . . If anyone had said to the plaintiffs and the defendants' directors and executives at the time when the licence was being granted: "Will the premises be sound and suitable for the plaintiff's purposes?" they would assuredly have replied: "Of course; there would be no point in the licence if that were not so." The term was required to make the contract workable.' (Judges Newey QC, p. 809)

Revocability

It used to be thought that the equitable remedies of injunction and specific performance would not be available if one party breached a contractual licence. The cases seemed to rule that the courts would not enforce a licence by granting an injunction or specific performance: to do this would mean that they were giving the licensee an interest in the land itself, not merely a personal right. The only remedy available for a breach of the contract (for example, for a wrongful revocation) was damages. In *Hurst* v. *Picture Theatres Ltd* [1915] 1 KB 1 for example, a cinema customer was physically removed because the owner (wrongly) believed he had not paid for his ticket. The Court of Appeal decided that the licensor should not have turned the licensee out: he was entitled to damages for false imprisonment and breach of contract.

In the *Winter Garden Theatre* case above, there was a contractual licence to sell refreshments in a theatre foyer; the licensee could revoke it by giving one month's notice but there was no provision for the licensor, the theatre owner, to do so. The licensor tried to revoke it but the licensee argued that he could not. The House of Lords decided that the licensor could revoke the contract, but only on giving reasonable notice; one month was reasonable in these circumstances.

However, in *Errington* v. *Errington & Woods* [1952] 1 KB 290, a father paid the deposit on a house and told his son and daughter-in-law that if they paid the mortgage the house would be theirs. When the father died, the son moved in with his mother, who had inherited the house, and they tried to get his wife out. The Court of Appeal held that the arrangement was a contractual licence: if the licensees paid the whole of the mortgage, the father would have been ordered to transfer the house to them. This contractual licence could not be revoked (by the licensor's heir) so long as one of the licensees kept their side of the bargain:

'The couple were licensees, having a permissive occupation short of a tenancy, but with a contractual right, or at any rate, an equitable right to remain as long as they paid the instalments, which would grow into a good equitable title to the house itself as soon as the mortgage was paid . . . contractual licences now have a force and validity of their own and cannot be revoked in breach of contract.' (Lord Denning MR, pp. 296, 298)

One of the clearest cases of enforcement of a contractual licence is *Verrall* v. *Great Yarmouth BC* [1981] 1 QB 202. A local council tried to revoke a licence which had been granted to an extreme right-wing political organisation to use a hall for a two-day conference. It was held that the council could not do so. Damages for breach of contract would not be sufficient remedy, so the Court of Appeal unanimously held that the contract should be specifically enforced. Lord Denning MR said:

'An injunction can be obtained against the licensor to prevent his [the licensee's] being turned out. On principle it is the same if it happens before he enters. If he had a contractual right to enter, and the licensor refuses to let him come in, then he can come to the court and in a proper case get an order for specific performance to allow him to come in.' (p. 216)

Transferability

Whether a contractual licence can be transferred to another person depends on the terms of the contract. Probably, a contractual licence under a theatre ticket would be transferable, but in *Errington*'s case it is likely that the daughter-in-law would not be able to sell her interest, at least until she had completed paying off the mortgage. In *Verrall*'s case, it is harder to say whether the contract would allow the licence to be transferred to another person; a less controversial organisation might not get specific performance because it would not have such difficulty finding an alternative venue.

Effect on buyers of land

The question here is, what will happen to a licence if the land-owner transfers her interest? In *Errington*'s case, the licence did bind the licensor's heir, but an heir is not in the same position as a buyer of land. The House of Lords' decision in *King* v. *David Allen & Sons Billposting Ltd* [1916] 2 AC 54 is an example of the traditional view that such licences cannot affect third parties, because they are merely personal interests. The licence in this case was to fix advertising posters to the licensor's wall. The licensor then granted a long lease of the building to a cinema which stopped the licensee fixing the posters. It was held that the licensor was liable to pay damages for breaching his contract. The cinema lessee was not a party to the case but Lord Buckmaster LC several times referred to the licence as a purely personal right, not an interest in land.

This case was decided before the House of Lords' decision in the *Winter Garden Theatre* case. In later years it was Lord Denning's view that equity would enforce a contractual licence against anyone who ought fairly to be bound by it. In *Binions* v. *Evans* [1972] Ch 359, for example, a contractual licence bound a buyer of unregistered land who had express notice of her existence. Because they had agreed to take the land subject to her rights, they were bound by a constructive trust:

> 'Wherever the owner sells the land to a purchaser, and at the same time stipulates that he shall take it "subject to" a contractual licence, I think it plain that a court of equity will impose on the purchaser a constructive trust . . . It would be utterly inequitable that the purchaser should be able to turn out the beneficiary.' (Lord Denning MR, (p. 368)

This case is similar, in some ways, to *Lyus* v. *Prowsa Developments Ltd* [1982] 1 WLR 1044 (see 10.6 above), but the use of a constructive trust as a remedy may now be more limited (see 11.5 above). It is possible that a contractual license will today bind a third party provided that a constructive trust is an appropriate remedy. The suggestion by the Court of Appeal in *Ashburn Anstalt* v. *Arnold* [1989] that in registered land a contractual licence might be the basis of a 'right subsisting in reference to land' for an overriding interest under s.70(1)(g) LRA was overwhelmingly rejected by the House of Lords in *Prudential Assurance* v. *LRB* (1992) (see 5.3 and 10.5 above). However, if the contractual licence gave rise to a constructive trust this would be sufficient basis for an overriding interest in registered land.

13.6 Estoppel Licences

Definition and revocability

The doctrine of estoppel was explained in 2.6 above. It is the essence of estoppel that a land-owner who has given a licence in return for some act by the licensee cannot simply change her mind about the licence and revoke it if to do so would be 'unconscionable and unjust' (Scarman LJ in *Crabb* v. *Arun District Council* [1976] Ch 179, and see below).

One example is *Inwards* v. *Baker* [1965] (see 2.6 above). A second is *Crabb*'s case (above), where Crabb and the local council agreed that he could use an access to a road. He sold a part of his land in reliance on the agreement as his remaining land was completely inaccessible without the new access. The council knew of his plans to sell part of the land but they nevertheless closed his access. The Court of Appeal were unanimous that it should be restored.

In *Coombes* v. *Smith* (13.5 above) the cohabitee had also claimed an estoppel licence but this failed, as had her contractual claim. The judge took a very strict view of estoppel here, but it may be significant that the man had already undertaken to the court to keep a roof over her head, at least until their child reached seventeen; a less responsible licensor might have received different treatment from the court.

Recently the Court of Appeal found a licence by estoppel in *Matharu* v. *Matharu* [1994] 2 FLR 597 (and see 2.5 above). The house was occupied by the widowed daughter-in-law of the legal owner, and he now wanted to live there himself. She claimed that she had a right to the house; believing in her right to the land, she had spent money improving it, with the legal owner's knowledge, and had also dropped court proceedings against her husband. The Court held by a majority that she did not have an equitable share in the land, but a licence under estoppel to remain there for the rest of her life.

Transferability

The traditional view is that an estoppel right is purely personal and cannot be transferred; in *Inwards* v. *Baker* it would seem that the right to stay there could be enjoyed only by the son, and in *Matharu*, only by the daughter-in-law. However, it is possible that the extent of the licensee's right might depend on the terms of the expectation aroused by the licensor; if, for example, she encouraged a belief that the licensee could sell her rights and if the licensee acted to her detriment in reliance on this, a buyer of the licence might be able to rely on the licensee's estoppel. This is an alternative explanation of the decision in *Ives* v. *High;* in such a case, the successors in title of the estoppel licensee were able to enforce the equitable claim.

Effect on buyers of land

Lord Denning MR clearly felt that estoppel licences were capable of binding a buyer of the land. In *Inwards* v. *Baker*, for example, he said, 'any purchaser who took with notice would clearly be bound by the equity.' (p. 37). In *Re Sharpe (a bankrupt)* [1980] 1 WLR 219, an old lady lent £12 000 to her nephew to buy a maisonette on the basis that they would live there together. He became bankrupt, and the trustee in bankruptcy went to court for a possession order against her. The money was held to be a loan so she did not have an interest under a resulting trust. However, Browne-Wilkinson J. said:

> 'If the parties have proceeded on a common assumption that the plaintiff is to enjoy a right to reside in a particular property and in reliance on that assumption the plaintiff has expended money or otherwise acted to his detriment, the defendant will not be allowed to go back on that common assumption and the court will imply an irrevocable licence or trust which will give effect to that common assumption.' (p. 223)

The most equitable solution was that she should be entitled to remain there until the loan was repaid: her right bound the licensor's trustee in bankruptcy. Brown-Wilkinson J went no further than this in his judgment. However, there was a buyer with an enforceable contract for the sale of the land (currently living in a caravan nearby) and of him he said:

> 'I am in no way deciding what are the rights of a purchaser from the trustee as against [the licensee]. It may be that as a purchaser without express notice in an action for specific performance of the contract his rights will prevail over [hers]. As to that I have heard no argument and express no view.' (p. 226)

Whether an estoppel licence does bind third parties is therefore not yet clear. It seems likely that – as in contractual licences – if the courts decide that a constructive trust is appropriate, then a third party may be bound, depending on the doctrine of overreaching, and the rules of notice in unregistered land, and overriding interests in registered land.

13.7 Comment

If one thing is clear about licences, it is that there is not one answer to the question, 'Are licences interests in land? Are they property?' The probable conclusion to be drawn from the brief summary in this chapter is that *some* contractual and estoppel licences are, but that most licences are not.

These issues have frequently been investigated by academics. Some seem to welcome licences as interests in land, often quoting Megarry and Wade's remark:

'The courts seem to be well on their way to creating a new and highly versatile interest in land which will rescue many informal and unbusinesslike transactions, particularly within families, from the penalties of disregarding legal forms. Old restraints are giving way to the demands of justice.' (1984, p. 808)

These writers would enthusiastically embrace the idea that twentieth-century land lawyers have produced a new interest in land, equivalent to the development of the restrictive covenant in the nineteenth century. From this viewpoint, the licence, or, more accurately, *some* licences are symbols of a new form of property, a right to share, which will take its place beside the traditional private and exclusive right.

Dewar (49 MLR (1986) 741) claims that the licence represents a 'unique category of rights over land' in which the judges 'impose their own views of the parties' needs':

'The licence is, simply, a different, but not a "new", form of right in land that does not conform to the model of a freely alienable right of exclusive benefit.' (p. 153)

However he goes further than most, claiming that the traditional concern of writers on land law, that is, forcing the judges' views of ordinary people's activities into the moulds of 'interests in land', has actually obscured the activities of the courts. The traditional academic concern with the abstract concepts of land law – which he calls 'conceptual formalism' – results from the evolution of land law as an academic subject: the domination of the requirements of conveyancers means that many courses 'cannot offer undergraduates a realistic view of the relationship between land and law'. The academic habit of fitting every case into a pre-formed mould is a result of the fossilisation of land law teaching over several generations. Categorisation can be a convenient way to achieve order out of chaos, but when the analysis obscures rather than illuminates the underlying patterns it is time, as Dewar argues, to start from the beginning again. And that seems a good point on which to end this book!

Summary

1 A licence is a permission to be on land: it covers a wide variety of permissions – bare, mutual, coupled with an interest, contractual and estoppel.
2 A bare licence can be revoked at any time.
3 A mutual licence binds everyone who comes to the land: so long as they enjoy the benefit, they must suffer the burden.
4 A licence coupled with an interest in land depends on the interest in question.
5 A contractual licence depends on its terms.
6 A licence by estoppel may arise when a person acts to her detriment relying on a promise that she will gain an interest in land.
7 Some contractual and estoppel licences seem to be becoming 'interests in land': they may bind a buyer of land.

Exercises

1 What is an 'interest in land'?
2 Can contractual licences be revoked on reasonable notice?
3 What remedies may be appropriate to an estoppel licensee?
4 What is land law about?
5 Paul and Linda are the registered proprietors of a very large house. When they bought it 15 years ago, it was very run-down and they did not have the time or money to do it up all by themselves. They therefore agreed with Cassie and Sam (Linda's sister and brother) that they would move in and help with the work; they said Cassie and Sam would be able to make their home there, with their disabled son. Cassie won £15 000 in the lottery and part of the money was used to pay for a new roof. Sam gave up his job to work on the house and look after Paul and Linda's children. He has been in hospital since falling off a ladder when mending one of the chimneys last year.

Paul and Linda are now going to separate. They have transferred the land to Damien who has been registered as proprietor. Advise Cassie and Sam.

Further Reading

General

Burn, E. H. (1994) *Cheshire and Burn's Modern Law of Real Property*, 15th edn (London: Butterworth) ('Cheshire').

Gray, K. (1993) *Elements of Land Law*, 2nd edn (London: Butterworth).

Lim, H. and Green, K. (1995) *Cases and Materials on Land Law*, 2nd edn (London: Pitman).

Mackenzie, J. A. and Phillips, M. (1994) *A Practical Approach to Land Law*, 5th edn (London: Blackstone Press).

Martin, J. E. (1989) *Hanbury & Maudsley's Modern Equity*, 13th edn (London: Stevens) ('Hanbury and Maudsley').

Megarry, R. and Wade, H. W. R. (1984) *The Law of Real Property*, 5th edn (London: Stevens).

Murphy, W. T. and Roberts, S. (1987) *Understanding Property Law* (London: Fontana).

Riddall, J. A. (1996) *Introduction to Land Law*, 4th edn (London: Butterworth).

Simpson, A. W. B. (1986) *History of the Land Law* (Oxford: Clarendon).

Chapter 1

Baker, J. H. (1990) *An Introduction to English Legal History*, 3rd edn (London: Butterworth).

Milsom, S. F. C. (1981) *Historical Foundations of the Common Law*, 2nd edn (London: Butterworth).

Chapter 2

Baker, P. U. and Langan, P. St. J. (1990) *Snell's Equity*, 29th edn (London: Sweet & Maxwell).

Consumers' Association (1986) *The Legal Side of Buying a House* (Consumers' Association).

Chapter 3

Hardy, D. and Ward, C. (1984) *Arcadia for All* (London: Mansell).

Chapter 5

Bright, S. and Gilbert, G. (1995) *Landlord and Tenant Law: the Nature of Tenancies* (Oxford: Clarendon Press).

Carrott, S. (1990) *Arden and Partington on Quiet Enjoyment*, 3rd edn (London: LAG)

Partington, M. (1980) *Landlord and Tenant, Text and Materials on Housing and Law*, 2nd edn (London: Weidenfeld & Nicolson).

Yates, D. and Hawkins, A.J. (1986) *Landlord and Tenant Law*, 2nd edn (London: Sweet & Maxwell).

Chapter 6.

Fairest, P.B. (1980) *Mortgages*, 2nd edn (London: Sweet & Maxwell).

Chapter 7

Jackson, P. (1978) *The Law of Easements and Profits* (London: Butterworth).

Chapter 8

Harte, J.D.C. (1984) *Landscape, Land Use and the Law* (London: Spon).

Preston, C.H.S. and Newsom, G.L. (1991) *Restrictive Covenants Affecting Freehold Land*, 8th edn (London: Sweet & Maxwell).

Chapter 9

Offer, A. (1981) *Property and Politics 1870–1914* (Cambridge: Cambridge University Press).

Ruoff, T. (1974) *Searching Without Tears: The Land Charges Computer* (London: Oyez).

Chapter 10

Joseph, M. (1989) *The Great Conveyancing Fraud*, 3rd edn (Woolwich: M. Joseph).

Shick, B.C. and Plotkin, I.H. (1978) *Torrens in the United States* (Lexington Mass.: Heath).

Chapter 11

Dewar, J. (1992) *The Law and the Family*, 2nd edn (London: Butterworth).

Gardner, S. (1990) *An Introduction to the Law of Trusts* (London: Clarendon).

Oakley, A. J. (1987) *Constructive Trusts*, 2nd edn (London: Sweet & Maxwell).

Sydenham, A. (1996) *Trusts of Land: The New Law* (London: Jordan).

Index